RESEARCH IN
SOCIAL PROBLEMS
AND
PUBLIC POLICY

Volume 1 • 1979

RESEARCH IN SOCIAL PROBLEMS AND PUBLIC POLICY

A Research Annual

Editor: MICHAEL LEWIS
Department of Sociology
University of Massachusetts

VOLUME 1 • 1979

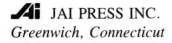 JAI PRESS INC.
Greenwich, Connecticut

CONTENTS

PREFACE

This volume inaugurates the annual series, *Research in Social Problems and Public Policy*. The papers I have chosen to publish cover a wide range of contemporary problems and are executed in a variety of methodological styles. Although I have methodological preferences, the reader will not find them imposed upon this volume or the others that will follow in this series. Each author speaks, as it were, in his or her own voice; and because in sociology there is no consensus about "correct" methodology, it should come as no surprise to the informed reader that the voices of the thirteen contributors to this volume do not always sound the same.

Despite the variety of substantive concerns and methodological styles, this collection of papers does possess a certain unity. Its basis is the fact that each of the contributors approaches the promulgation of public policy as a problem. Contrary to a large body of policy-relevant scholarship, the papers in this volume are not premised on a conception of public policy formulation which assumes high purpose and rational intention on the part of policy makers, a conception which consequently places policy determination beyond the sphere of analytic attention and relegates policy scholarship to a form of intelligence in service to presumably unassailable ends. In each of the papers collected here, policy formulation is itself regarded as a problem necessitating disciplined analysis. In some of the papers public policy is the center of attention; in others policy issues are considered in the context of broader analyses of particular social problems. But in all of the papers public policies are conceived of as products of the play and sometimes the clash of social interests, and consequently as products which do not invariably imply the greatest good for the greatest many. For each of the contributors whose work appears in these pages the central issue is not how to make a given policy initiative work; it is, rather, whether or not the initiative in question is *justified* when analyzed from the perspective of the author's value commitments and what is known about the behaviors and conditions the initiative is intended to address.

The intent of this volume is to move contemporary policy discourse from the assessment of means given an uncritical acceptance of ends to a holistic assessment in which both ends and means receive their share of appropriate critical attention. It is my firm conviction that only by doing so can we hope to create the conditions necessary for the development and adoption of public policies whose purposes truly contribute to maximized human serviceability in contemporary society. In my view the contributors to this volume have served its purpose admirably. I hope that you, the reader, will agree.

Michael Lewis
University of Massachusetts

THE LIMITS OF DEINSTITUTIONALIZATION

Bernard Beck, NORTHWESTERN UNIVERSITY

In recent years many well-meaning people have come to believe that the institutionalization of the mentally and emotionally incapacitated has proven to be counterproductive to their well-being. In their zeal to correct the abuses frequently characteristic of large-scale custodial institutions the reformers have often championed deinstitutionalization—or the release, under supervision, of patients into the community. In his provocative paper Bernard Beck challenges the efficacy of this reform strategy. He analyzes the origins of deinstitutionalization in anarchist sentimentality and indicates why it is that this presumably humane reform may not be so humane after all.

The field of social policy is often the meeting ground of practical officials conducting conventional organizational business and idealistic planners pursuing large scale visions of social transformation. Their encounters may result in mantling programs of pedestrian origin in the rhetorical colors of radical sentiment. I intend to show how an important recent movement in the treatment of social problems, deinstitutionalization, acquired a rationale based on the anti-institutional sentimentality of the 1960s. This rationale invited the participation

Research in Social Problems and Public Policy—Vol. 1, 1979, pages 1–14

and support of people with benevolent, idealistic intentions and obscured some serious implications of this treatment approach. This case can serve as an example of the dangers in bringing sentimentality to the formation of social problems policy.

THEORY AND SENTIMENTALITY

The modern world has seen the development of a number of theoretical systems analyzing society, its fundamental contradictions, and directions for transforming it positively. Such systems include a variety of Marxist and other socialist analyses, fascism, anarchism, and several forms of conservative thought. Close familiarity with these systems of thought is found among rather small groups and circles. Organized political groups with a basis in such systems include larger numbers of participants. Most inclusive of all are the large aggregates of people who are sentimentally influenced by the best-known themes found in such a system. It is possible for a little-known and less understood theory eventually to affect whole populations by the popularization of characteristic ways of labeling problems or seeking solutions. Ordinary people whose ways of thinking may be quite conventional and uninfluenced by the basic premises and logic of an abstruse theory may adopt convenient pictures of social life provided by the theory, but without the accompanying intellectual structure. Such casual borrowings from a complex theory come to be called "vulgar" versions of the theory and are often held in contempt by serious students of the original theory.

Nevertheless, they continue to be used as models for understanding social life by many people in many practical situations. They endure as forms of sentimentality that color people's approach to social action. In calling these simple models forms of sentimentality, I mean that people are predisposed to understanding many situations as instances of these models and to forming their own loyalties and strategies for action on the basis of the generalized sentiments they feel about the model. For example, people who in general feel sympathy for the underdog or respect for symbols of authority are acting in particular situations on the basis of global attitudes formed prior to their encounter with those particulars. All they need do is determine in each case who is the underdog or who is in authority; once that determination is made, their response can follow automatically.

Although a form of sentimentality may have roots in an elaborate theoretical scheme, the spread and popularity of the simplified models probably has more to do with the practical needs for rhetoric of people experiencing a major social development in their daily lives than with their interest in a thorough analysis of societal structure. For example, when many people are engaged in specific labor-management struggles, a kind of Marxist sentimentality may become popular, without many of them feeling impelled to inquire more deeply into the system of Marxian thought. In a period when a certain sentimentality is popular, the success of detailed social policies may depend on the degree to which they can enlist active participation and passive public acceptance by means of an ideological presentation in terms of the current sentimentality. This requirement of sentimental acceptability applies not only to general public opinion but also to the deeper involvement of professional social critics, commentators, academic observers, and independent practitioners, whose work frequently has sentimental bases as well.

ANARCHIST SENTIMENTALITY

One of the notable social theories that has given rise to this process is anarchism. Anarchism is an attractive proposition whose simple form and grand scope have moved thinkers for generations, even centuries, although very few have managed to hold to it for very long. Even when no one can convincingly show how it may be achieved or what exactly it would look like if it came, it still serves as the ultimate objection to all theories of social organization.

Anarchism is more than a utopian proposal or a critical theory, however. It is also a form of sentimentality. By now it is a fairly popular one. Anarchist sentiments are reflected in plans and decisions on an ordinary day-to-day level, in circumstances that may not remotely admit the possibility of an anarchist transformation of society. Embattled American children have uttered the patriotic slogan, ''It's a free country!'' for a long time. Although this cry is unmatched in its eloquence and passion, it is not often meant as a call to smash the state, fracture the cultural hegemony of the ruling class, or tear down the walls and free all political prisoners. Nevertheless, it has its roots in a conception of social life that is fundamentally anarchist. To the extent that it succeeds in winning a moment of liberation for its young partisan, it demonstrates how susceptible its audience is to anarchist appeals.

In the sixties we were witnesses to an abundance of small social experiments. Under a profusion of labels (alternative living arrangements; free schools, theaters and festivals; communes; people's parks, streets, newspapers, law offices and medical clinics; to name only a few), groups of people attempted seriously to realize anarchist values, even though the conditions of American society were in no sense propitious and the acknowledged requirements of transformation of economic and political institutions had not been fulfilled. These were anarchist enterprises conducted, in the quaint jargon of the times, ''inside the belly of the monster.''

In whatever form and with whatever central item of business, these ventures usually participated in a common view of collective action: that large-scale organizations acting under rigidly imposed rules are inimical to human purposes, destructive of character, fundamentally aimed at the limitation and control of the people involved in them, and tailored to suit the interests of ruling elites under an ideological camouflage of maintaining order for the sake of all; and that smaller groups of people acting in behalf of common interests, making decisions by consent based on equality of participation could produce greater creativity, responsiveness, freedom, and escape from subservience to corrupt engines of power. At the very least, the participants hoped, liberated zones could be established, sanctuaries where humane living could take place day to day, even if the larger social environment remained oppressive. At the most, these small scattered enterprises could be the beginning of a pervasive network of interrelated sites of change that would ultimately bring down the petrified structures of modern American hyperinstitutional life.

Some of these communal attempts have survived and flourished until today. Rural communes, urban collectives, and alternative institutions were often short-lived and had a high rate of failure, but under favorable circumstances there were those that endured. There are still small networks of people pursuing the original aims and seeking new organizing forms and new settings. But a great number of the communal enterprises experienced problems that are instructive about the fruits of anarchist sentimentality. Communalism showed itself vulnerable to larger social events, by reason of its marginality. In this respect, its history is comparable to the history of bohemianism and reveals the same kinds of contradictions evident in bohemian communities. In both cases, the survival of the enterprise becomes dependent on one of several circumstances that compromise its ideological stance. These circumstances include: elite sponsorship (if it is amusing or exploitable) by grants from public agencies, private foundations or individual benefactors, and private incomes of participants who can afford to undertake life-style experiments; gaps in the marketplace (which is in general tightly organized) that permit a meager living from day-labor or providing marginal goods and services; ascetic isolation, in which contact with the social environment and productive activity by members is kept to a minimum, a kind of voluntary poverty; or evolution into a profitable business, such as marketing handicrafts, promoting rock concerts, or serving health food.

In addition to dependency on some favorable circumstances, communal enterprises are vulnerable to internal loss of participation, often on the same ideological grounds that led to the establishment of the enterprise. Members sometimes withdraw from the common effort because they find it abridging their freedom. The solidarity and mutual commitment that must exist in a nonrepressive setting apparently rest on strong sacred elements of culture. Such elements are hard to build and make effective to order. In their absence, consensus is always on the brink of seeming arbitrary. Solidarity is easier to attain when there is no alternative, but the defining condition of alternative communal forms within our conventional social structure is that members can usually choose to return to the conventional realm. Finally, the continuation or demise of communal ventures often hinges on the tacit permission of powerful environing agencies. Local authorities like health and fire inspectors, zoning boards, state departments of registration, commerce and labor must be tolerant or inattentive to allow communalists to continue operating without obeying a multitude of regulations and institutional rules. That permission is often affected by events having nothing to do with the character of the ventures themselves, such as party politics, real estate markets, and budget-making in state departments.

In all these respects, the communal alternative institution, like the bohemian artist, arrives at the position of a sentimentalized small business, a mom-and-pop grocery store with a grandiose ideology. Sentimental anarchism leads to a search for alternative social forms that eventuates in the rediscovery of the petit-bourgeois mode of adaptation. In spite of the ambitious goals at the start, this sentimentality converges with the conventional kind found among generations of factory workers and organization men, sometimes called the American Dream (Chinoy, 1955).

Whatever the dilemmas of communalism in the sixties, it was basically an attempt by autonomous persons to reconstruct a free collective life for themselves. But the seventies have seen the flowering of a far more perplexing bud of sentimental anarchism, a growth that could be called "third-party anarchism." In this form, anarchist sentiments are invoked not in behalf of oneself and fellows but in behalf of some identifiable group of others who will receive the benefits of the vision. In the most curious version, these others come to notice as official targets of state activity, and the anarchist treatments are applied to them under state auspices. This version is known as "deinstitutionalization" in a variety of fields organized around ministering to the wretched.

ANARCHIST SENTIMENTALITY AND DEINSTITUTIONALIZATION

The process of deinstitutionalization is occurring today in many different fields, under the jurisdiction of many official and quasi-official agencies and collegia of professional experts. In fact, it is appearing in virtually every area where the establishment of institutions was the path of progressive meliorism a half century ago (Rothman, 1971). We are to be breaching the walls of prisons, hospitals, asylums, correctional centers, reformatories, and homes for the handicapped, retarded, neglected, abused, abandoned, dependent, incompetent, misguided, not yet productive, no longer productive and never could be productive.

The benign terminology of institutions expresses a view of overwhelming generosity, that places of nurturance and healing are to be provided to those who are victimized and unequipped to survive out in the cold. But the last generation achieved a shattering insight and broadcast it to the popular ear. These were not havens but places of incarceration, whose inmates paid for the crime of appearing troublesome by being held in close arrest, physically mortified and morally abased. Among those who brought the news were Edgar Friedenberg (1967);

Erving Goffman (1962); Paul Goodman (1962); John Holt (1964); Ivan Illich (1971); Ken Kesey (1962); Herbert Marcuse (1964); and Thomas Szasz (1965). To this indictment specifying means and opportunity, recent historical and structural research has added some account of motive, thus completing the corpus delicti (Piven and Cloward, 1972). We now have the outline of the role played by institutional incarceration in the tutelage of a disciplined modern labor force paying taxes to the rational organization of work. Commitment to a facility was the lot of those who failed the labor force test. Only in the area of social welfare was this approach replaced early. In welfare, we have a model of the new ideas of deinstitutionalization in the other custodial fields, where surveillance replaces custody (Piven and Cloward, 1972).

The implicit anarchist criticism of custodial institutions that became popular in the sixties had its greatest sentimental impact in a bitter revulsion against the lowest level of custodians. The institutional walls empowered brutalized and brutal guards, orderlies, ward nurses, supervisors, teachers and counselors to assault the integrity of inmates under cover of bureaucratic paperwork and institutional pieties. The higher levels were charged with indifference. Although prison lore told us that ''We're all prisoners here, even the screws,'' custodians were not ordinarily regarded with sympathy by sentimentalists. Although there was no necessary vindictiveness in the anarchist analysis of institutions, when the complex struggles for change were joined and custodians were found in opposition to anti-institutional reforms, the response was moral outrage. Then the scene was played out of the battle between those trapped in their work and those excluded from work. This sentimental understanding meant that the upper levels of decision makers were largely overlooked and the environing institutional forms were not made an immediate order of business.

Starting in the mid-fifties and continuing all through the period of development of contemporary anarchist sentimentality, public officials became increasingly aware of a growing problem in operating institutional facilities for the custody of public clients. There was a rapid increase in the numbers of clients, the extent of services that had to be provided, the cost of services, the numbers of public workers needed to provide services, and the scale of administrative organization to manage these activities. Over the same period, there was an increasingly severe crisis in the supply of resources, especially funds, to meet these demands. Officials came under great pressure to reduce the cost of such public institutional services (O'Connor, 1973; Scull, 1977). In the sixties, officials who attempted such reductions were labeled as fiscal conservatives and met opposition from groups concerned with the needs of the unfortunates who became public clients. They were also defined as adversaries by anarchist sentimentalists, often the same concerned people.

This situation prepared the ground for a novel development of the seventies, the appearance of a ''new'' generation of elite functionaries in state and private apparatuses who were able to present themselves as apostles of the anarchist creed in spite of their high offices. In contrast to the fiscal conservatives, the new officials laid claim to the anti-institutional ideology popular on the left. These governors, heads of departments, foundation directors, agency executives, management consultants and tenured professors persuasively enlisted the collaboration of a generation of sentimental anarchists, advocates for inmates, and uncertified job-seekers in an attack on the stones in the walls, the stacks of paper in the bureaucratic offices, and the licenses of job-holders.

This battle satisfies anarchist sentimentality in several respects. It confronts the visible physical and personal symbols of tyranny. It provides a spectacle of liberation as victims of incarceration are set free. It provides occasions to say "no," loudly and with conviction, to intricate and specious institutional apologies. Finally, it provides an opportunity for practical action, even livelihood, under the rubric of anarchist values, in this practical world where meaningful paying jobs are in short supply. But the cost of this sentimental indulgence was the neglect of rigorous anarchist analysis, which would produce greater skepticism and a more subtle understanding of the dilemmas of social life.

ANARCHISM VS. ANARCHIST SENTIMENTALITY

Deinstitutionalization does not dispense with, nor even materially affect, the problem of the control of populations certified inadmissible to the world of work. This problem is itself an aspect of the problem of imposing discipline on a labor force. These problems are fundamental to any proper anarchist perspective. In fact, it is the insistence on this problem that distinguishes anarchism from all other revolutionary theories. Deinstitutionalization does not address the processes by which target populations for social control are organized, labeled, segregated and made available for treatment. Sentimental anarchists have shown how institutions of social control have drummed up social control business for themselves, but they have not convincingly shown (nor is it, I believe, showable) that demands for social control would not arise if the institutions did not exist. Large concentrations of power do exist and can generate effective demand for social control of embarrassing residual populations. Moreover, socially helpless members of society are often in positions of such desperation that they must regard the existence of social control agencies as positive resources for resolving personal crises. Deinstitutionalization would not abate either of these major sources of candidates for control and custody (Beck, 1967).

Deinstitutionalization does not even excuse target populations from state supervision when it expels them from its campuses. The files are not closed when the gates are. Once again, a proper anarchism should focus on the compromised status of people, not merely on their housing arrangements. What made deinstitutionalization practically and politically possible in field after field was the development of technical novelties that permit extramural control by pharmacology, electronics, and accountancy. There is no reason to believe that such outpatient treatment represents a decrease in tyrannical supervision. It remains to be seen whether it even represents a decrease in physical suffering in the long run. What is common in these situations is that the invisibility of control that used to be accomplished by segregation behind walls and that was pierced by the courageous work of critics of total institutions is reconstructed by dispersing the embarrassing wretches in the numerous nooks and crannies of the larger social world that are disingenuously called the "community" and the "private sector" in the new jargon.

Finally, deinstitutionalization does not address the fundamental problem of how people, once identified as targets of state control, can gain readmission to ordinary citizenship status—that is to say, in a modern society, entrance to the labor force. The obstacles to free social participation that inhere in a selective, exclusive and alienated system of work are central to anarchist concern, but are neglected in favor of a sentimental identification with victims that often becomes a romantic admiration of their apparent "freedom" from work. The role of work in human life is a basic question, requiring extensive analytic treatment. It is the mark of sentimentality to express repugnance for the present organization of work by escaping it vicariously through the idleness of client populations.

Anarchist sentimentality in behalf of deinstitutionalization does not merely interfere with necessary anarchist criticism. It also produces susceptibility to a variety of fictions that cover realities abhorrent to anarchist theory. I wish to describe three of these in particular: the fiction of community, the fiction of alternative arrangements, and the fiction of advocacy. They are all routes to an unhappy outcome, that anarchist sentimentalists become the architects of a new tyranny, or rather, the continuation of tyranny by other means. The dreadful irony here is that sentimentality, instead of fulfilling one of its basic functions, to make resistance to errors instinctive, instead manifests one of its basic dangers, by desensitizing resistance through self-righteous complacency.

The fiction of community has a special place in the ideology of deinstitutionalization. The fact that institutional walls enclose scenes of brutality and negligence has never been enough, by itself, to cause walls to be torn down. The inmates are only allowed free when there is a setting that will receive them. If incarceration is a means of controlling a distinctive subpopulation with its own rich culture, then the freed inmates can return to their own world. For they were not necessarily troublesome within that world, but only in the interaction between that world and its conquerors. Thus, if the ills of institutions are sentimentally attributable to tyranny, the alternative to institutionalization is a return to "The Community." In fact, the word "community" is used in the jargon of deinstitutionalization in a facile and sentimental way to stand for this necessary next step in the argument. In order to make it persuasive, a patently false and idiosyncratic picture of ordinary life outside the walls is painted. Society is described as divided into recognizable, flourishing, self-conscious and responsible communities; clients and inmates are seen as having enduring or reconstructible ties to such communities; and the verdict of social incompetence that is the statutory implication of having a case file in a public agency is attributed wholly to whimsy and bigotry inherent in the process of official labeling. Although this happy vision of community pervades discussions of deinstitutionalization, there is very often nothing in reality that corresponds to the image, especially in the case of the most wretched inmates. The very fact that they have fallen among state officials is eloquent testimony to the lack of the social, political and economic resources that support the kind of household and community life that protects the individual from the hard edge of the state. Whether because of the conditions that led to state action or because of the fact of state intervention itself, most of the victims of institutional abuse cannot go home again. Although there is no particular ignorance about these circumstances, state agencies are able to operate routinely in terms of the illusory model of the community because the job of placement in the community and inspection of the quality of life in the community thereafter is the responsibility of other functionaries. That is, the reintegration in the community that is spoken of is defined operationally as the closing of institutional files. The "mainstreaming" of special education students, the "aftercare" of discharged mental patients, the adjustment of paroled convicts means that the task of failing is shifted to the less visible school psychologists, aftercare case workers and parole officers from the notorious ruins of state institutions that are in the limelight. In fact, far too often, the deinstitutionalized inmates end up reassigned to unofficial holding pens, commonly under private business proprietorship, as a result of enduring desperate stop-gap placement efforts that are made when there turns out to be no real community to accept the refugees. In this incarnation, the inmates appear on public welfare rolls, but they have disappeared from the files of the agencies that run institutions.

As a common result of communal thinking and of the absence of natural communities that can receive the discharged inmate, new forms of institutional life are emerging under the rubric of alternative institutions, once again with the curious sponsorship of the state. These arrangements are based on experiments in constructing communal living arrangements that multiplied in the sixties, although they have been a historical tradition in America for more than a century. They appear under a variety of names, including group care homes, residential treatment centers, sheltered workshops, and halfway houses. The most cherished of anarchist and other progressive ideas are invoked to promote these establishments, including the virtues of the extended family, the commune, the kibbutz and the encounter group. Although their immediate ancestors are experiments in minimum security arrangements aimed at humanizing institutions of incarceration, they now represent the obverse, attempts to structure and guide freedom (or eviction).

By contrast with the notion of community, these arrangements are organized and sponsored by the state; they have staff recruited and paid by the state; and they constitute the continuation of state supervision (in the juridical sense, if not de facto) and peculiar citizenship status. The characteristics of the staff are especially interesting. These are state custodians in plain clothes rather than uniform, for all the world like social service mod squads. Let me make clearer the fictitious character of the alternative institution story that covers these establishments. They do not come into existence by compact of the participants nor one at a time out of the interests of each group of comrades. Instead, they are created by edict at the highest level of policy making, and participants are assigned to them by case officers. Individual performance is then officially monitored. Although residents have considerable influence over their own staying or leaving (as veteran inmates always do to some extent) their institutional destiny is still officially in the hands of their custodians and is more influenced by official policies and politics than by their own personal circumstances. There is already reason to believe that inmates react to these new forms in the same way as to any other institutional placement, by a rational calculation of proximate costs and benefits (''It's in a good school district,'' ''There's a beach nearby,'' ''The food is lousy,'' ''I don't get along with the guy across the hall'') (Wittner, 1977, Chapter 8).

The third fiction, advocacy, is in some ways the most frightening and the most problematic from an anarchist point of view. For advocacy is the apology for the involvement of the third-party operative in this recent version of the relations between the state and the targeted person. In deinstitutionalization, the most notable anarchist exponent is not the inmate himself, resisting state custody in the name of his or her own freedom. Instead it is some other person, sympathetically identifying with the victim from a position of safety, asserting the general claims of liberation on behalf of the victim, and eventually achieving an accepted status within the institutional framework. By accepted status I mean particularly a defined office that includes the right to be regarded as a party of interest in the dealings of the system, to speak in behalf of the client, make claims and accept terms in his or her behalf, and to be funded and even rewarded out of public funds. This position has been dubbed ''advocate'' or ''ombudsman,'' accomplishing several functions: First, it linguistically distinguishes the role from those of custodian, caseworker and guard, which are so seriously discredited under the institutional system. Second, it disguises the difference in position between the client and the advocate, thus making it appear as though the client has a voice of his or her own in the new order and as though the advocate does not have a separate voice whose origins might be suspect. Third, it disguises the advocate's position as a servant of the state. Fourth, it prevents the advocate's activity from being defined as an imposition of an external plan on the client's future and an intrusion of an external interest into the client's life. It is the vocabulary of advocacy that allows the sentimental anarchist to be obtrusively present and willfully active in the system of state control without abandoning anarchist rhetoric. It is as though the anarchist were not there as a separate factor in the situation. Of course, this assumption of an aloof position, committed disinterestedly to the welfare of other people, is the most common camouflage of state tyranny in behalf of ruling interests. It is a camouflage that anarchists are endlessly trying to penetrate in their criticism of the state.

The wardrobe of fictions necessary to dress deinstitutionalization in anarchist clothes is now complete. When the walls are torn down and the inmates set free, they are now seen as free to rejoin communities (that either do not exist or have no organic relationship to the returnee), to participate in free living arrangements (which are neither free nor autonomous nor creatures of their participants) and to participate in arranging their own destiny by expressing themselves (in voices that are not theirs but the voices of third parties whose presentation of them will be more influential than their own real characteristics). The creators of this image are then able not only to assume the postures of anarchism in the eyes of others, but in their own eyes as well, thus avoiding the harsh light of self-criticism and the instinctive reactions that might inhibit their participation in developing new forms of tyranny.

CONSEQUENCES OF DEINSTITUTIONALIZATION

What then are the real, practical effects of deinstitutionalization, leaving aside pretensions to anarchist sentimentality? In *certain* circumstances, they might include a real and positive alleviation of severe forms of suffering in institutions. This possibility is made more probable when concrete improvements in forms of treatment accompany the general rhetoric of deinstitutionalization, such as the use of pharmaceuticals to help mental patients cope with life in noninstitutional settings or improvements in the transfer of funds that make it harder to victimize clients and rip off their support money in tenement hallways. But the verdict on these changes will have to be rendered on a case by case basis. Virtually none of the new systems will operate automatically to fulfill their own program promises, so each case must be scrutinized in terms of follow-up support through budget allocations, providing facilities, resources and personnel, warding off exploiters and rip-off artists, and reporting and evaluating actual results. Unfortunately, deinstitutionalization in fact and the apologies that surround it make these support activities harder, not easier, by making the target population far less visible, by dint of dispersal of the target population, even to institutional officers.

Another important effect is the transformation of important activities from the public to the private sector. This does not mean that the state or the public fiscal system ceases to pay the bill for social control, only that the money is disbursed to private contractors rather than expended by public agencies. Once again, anarchist sentimentality eventuates in petit-bourgeois reality. Worst of all, the shift from public to private activity may make a complete sham of deinstitutionalization when emancipated inmates wind up in private residential arrangements that dupli-

cate institutions of incarceration. Witness recent nursing-home scandals, expo-
sures of youth treatment centers and the growth of "psychiatric ghettos" in aging
apartment hotels, all bankrolled by welfare departments.

A third effect is the transformation of staff in the social service cum custodial
control fields. The war against bureaucrats and guards has not in general resulted
in significant declines in staff or in the overall costs of staffing. However, the
forms of staff recruitment and maintenance have changed. Even more significantly, so have the social origins of workers in these fields. For good or ill, the
growth of the social control fields has provided ordinary citizenship status
through work to large numbers of recently oppressed people, especially members
of subordinate ethnic and racial groups and mobile working-class members. The
historical irony is that the task of controlling labor-force outcasts has provided
opportunities for labor-force participation. Employment in the control fields has
provided some benefits of status and secure income and the protections of civil
service, universalistic hiring, and, recently, unionization. In the transformation
of staff arrangements, those forms of participation are subject to contraction,
while opportunities expand for consultants on the high end and for transient and
volunteer workers on the low end. The implication is that jobs will now be
created for Masters of Business Administration, specialists in public administration, and kindred workers, with a corresponding regressive effect on the class,
racial, ethnic (and probably gender) dimensions of employment. The use of young
people and other novices in advocate and other functionary roles will also increase
the possibilities of manipulation of sentiments and the imposition of centralized
policies. Since workers in the control system are custodians, any processes that
disguise this fact from those workers themselves is obscurantist and promotes in-
visible tyranny. In this light, recent attention to the phenomenon of "burn-out"
among workers in social service fields justifies personnel policies which evict
workers from their positions just when they develop a veteran's experiential sense
of the realistic parameters of the job (Freudenberger, 1974). Young volunteers are
then really akin to migrant agricultural workers, available for super-exploitation
for reasons having more to do with the disciplining of the labor force rather than
the control of those excluded from it.

A final practical effect, one which overshadows all the good intentions of the
original theorists of deinstitutionalization, is to improve the chances of politicians, especially but not only at the state level, who can make a show of cutting
costs and increasing efficiency in a period of scarce money and taxpayer revolts.
As an added unearned increment, they can persent themselves as liberal Aquar-
ians into the bargain.

Although I have undertaken to discuss the effects of anarchist sentimentality in
short-term policy making, I would like to add a few general comments about the
possibilities of authentic anarchist approaches to institutions of social control,
since my remarks have been so uniformly critical. I have posed the fundamental
problem of custodial institutions as an outgrowth of the system of achieving

citizenship through labor force participation in modern societies. People who by one means or another are detached from the labor force and thereby lose any claim to ordinary citizenship become the targets for special systems of social control, either as inmates or as outpatients. The fundamental resolution to the problem of their treatment must be found in the conferral of citizenship, either in the form of access to the labor force (a very tall order) or in the form of breaking the tight interdependence between labor-force participation and citizenship (an even taller order, especially in these gloomy times). To put it another way, when communities exist in reality that are willing to include our targeted people on some basis acceptable to those targeted people, the problem of control will be "solved." This proposition is as general and visionary as anything in the history of anarchist thought. I claim for it at least the sociological virtue that it focuses on the arrangements negotiated by people rather than on fruitless arguments over their essential nature. It means, furthermore, that anarchist attention must be focused on the general issues of the construction of community and the construction of citizenship, rather than on the residual issue of comforting the wretched. Comforting the wretched is a worthy act, under any system of social arrangements. But it is not I think, particularly associated with anarchist processes, except in current sentimentality.

CONCLUSION

I have attempted to outline the role of a current form of sentimentality in providing a rhetorical apology for a social policy based on a fiscal crisis in ways of dealing with custodial targets. This policy, born out of the pressures on public officials, became much more popular and acceptable, especially among social problems specialists, when it was presented in the trappings of a crude kind of anarchism. This sentimental version of anarchism is grossly at odds with the tradition of systematic anarchist thought, but the popularity of the sentimental version obscured both the practical problems of deinstitutionalization and the theoretical difficulties that its adherents might have noticed otherwise. This case suggests the importance of attending to the effect of sentimentality in general in predisposing students and practitioners in the fields of social problems and social policy to uncritical acceptance of initiatives and programs that require a harder, clearer look.

REFERENCES

Beck, Bernard (1967), "Welfare as a Moral Category," *Social Problems* 14 (3):258–277 (Winter).
Chinoy, Ely (1965), *Automobile Workers and the American Dream*. Garden City, N.Y.: Doubleday.
Emerson, Robert M. (1969), *Judging Delinquents*. Chicago: Aldine.

Freudenberger, H. J. (1974), "Staff Burn-out," *Journal of Social Issues* 30:1974, Pp. 159–165.

Friedenberg, Edgar Z. (1967), *The Vanishing Adolescent*. Boston: Beacon.

Goffman, Erving (1962), *Asylums*. Chicago: Aldine.

Goodman, Paul (1960), *Growing Up Absurd*. New York: Random House.

Holt, John (1964), *How Children Fail*. New York: Dell.

Illich, Ivan (1971), *Deschooling Society*. New York: Harper and Row.

Kesey, Ken (1962), *One Flew Over the Cuckoo's Nest*. New York: Viking.

Marcuse, Herbert (1964), *One-Dimensional Man*. Boston: Beacon.

O'Connor, James R. (1973), *The Fiscal Crisis of the State*. New York: St. Martin's Press.

Piven, Frances Fox, and Richard A. Cloward (1972), *Regulating the Poor*. New York: Vintage.

Rothman, David J. (1971), *The Discovery of the Asylum*. Boston: Little, Brown.

Scull, Andrew (1977), *Decarceration*. Englewood Cliffs, N.J.: Prentice-Hall.

Szasz, Thomas S. (1965), *Law, Liberty and Psychiatry*. New York: Macmillan.

Wittner, Judith Ginsberg (1977), "Households of Strangers: Career Patterns of Foster Children and Other Wards of the State." Unpublished Ph.D. dissertation, Northwestern University.

SMALL WINNINGS:
BLUE COLLAR STUDENTS IN COLLEGE
AND AT WORK[1]

Eve Spangler, AMERICAN BAR FOUNDATION

It is an article of liberal faith that education is the most important mobility ladder in contemporary American society. In particular it has been facilely assumed that access to higher education opens up important mobility opportunities for the less advantaged. In her well-researched and carefully reasoned paper Eve Spangler calls both of these beliefs into serious question. She takes a systematic look at who goes to college, and what happens to them once they enroll. Her conclusion that, on the whole, social and economic inequality is maintained by the higher education experience is not likely to bring comfort to those policy makers who have been espousing education as a counter to ascribed inequality.

Since the time of Jefferson, the ideal of equality has been a part of the American political creed; it's primacy undisputed. Yet, there is little agreement about either its definition or its proper implementation. Generally, American society poses equality of opportunity as a value and a goal. Perhaps because the environment once seemed to offer limitless opportunity, equality of condition has not often been

Research in Social Problems and Public Policy—Vol. 1, 1979, pages 15–41
Copyright © 1979 by JAI Press, Inc.
All rights of reproduction in any form reserved.
ISBN 0-89232-068-0

addressed. Egalitarian reform efforts stress opportunity and ignore, if they do not actually deny, the desirability of equality of condition. Dwight Eisenhower's dictum that "in the economic race, every man should have an equal place at the starting line" (Albertson, 1963, p. xv) reflects the universal consensus, shared by conservatives and liberals, that minimal economic opportunity for all is a desirable goal.

The list of those entitled to equality of opportunity has grown consistently more generous over the course of American history. First, property ownership, then religion, then race, and more recently ethnicity and sex have been invalidated as categories by which anyone may be denied access to valued social goods. Yet, despite the ever-growing number of people entitled to "an equal place at the starting line" equality of opportunity remains an elusive goal.

Before the Industrial Revolution, land was the essential means of production—its possession therefore determined economic and social position. The relatively easy access to land characteristic of preindustrial America seemed to establish equal opportunity and to guarantee it for posterity. But the development of industrialism introduced the distinction between productive and consumer property. This made landholding a very much less important determinant of position, and undermined both the political and economic benefits thought to be associated with it. In this context, reformist theory discarded the idea of land redistribution (an idea which still animates reform efforts in nonindustrial societies) and came to depend more and more on the leveling potential attributed to schooling to guarantee equal opportunity. In fact, education is currently depicted, rightly or wrongly, as the crucial, indeed the only, means of breaking hereditary cycles of poverty and wealth.

The theory which makes education responsible for creating equality of opportunity rests on two assumptions: first, that citizens are capitalists increasing their productive capacity through education (and not merely powerless workers seeking employment); and, second, that schools, like the state itself, are an intrinsic part of the social contract—a neutral agency which is equally responsive to all segments of an industrial society. According to this vision, students are young people investing their efforts in self-improvement. Educators are experts whose services are available to them, and whose evaluations are binding upon privileged and underprivileged alike. Schools are thus said to fulfill several functions: to educate, to allow talented but needy students to secure credentials for economic advancement, to identify the most able among the oncoming generation of workers for the benefit of the larger community.

Discussion of the potential of schools to equalize opportunity currently focuses on higher education. College is presumed to provide those skills which will give access to the most desirable sectors of the labor market—with life-long advantages for both college educated individuals and for society. However, public optimism about the benefits of a college education rests on a series of interlocking, plausible, yet misleading assumptions about the extent and consequences of college attendance. The assumptions which, together, undergird public support for higher education can be stated as follows:

First, it is said that more people than ever before are going to college. Since the Second World War college enrollments have risen enormously. Authorities on higher education, like Martin Trow, maintain that nearly half of all the American college-age population is in college. "As recently as 1940," wrote Trow in 1961, "the total number of students enrolled in college comprised only 15 percent of the college age group.... By 1954, that proportion was up to 30 percent and by 1960 it was around 37½ percent.... If that rate of increase is maintained, and that is a conservative forecast, then by 1970 college enrollment will comprise about half of the college age group" (Trow, 1961, p. 151).[2]

Second, it is said students currently are being drawn into higher education from all sectors of society. Working-class children are going to college in increasing numbers. The rise in their college enrollments suggests not merely a growth, but a *democratization* of educational opportunity. Herman Miller, of the U.S. Bureau of the Census, concludes therefore that "College students are drawn from all segments of American life.... It is clear that our colleges are not rich boys' clubs. Large numbers of low income families are represented on the campuses" (Miller, 1964, p. 162).

Third, it is said that the American occupational structure changed to increase the demand for more educated workers at the same time that college enrollments were increasing. Indeed, the economy's need for highly educated labor is seen as the principal stimulant to increased college attendance. The technical and professional sectors of the labor force are growing most rapidly, thus providing a ready market for college graduates.

Between 1940 and 1950, the number of engineers in the country doubled; the number of research workers increased by 50 percent. Even more striking, between 1950 and 1960 the total labor force increased by only 8 percent; but the number of professional, technical and kindred workers grew by 68 percent—and these, of course, are the occupations that call for at least some part of a college education" (Trow, 1961, p. 154).

Finally, unprecedented opportunities for upward mobility are said to have been produced by the felicitious combination of more good jobs and more college graduates. "Room at the top" is said to be expanding in American society and to be increasingly available to the college-educated.

Unfortunately, however, all four crucial assumptions of this widely accepted model are vulnerable.

The increases in college enrollments have been overstated (Table 1). The projections which indicate that nearly half of the eligible age group will go to college are based on the enrollment statistics of eighteen- and nineteen-year-olds. These statistics are unreliable because they include a sizable number of high school students. Figures on the school enrollment of twenty- and twenty-one-year-olds provide a more reliable picture of sustained college attendance. These figures indicate that college enrollment encompasses slightly less than one third, nowhere near one half, of the college age population.[3]

Table 1 also indicates that the growth in college enrollments has not been continuous. Rather, college attendance has increased to its present level in two separate steps, between 1955 and 1960, and again between 1960 and 1965, most likely in response to specific short-term events of those two periods. It seems sensible to suppose that the post-Sputnik spate of funding for college study and the draft exemptions accorded students during the Vietnam war gave rise to dramatic increases in college enrollments. In any case, the idea that "social system needs" will inevitably generate slow but steady increases in college attendance is not supported.

If the growth of college enrollments has been overstated, so, too, has its democratic character. According to Table 2, children from the least educated strata in society are going to college in increasing numbers. However, more of them are enrolling than are graduating. Moreover, whatever the educational gains of the least privileged students may be, it is important to note that they are outstripped by the educational gains made by youngsters from more privileged homes. While virtually all children from advantaged homes go to college, only a portion of those from less privileged homes do so. The result is that the achievement gap between sons of the least educated and sons of the most educated parents has more than doubled. According to a study by David Riesman and Christopher Jencks (1962, pp. 95–96):

> In some ways the most startling fact to emerge from the historical data, and the one that fits least well with the conventional wisdom about higher education, is that until relatively recently even the sons of college-educated parents were not very likely to go to college.... This meant there was lots of room for growth in upper middle class enrollment rates. This

Table 1. Percent of the Population of a Given Age Enrolled in School, by School Type, October, 1950 to October, 1975.

Year School Type:	18–19 Years Old		20–21 Years Old		22–24 Years Old	
	All Enrollment	College Enrollment	All Enrollment	College Enrollment	All Enrollment	College Enrollment
1950	29.4	18.1			9.0	8.4*
1955	31.5	19.1			11.0	10.2*
1960	38.4	27.5	19.4	18.8	8.7	8.3
1965	50.4	36.3	30.2	28.9	17.9	17.3
1970	49.4	36.5	31.1	30.7	18.2	17.7
1975	46.9	36.7	31.2	30.2	16.2	15.7

*Prior to 1960, school enrollment is reported only for the age groups 18–19 years old, 20–24 years old.

Source: U.S. Department of Commerce, Bureau of the Census. *Current Population Reports.* Series P-20. 1950-#34; 1955-#66; 1960-#110; 1965, 1970-#260; 1975-#294.

Table 2.   Educational Mobility, from Father's Education to Son's Education for Sons of Different Ages.

Son's Age (in 1962)	Father's Education				
	Less than Eight Years (1)	Some High School (2)	High School Graduate (3)	Some College (4)	Attainment Gap (Col. 4–Col. 1) (5)
	Percent of Sons Obtaining at Least One Year of College Education				
25–34	14.2	27.8	44.1	78.0	63.8
35–44	14.4	22.0	44.9	70.4	56.0
45–54	11.0	19.1	33.2	62.3	51.3
55–64	8.4	15.0	31.4	47.3	39.8
	Percent of Sons Graduating from College				
25–34	6.5	16.6	24.9	51.7	45.2
35–44	5.8	11.0	27.5	53.1	46.3
45–54	5.4	8.9	14.5	37.7	32.2
55–64	5.4	8.5	16.9	27.6	22.2

Source: William Spady, 1967, 276.

growth was probably concentrated among the less academically competent middle-class students, almost all of whom now go to college. This rise of enrollment of middle-class mediocrities evidently offset the parallel rise among able lower-class students.

Thus, while conventional wisdom holds that a growth in college attendance must narrow the educational gap between classes, Riesman and Jencks's research concludes that precisely the opposite is true: college attendance is increasing and, simultaneously, the class gap in education is also increasing. The equally conventional assumption that the occupational structure is changing to accommodate the highly trained personnel produced by the educational system may be equally open to question.

The changes in the American occupational structure (as indicated in Table 3) reveal a genuinely expanded market for college-educated labor. The statistics, however, tend to be misleading, because the growth in the professional sector is more impressive in percentage terms than in absolute numbers. Even in the most recent census data, professional and technical workers still comprise less than 15 percent of the entire labor force. Thus, the enormous growth rate of the professional sector has relatively little impact on the national employment picture. The number of jobs at the top of the occupational system remains small.[4]

If the number of college graduates is expanding significantly and the growth in occupations requiring college-educated labor is not keeping pace, then it is reasonable to ask how increasing college education is affecting the labor force. What are college graduates doing with their education? The research of Folger and Nam suggests that, for the most part, they are competing for the same jobs once held by their parents without college degrees but now no longer accessible

Table 3. Major Occupational Groups of the United States Labor Force, 1900 to 1970.

	1900	1930	1940	1950	1960*	1970**
WHITE COLLAR	17.6	25.4	31.1	36.6	40.1	44.8
Professional & Technical	4.3	6.8	7.5	8.6	10.8	13.7
Managers, Officials & Proprietors	5.8	7.4	7.3	8.7	8.1	7.7
Clerical	3.0	8.9	9.6	12.3	14.1	16.7
Sales	4.5	6.3	6.7	7.0	7.1	6.7
MANUAL	35.8	39.6	39.8	41.1	37.7	33.9
Craftsmen	10.5	12.8	12.0	14.1	13.6	12.9
Operatives	12.8	15.8	18.4	20.4	18.9	16.6
Laborers	12.5	11.0	9.4	6.6	5.2	4.4
SERVICE	9.0	9.8	11.7	10.5	11.2	11.9
Private	5.4	4.1	4.7	2.6	2.7	1.4
Other	3.6	5.7	7.1	7.9	8.5	10.5
FARM	37.5	21.2	17.4	11.8	6.0	2.9
Owners, Managers	19.9	12.4	10.4	7.4	3.7	1.7
Laborers	17.6	8.8	7.0	4.4	2.3	1.2

*1960 Statistics do not total to 100% because no occupation was recorded for 3,453,000 unemployed persons, totaling 5% of the labor force.
**1970 Statistics do not total to 100% because no occupation was recorded for 5,180,000 unemployed persons, totaling 6.5% of the labor force.
Source: U.S. Department of Commerce, Bureau of the Census, *Historical Statistics of the United States from Colonial Times to 1970,* Part I, Series D, 102–232, p. 139.

to high school graduates. For example, at least junior college level technical certification is currently required to enter such occupations as hair dressing and television or refrigerator repairing. Between 1940 and 1960, Folger and Nam conclude that "Overall, about 85% of the rise in educational attainment may be attributed to increased educational levels within occupations, and only 15% to shifts in the occupational structure from occupations requiring less to occupations requiring more education" (Folger and Nam, 1964, p. 29).

Finally, the traditional liberal optimism that education is an investment that pays off in income and status proves to be equally unfounded. Income distribution (Table 4) and intergenerational occupational mobility rates (Table 5) turn out to be remarkably insensitive to educational upgrading. The traditional ties between the occupation of father and son remain intact (Table 6). This research in no way indicates that American society is becoming more egalitarian or that education in general is a key to economic opportunity.

In terms of higher education in particular, inequality is clearly increasing. Its principal source is the sharply limited number of working class children who go to college. The more flagrant forms of race and class tracking occur primarily in high schools (Cicourel and Kitsuse, 1963) and in junior colleges (Clark, 1960a, b).

Table 4. Family Income Distribution (%) by Income Quintiles for Selected Years, 1947–1975.

	1947	1950	1955	1960	1965	1970	1975
Wealthiest 20%	43.2	42.8	41.8	41.3	40.9	40.9	41.1
2nd Wealthiest 20%	23.1	23.4	23.4	24.0	23.9	23.8	24.1
Middle 20%	17.0	17.4	17.7	17.8	17.8	17.6	17.6
2nd Poorest 20%	11.8	11.9	12.2	12.2	12.2	12.2	11.8
Poorest 20%	5.0	4.5	4.8	4.8	5.2	5.4	5.4

Source: 1975: U.S. Department of Commerce, Bureau of the Census. *Statistical Abstracts of the United States,* 1976, Table 651, 406.

1947 to 1970: U.S. Department of Commerce, Bureau of the Census, *Historical Statistics of the United States from Colonial Times to 1970,* Part I, Series G 85–90, 293.

Four-year colleges and universities therefore can influence only preselected students from relatively privileged homes. Class differences in the rate of college attendance will be documented in greater detail below.

But the problem of inequality in higher education is not limited to class differences in access to college. It is compounded by four additional considerations: 1) the bulk of college enrollment is heavily concentrated in public institutions[5]; 2) public colleges and universities are financed by tax dollars; 3) the real

Table 5. Intergenerational Mobility, from Fathers' Occupation to Sons' First Occupation within Broad Occupational Groups, for Sons of Different Ages.

		Sons' First Occupation		
Occupation of Fathers with Sons Born:	Total	White Collar	Manual	Farm
1927–1936				
White Collar	100.0	57.6	40.6	1.8
Manual	100.0	24.7	71.6	3.7
Farm	100.0	15.1	45.6	39.3
1917–1926:				
White Collar	100.0	54.4	43.1	2.5
Manual	100.0	22.6	72.5	4.9
Farm	100.0	10.5	41.6	47.9
1907–1916:				
White Collar	100.0	54.5	42.6	2.9
Manual	100.0	25.5	69.2	5.3
Farm	100.0	9.1	36.1	54.8
1897–1906:				
White Collar	100.0	58.3	38.4	3.3
Manual	100.0	27.5	66.3	6.2
Farm	100.0	10.0	33.8	56.2

Source: Peter Blau and Otis Dudley Duncan, 1967, Table 3.8, p. 107.

Table 6.   Relationship of Fathers' Education to Sons' First Occupation;
Relationship of Respondent's Education to Respondent's First Occupation.

A. Correlation Between Fathers' Occupation and Sons' First Occupation, for Sons of Different Ages

Sons Born in Years	Correlation: Father's Occupation with Sons' First Occupation
1927–1936	.380
1917–1926	.377
1907–1916	.388
1897–1906	.384

B. Correlation Between Respondents' Education and Respondents' First Occupation, For Respondents of Different Ages

Respondents Born in Years	Correlation: Respondents' Education with Respondents' First Occupation
1927–1936	.574
1917–1926	.532
1907–1916	.554
1897–1906	.557

Source: Peter Blau and Otis Dudley Duncan, 1967, Table 5.3, p. 178.

burden of taxation falls more heavily upon the poor than upon the rich (Hansen and Weisbrod, 1969); and 4) the principal economic benefits of a college education are retained by private individuals in the form of added income. Together, these facts suggest that the poor not only are denied access to a valued social service, but that they underwrite this service for the affluent. In Christopher Jencks's terms: Auto workers pay taxes so that the sons of lawyers may go to college and to law school, one day to charge auto workers fat fees for legal services (1972, pp. 259–260). The net impact of college, like the rest of the educational system, therefore, is to increase and not to diminish inequality.

The persistence of inequality of income and job opportunities in the face of a greatly expanded educational establishment has led to a radical reformulation of theories about the functions of education in a democratic society. "Revisionists" assert that, in truth, schools are coercive, order-legitimating organizations devised by economic and political elites for their own advantage (Bowles and Gintis, 1976; Katz, 1971); that schooling serves to inculcate loyalty to the established order; thus, that schooling profits the beneficiaries, but not the victims of the status quo. Working class students seeking middle-class status through college degrees succeed only in setting off a competitive cycle. They pressure other working class students also to acquire more schooling. Employers, in turn, are permitted to inflate their minimum educational demands whether these are task-relevant or not. A variant of this theory holds that the apparently meritocratic competition found in schools masks the true nature of class conflict: the manipulation of educational requirements and credentials deflects attention from the fact that the upper strata of society derive their privileges not from wages but from the profits of property ownership (Collins, 1975).

It is the purpose of this study to examine the competing claims of liberal and radical theories of education with information about a recent generation of college students.

Although schools in general, and colleges in particular, do not generate equality of opportunity, they continue to enjoy a high degree of legitimacy. Families struggle to secure for their children the presumed benefits of a college education. Why? Is the public simply massively misinformed about the equalizing potential of a college degree? Is a college education prized for reasons apart from its economic value? Or, do a large enough number of working class individuals advance their economic and social position by going to college to obscure the fact that, in the aggregate, college is not an equalizing force?

These questions are not often posed. It simply has been assumed that when working class children become full-time university students, assimilation and upward mobility automatically follow. (It may be that, because students who are drawn into college from working class homes are often exceptionally able and ambitious, their outstanding qualities bolster the assumption that college attendance among the poor automatically generates upward mobility).

If this assumption about education's equalizing potential, at least for those who have access to it, is to be examined, two questions must be answered by both liberal and radical theorists. What happens to the working class student in the university? What happens to the working class graduate in the labor force? If working class college students do become assimilated into the middle class on campus and later at work, then liberal theory finds some support. Education would be shown to equalize opportunity in certain cases. The significant political agenda would then be to insure wider access to college education. If, on the other hand, working class students remain distinctively isolated on campus and later at work, then radical theory is sustained. Education would fail to promote working class students into the middle class in almost all instances. In this case a whole new political agenda would have to be developed. Working class families would need to recognize that college does little to improve their children's life chances. They might, then, be moved to consider collective rather than individual solutions to the problems of inequality.

Some light is shed on these questions by data now available from the American Council on Education (ACE), a research organization which conducts studies designed to meet the planning needs of American colleges and universities. In a ten-year longitudinal survey of the educational and career development of college students ACE studied a nationally representative sample of 16,674 individuals. Respondents in the ACE study were first-time, full-time college freshmen enrolling at four-year colleges and universities in the fall of 1961. They provided information about their educational and occupational goals and experiences at college entry (1961), four years after college entry (1965) and ten years after college entry (1971).

Although the ACE research was not originally designed to answer questions about working class social mobility it nevertheless indicates significant class differences in access to and graduation from college. Unequal access to higher education is graphically documented by a comparison of the social origins of the 1961 freshman class with those of the population at large (Table 7). White-collar families with incomes at or above the national median comprise approximately one fifth of the general population, but account for three fifths of all college students. Blue-collar families, especially those whose income falls below the national median, are correspondingly underrepresented on campus. They comprise approximately one third of the American population, but account for less than one tenth of the freshmen in college.

Not only do fewer children from working class homes enter college, but, of those who do go, fewer complete it. A consistent class difference in college graduation rates can be seen among men. Four years after entering college 70 percent of the men from affluent white-collar families have completed a bachelor's degree, while only 60 percent of men from low-income blue-collar families have done so.

A 10 percent difference in degree completion rates indicated by the ACE study might seem insignificant, even to offer comfort to liberals arguing that working class students can surmount disadvantaged backgrounds by going to college.

Table 7.   Percent Distribution of Social Classes, in the United States, Male Labor Force According to the 1960 Census, and among Fathers of the ACE 1961 Sample of College Freshmen.

	Social Classes in the Male Labor Force, 1960 Census Data	Social Classes in the College Freshman Class, 1961 ACE Data
White collar	34.8%	70.2%
median income or above	22.0	59.1
below median income	12.8	11.1
Blue collar	55.1	21.3
median income or above	24.7	13.3
below median income	30.4	8.0
Farm	10.1	8.5
median income or above	3.4	4.4
below median income	6.7	4.1

Source: United States Bureau of the Census. *U.S. Census of Population,* 1960. Subject Reports: Occupational Characteristics, Final Report PC(2)7-A. Table 25, pp. 232ff and American Council on Education 1961–1965–1971 Longitudinal Panel.

However, such a conclusion would be premature. For several reasons significant to the present study, but not to the ACE's original research purpose, the ACE findings understate class differences in college graduation rates.

First, as is inevitable in longitudinal studies, the ACE survey lost a great many respondents over the ten year period of the research. The final set of respondents represent only 28 percent of the originally targeted group. Individuals who dropped out of the study tended to come from low-status homes and to be academically unpromising students (Astin and Panos, 1969). As a result the final ACE report overestimates academic success, understates academic failure and underestimates true middle class/working class differences in achievement.

Furthermore, the ACE survey was conducted between 1961 and 1971, a period in which the labor market for college graduates was booming: the direct cost of a college education was relatively low, and, on the average, the returns in wages and occupational status were high (Freeman, 1976). The Vietnam war added still another dimension to college attendance. Draft deferments for male college students increased the incentive for young men to stay in college. These two historical features—the favorable labor market and the war—kept many marginal blue-collar students in school. The dropout statistics from this period are therefore unusually low and unlikely to be applicable to any other ten-year period in American history.

Another factor, in this case methodological, tends to limit the conclusions to be drawn from the ACE data. A traditional sociological definition of class background is used in this study: all white collar workers are considered to be middle class, and only blue collar workers are classified as working class. Such a definition tends to underestimate possible working class/middle class differences because a great deal of lower-level white collar labor, particularly in clerical and retail jobs, is so proletarianized that people employed in these fields could be termed working class (Bravermann, 1974; Hamilton, 1972; Vanneman, 1977). A nontraditional definition of class which included clerical and sales families in the working class would indicate a far larger disparity between the college performance of working class and middle class students. The more traditional definition was selected precisely to avoid stacking the deck in such a way as to maximize class differences in college success.

Because of the above factors, the 10 percent differential in college graduation between the middle class and the working class students takes on a more problematic cast. The advantage of being middle class in college is not merely, as liberals tend to argue, an easily correctable holdover from a less egalitarian age (Bowles, 1971). Instead, the evidence strongly suggests that working class students continue to suffer a disadvantage in college graduation even at that moment in history most propitious to their advancement. Schooling is no guarantee of "an equal place at the starting line." On the contrary, the 10 percent class differential in college graduation in the mid-1960s reveals a resilient core of class inequality. With increasing economic pressures, the fault lines of class inequality can only become more visible.

PERSISTENT CLASS DIFFERENCES IN COLLEGE AND VOCATIONAL EXPERIENCES

How are these persistent differences in college achievement between white collar and blue collar college students to be explained? Can they be attributed to deficiencies in talent or ambition among working class students, or to the effects of social discrimination and exclusion by more privileged students? How much weight must be given to factors like the quality of the educational institution, the availability of professors to students, to the pressure of financial need?[6] What interaction of these factors produces the existing pattern of class differences in the rate of college graduation?

Nothing in the ACE data indicates a deficiency of talent or ambition in working class students. The correlations of class background with ability (r = .04) and with educational aspirations (r = .06) are small. In these respects the students from working class families resemble their college classmates more than they resemble people from their old neighborhood. Since the data do not indicate that working class students are less able or ambitious than middle class students, the limitations on their success must have other sources.

One such source lies in the pattern of college social life. Students of all sorts tend to be about equally interested in dating and extracurricular activities, irrespective of their educational plans or the type of college they attend (the correlation of peer integration with educational aspirations is .06; with school prestige it is .07).[7] Yet, the ACE data indicate that working class students participate less than middle class students in the informal social life of the campus. (The correlation between social class and peer integration is .13). Nearly half of the students from low-income working class families (48 percent) show low peer integration as compared to one quarter of the students from affluent middle class families (26 percent). Conversely, 19 percent of the less privileged students and 37 percent of the more privileged students enjoyed high peer integration. Put differently, middle class students generally have more dates, play more ball, join more clubs and know more people on campus than working class students. These class differences in peer integration may help explain the class differences in the rate of college graduation.

The ACE research turns out to be inconclusive about the relationship between school quality and academic performance.[8] It recognizes that middle-class students generally attend more prestigious colleges than working class students (the correlation between social class and college quality/prestige is .14). But it also shows that the advantages conferred by prestigious colleges are somewhat undermined by a pattern of limited student-professor interaction. Students at prestigious schools have less contact with professors than at more modest schools (r = −.18). Professors everywhere concentrate most on their brightest students, irrespective of socioeconomic standing (the correlation of teacher contact with ability is .11; with socioeconomic standing of students it is −.03). Able working class students at "local" colleges therefore may actually have an advantage in the correlation between student performance and teacher contact. In any case, class differences in degree completion cannot be attributed to faculty availability because there is no evidence that faculty discriminate against blue collar students.

Finally, financial pressure might seem to explain both the restricted campus life of working class students and the greater likelihood of their leaving college without a degree. Indeed, working class students are somewhat more likely to hold jobs during the school year than middle class students. (The correlation between social class and employment is −.11). Such employment, in turn, inhibits peer integration (r = −.22). However, a significant number of blue-collar students do not work during the school year—fully half of all the male respondents in the ACE survey did not. Working class students meet the financial demands of college through scholarship aid (more readily available during the period of the ACE study than at present), student loans and summer employment. Those who hold jobs during the semester are as often at the low end of the ability or interest spectrum as they are at the low end of the income scale.

Moreover, even when middle class students hold jobs during the term, they maintain a more active campus life than similarly employed working class students. (The zero-order correlation between socioeconomic background and peer integration is .13; the partial correlation between these two variables controlling for work history is .12). Thus, although economic pressures undoubtedly caused some working class students to seek employment and to defer college graduation, financial need alone does not explain why working class students have low peer integration or why they have a poorer college completion record than middle-class students.

None of these factors, taken individually, can explain class differences in college completion rates. But considered together, they provide a substantial basis for predicting which students will complete college, and for explaining why working class students and middle-class students differ in this achievement. Table 8 summarizes the contribution of each element—class background, ability, ambition, peer integration, school quality, teacher availability and financial need—to degree completion when the presence of all the other elements is statistically taken into account.[9]

In demonstrating that ability is the single most important determinant of success in college, the ACE data supports liberal theory: the university appears to be a meritocratic proving ground, *at least for those who have access to it.*

High educational aspirations also increase the likelihood of college graduation, although not as strongly as ability. This, too, is consistent with liberal theory which holds that achievements are largely a product of individual ability and

Table 8.   Undergraduate Degree Completion Four Years After College Entry,
Discriminant Function Analysis.

Dependent Variable: Degree Completion: 0 = no; 1 = yes; N = 10,906

Predictors:	Standardized Discriminant Function Coefficients
Social Class	.10797
Ability	.79341
Educational Aspirations	.15864
School Quality/Prestige	−.14802
Teacher Contact	.18644
Work History	−.10075
Peer Integration	.61258

Canonical R: .38279 (p ≤ .001)

Actual Group	Predicted Group			
	No Degree	B.A. or B.S.	Total	(n)
No Degree	67.2	32.8	100%	2,467
B.A. or B.S.	29.7	70.3	100%	8,437

69.6% of known cases correctly classified.

Source: American Council on Education 1961–1965–1971 Longitudinal Panel.

motivation. Since *in this study* neither ability nor motivation depends upon socioeconomic status, their effects on academic achievement cannot be dismissed as mere proxies for a hidden relationship between social standing and college graduation.

The ACE data also suggest that the impressive record of prestige schools in graduating most of their entrants is more a function of the socioeconomic advantages and ability of the entrants than of the school itself. Discounting these advantages "at the starting line," school prestige alone does not enhance the probability of graduation. Prestigious schools (as defined in this study) are highly competitive and large in size. Both of these features tend to inhibit academic achievement.

But, if school prestige does not promote academic success, contact with professors does. Students who had frequent contact with faculty, irrespective of the prestige of the college, were more likely to complete college within four years than students who had little contact with the faculty. Here, the ACE study is consistent with studies of academic achievement among elementary and secondary school students (e.g., Coleman et al., 1966) which show that teachers are more important to achievement than any other school characteristic.

Thus far the factors which are clearly associated with college completion— ability, motivation, teacher contact—are not strongly related to socioeconomic background. They therefore cannot explain why working class men do not complete college as often as middle class men do.

Among the respondents in the ACE study peer integration is the factor which is

most clearly related both to socioeconomic background and to college graduation. It is second only to ability as a factor explaining who graduates from college
and who drops out. Even social class origins and school year employment do not
appear to have much impact on college graduation apart from their influence on
peer integration. Further, the most significant difference between middle-class
and working class students is the extent of their integration into the informal
social life of the campus. And, these differences between blue collar and white
collar students occur despite the substantial similarities between them in ability
and aspirations. Such findings support radical theories which hold that the educational system is a tool for maintaining and legitimating privilege. They undercut
the liberal theory that education equalizes opportunity.

The crucial role collegiate social life plays in promoting college completion is
surprising since professors often depict collegiate social culture as a hindrance to
serious study. At best, extracurricular activities are perceived as a necessary form
of relaxation; at worst, as an anti-intellectual drain on student energy. Yet the
data suggest that this is a misleading analysis, for participation in collegiate
activities clearly contributes to the likelihood of college graduation, while exclusion from peer culture makes dropping out more likely.

The ACE data themselves do not explain why peer integration is so necessary
to college performance. However, ethnographic studies done from the students'
perspective concur in finding that social factors are as important as individual
ability and motivation in determining academic achievements (Becker et al.,
1961; Becker et al., 1968; Bucher and Stelling, 1977; Olesen and Whittaker,
1968).

Student behavior is group behavior—never entirely explicable in individual
terms. Definitions of appropriate student behavior are collectively formulated
and commonly held. It is only within a framework provided by such definitions
that individual talent and commitment can manifest themselves. From the students' point of view, faculty expectations appear open-ended and mysterious. No
student can ever be sure when an assignment is completed that the professor's
demands have been correctly interpreted and applied. Even able and ambitious
students face multiple uncertainties: materials of unknown complexity, faculty
expectations which are clearer to the professors voicing them than to the students
hearing them, limitations of time and energy. Students need integration into peer
culture because it is through interaction with their peers that individuals learn
how to organize their own efforts (Becker et al., 1961). At a bare minimum, peer
culture provides nuts and bolts survival information: which courses are "guts,"
which teachers will extend deadlines on required work, where on campus you
can find a quiet place to study, who has files of old exam questions.

But peer culture also has the subtler function of creating a climate for student
self-definition. As students see it (Becker et al., 1968), the college years are
important for accomplishing the transition from childhood to adulthood. Although this transition requires some academic learning, its main object is to

demonstrate social as distinct from intellectual maturity. Being socially mature, in turn, means keeping academic work in its "proper perspective" and devoting substantial time and energy to being a "well-rounded person." Extracurricular activities are significant in this enterprise because, through them, students demonstrate their competence in the management of time and responsibility. An active social life validates one's claim to well-roundedness. Thus, peer integration provides the student not only with practical information, but also with an arena for self-definition which is more attractive than the world of work available to high school graduates.

In sum: the ACE survey shows, as common sense would predict, that both talent and motivation are required for successful performance in college. Somewhat less obviously, the study also shows that blue collar and white collar students are highly similar in these characteristics. Most unexpectedly, the ACE data demonstrate that peer integration is almost as important as talent in a successful college career. Further, it is primarily in peer integration that working class students differ from middle class students. The political and educational implications of these facts have, thus far, received scant attention.

Moreover, the exclusion of working class students from informal sociability may have lasting, adverse effects on their achievements, even beyond college. Social isolation on the campus can handicap working class students in developing networks of personal contacts useful for later access to business jobs.

The literature on job-seeking behavior argues that job satisfaction is often related to the job's source: positions obtained through the mediation of friends and family tend to be more desirable—better paid and more challenging—than positions obtained through impersonal channels (Granovetter, 1974). Both family connections and friendships established in college are useful for securing information about and referrals to attractive jobs. Working class graduates do not have family networks which can provide crucial information on professional jobs. College friendships with the middle class students who enjoy such connections, therefore, would be particularly valuable to working class graduates struggling to convert educational credentials into occupational success. But the ACE data on college experiences suggest that working class students often are unable to establish such connections. It follows, therefore, that working class college graduates are likely to be less successful than their middle class counterparts at least partly because of their lack of peer integration in college.

The information on career development provided by the later portion of the ACE survey can be used to explore the job-seeking techniques and work patterns of college graduates. Such explorations must be limited, however, by the tentative nature of the data: many of the potentially most successful respondents were still in graduate or professional training when the last wave of the survey was conducted; among those who were employed, early career information may not adequately reflect lifetime patterns of income and work satisfaction; and, information on a single job search (explaining how the respondent acquired his or her 1971 job) cannot reflect all the advantages conferred by friendship networks.

With all of these limitations in mind, the study nevertheless indicates class differences in postcollege career development. Business and education, the two largest sources of employment for college graduates, constitute a fork in the road: white collar graduates find most of their jobs in the business world; blue collar graduates largely head toward jobs in education. In 1971, among B.A.s, 25 percent of the men from low income blue collar homes were employed as teachers, as opposed to only 12 percent of the men from affluent white collar families. Among M.A.s, 49 percent of the men from low income working class backgrounds but only 31 percent of the more advantaged men were so employed. Conversely, among the poorer working class men with B.A.s, only 24 percent were following business careers, as opposed to 36 percent of comparably educated affluent middle class men. Among M.A.s, 14 percent of the low income blue collar men are in business, compared to 26 percent of the affluent white collar men. These divergent career paths strongly suggest substantial class differences in lifetime income, even among men with the same educational credentials.

These trends are reflected in Table 9 which compares the net impact of social origins, collegiate peer integration, educational achievements and job searching strategies on teaching and business careers.[10]

According to Table 9, businessmen seldom held more than a bachelor's degree. Their jobs were secured primarily through the mediation of friends and family. They had extensive friendship networks in college. They were unlikely to have applied directly for their current positions or to have profited from a professor's reference.

Public school teachers differ from businessmen in virtually all of these features. Their teaching positions were secured either by direct application or through the mediation of a professor, not through the mediation of friends and family. Generally, men who became teachers had a restricted social life in college. Many had done graduate work beyond a bachelor's degree.

The ACE material shows the continuing impact of both social origins and collegiate peer integration on early career development, even among college graduates. Exclusion from campus social life appears to be highly consequential beyond college graduation into the early career years.

This study therefore supports the conclusion that in the mid-1960s working class students received only modest benefits from a college education. By going to college they could get ahead of their blue collar age mates, but they were unlikely to catch up with their white collar classmates either in occupational status or income. Even their relatively modest toehold in the middle class was dependent upon the availability of jobs in the public service sector. If this pattern holds in an era of declining school enrollments and general retrenchment in

Table 9.   Careers in Public School Teaching and Business, Predicted from Socioeconomic Background, Collegiate Peer Integration, Educational Attainment and Job-Searching Strategies.

Dependent Variables: Public School Teaching: 0 = no; 1 = yes; N = 10,886
Business Employment: 0 = no; 1 = yes; N = 10,886

Predictors:	Standardized Discriminant Function Coefficients	
	Teachers	Business
Social Class	−.26594	.14061
Collegiate Peer Integration	−.11610	.31147
Educational Attainment	.06116	−.69005
Job Searching Techniques		
Referrals by Friends, Family	−.24654	.46679
Direct Application	.62020	−.29699
Referral By Professor	.69077	−.19359
Canonical R:	.24605 (p ≤ .001)	.25386 (p ≤ .001)

Actual Group		Predicted Group		
	Not Teaching	Teaching	Total	(N)
Not Teaching	60.6	39.4	100%	7,861
Teaching	37.4	62.6	100%	3,025

61.2% of known cases correctly classified

Actual Group		Predicted Group		
	Not Business	Business	Total	(N)
Not Business	63.7	36.3	100%	9,082
Business	38.0	62.0	100%	1,804

63.4% of known cases correctly classified.

Source: American Council on Education 1961–1965–1971 Longitudinal Panel.

public spending, then the vocational destiny of working class graduates looks murky indeed.

A college education in these circumstances provides only a precarious and circumscribed entree into the middle class. These results can be explained by distinguishing between cultural and structural assimilation (Gordon, 1964). Cultural assimilation refers to convergence between two groups in cultural matters—i.e., in matters of values, aspirations and attitudes. Structural assimilation (loosely defined) refers to the permanent inter-mixing of two populations on a behavioral level—i.e., in such matters as club membership, friendships and intermarriage. It is important to differentiate the two precisely because the one does not lead automatically to the other. This appears to be the case for working class students. They have the same cultural aspirations as middle class students. Their educational plans, for example, are indistinguishable. Yet, structural assimilation into the mainstream, business sector of the middle class often eludes them. And, the ACE survey suggests that this pattern of limited mobility could continue indefinitely. Indeed, the downturn in the economy for college graduates of the past decade (Freeman, 1976) implies that structural assimilation will become even more elusive for working class graduates, irrespective of their cultural conformity.

The following questions are also implicit in the distinction between structural and cultural assimilation: Under what conditions does structural assimilation follow cultural assimilation? At what point is structural assimilation likely to be blocked? One hypothesis (Gordon, 1975) suggests that structural assimilation occurs most readily when groups differ only in what sociologists call achieved characteristics. Achieved characteristics are those which individuals can change. Conversely, structural assimilation is most resisted when groups differ in as-cribed characteristics—those characteristics which are affixed at birth and cannot be changed. According to this theory, structural assimilation would occur more easily between groups which differ primarily in language (as seems to have occurred among American Catholics of different national origins) than between groups which differ in race (as is also borne out by the American experience).

Social scientists have generally described adult social class identity as an achieved rather than as an ascribed characteristic. In this society, socioeconomic standing is not presumed to be fixed at birth with nearly the same degree of finality as racial and sexual identity. Indeed, the possibility of upward mobility has been a major shibboleth of American life. Yet the ACE study suggests that, as a group, even those exceptionally able and ambitious working class youths who complete college achieve only limited structural assimilation into the middle class. Similarly, a more recent national survey of occupational mobility supports the ACE study in concluding that the prospects for social mobility are declining.

> The historical tendency toward upward mobility among U.S. men ... is neither uniform nor inevitable. The continuation of historical trends of occupational mobility is strictly limited by the depletion of occupation groups—service workers, laborers, farmers—which have earlier served as sources of recruitment into higher status occupations'' (Hauser and Featherman, 1973 p. 309).

It appears, therefore, that our society may be entering a period in which socio-economic origins increasingly take on the character of an ascriptive trait and in which the prospects for structural assimilation into the middle class are growing increasingly dim.

IMPLICATIONS AND CONCLUSIONS

American society has long proclaimed itself to be egalitarian, despite the man-ifest existence of great social and economic inequalities. The contradiction has been rationalized by the belief that egalitarianism can be defined not as equality of condition but as equality of opportunity, with education as the great equalizer. In this light, data showing that education is not an effective leveler leave sociologists, ordinary citizens and political activists who look for social justice through broadening opportunity equally stranded. Students of social stratification must revise their theories to account for the fact that education does not break down social barriers, but actually strengthens them. Working class families must recognize that the power structure which excluded their parents will not automatically include their children because they have earned a college degree. Political activists committed to egalitarianism must recognize that the comfortable program of attaining social equality by the relatively painless method of providing more higher education is inappropriate.

Numerous studies have now established that college attendance has become an increasingly middle class prerogative since World War II. The ACE material goes further in showing that even among college students each generation re-creates social and economic inequalities. Informal college life is pinpointed as a significant source of class stratification: the campus environment, supposedly blind to socioeconomic differences is, in fact, charged with class distinctions.

Because the ACE study is a survey, it does not capture those subtle face-to-face interactions which, when aggregated, harden into class divisions. However, an experimental study of stratification undertaken by Robert Leik and his associates (1975) suggests how stable patterns of inequality can sometimes be created. Leik found that in an open social system with unevenly distributed resources, almost all individuals quickly choose to interact with those persons who have the most resources. Highly attractive people with ample resources then select others like themselves as interaction partners and exclude less privileged actors from their exchange networks. This pattern of privileged persons choosing similar partners proceeds down the scale of resources until stable interaction groups emerge, each group composed of persons with similar resources. The boundaries of the groups remain relatively fixed and each group can be ranked among the others by the resources which its members typically command.

The analogy between this experimental research and campus social life is striking. When freshmen arrive on campus they find a relatively open social system without obvious race, class or sex etiquette dictating friendship choices. Nevertheless, students sort themselves into relatively stable friendship groups in a short space of time (Wallace, 1966). Both the ACE survey and Leik's experiments suggest that these friendship groups might well consist of persons of relatively similar socioeconomic standing.

However, since campuses are not laboratories, the transposition of Leik's work from experiment to observation raises questions about which resources actually have the strongest gravitational pull: brains, money, social charm, sexual attractiveness. Can intellectual skills attract friends as reliably as social graces? Do working class students have few friends (as the ACE data would imply) or only few *middle-class* friends (as Leik's work suggests)? Which characteristics are consciously used by students in selecting their friends?

Even if all these questions were answered, and the implications of the ACE survey and Leik's experiments accepted, the behavior of individuals committed to the educational system would probably not change significantly. Parents, students, professors and administrators all have available only a limited number of options in a society whose basic features are beyond their control.

Blue-collar families might well understand that only relatively modest economic gains are to be derived from college attendance and still struggle to send their children to college. The alternative is to send their children directly to work from high school while neighboring working class families are sending their children to college. To be willing to take such a chance would be to assume that union protection and company benefits are as valuable in the long run as a college degree. But the general inflation of educational demands for even the most modest of jobs makes this an implausible assumption. If a college degree does not guarantee that its recipient will get ahead it may at least keep him from falling further behind others in his generation. For blue collar families, then, even the best personal investments open to them are likely to yield low returns.

Students are equally unlikely to change their social life in the interest of egalitarianism. They probably do not perceive that their informal college life reflects considerable sensitivity to the social origins of their classmates. Further, informal socializing is prized by students precisely because it is the one area of the university in which they can run their own lives. Therefore, administrative attempts to insure that appropriate numbers of working class students be included in extracurricular activities would certainly be resisted as an invasion of privacy.

Nor can administrators be expected to force upon students a standard of equity which the general community has not endorsed. Administrators might be expected to censure clubs and teams which flagrantly discriminate against racial minorities. But social class is not similarly suspect and administrators are unlikely to intervene in the relative isolation of working class students.

College teachers are the only members in this system who, out of the logic of their own work, might genuinely like to see many more able (blue collar) students and fewer (white collar) mediocrities in their classes. Professors, however, have little power. In recent years, declining enrollments and retrenchments in hiring and general funding for universities have made teaching careers increasingly precarious. Despite their individual preferences, teachers as a group are unlikely to call for policies which would alienate public support or lead to further declines in student enrollments.

For similar reasons university administrators are loath to discourage potential clients and supporters from projecting their hopes, however unrealistic, onto higher education. Chancellors and deans have very little control over the economic realities of higher education: they can alter neither the fact that the taxes which support their institutions are often paid by families who do not send their children to college nor the fact that students are drawn largely from privileged families who use tax-supported public services for their own advancement. Even concerted recruitment efforts among low-income families do not change the middle-class character of enrollments very much. All that administrators and professors can do to equalize this situation and yet remain consistent with their own interests is to call for greatly expanded public support for education. But were large numbers of blue-collar students to be drawn to the campus, the problem of converting educational credentials into good jobs would only be exacerbated by the increased competition for the most desirable positions.

This study contends that the major participants in the university, individually and together, lack the power to make hgher education substantially more egalitarian. It is also argued, however, that working class families nevertheless will seek upward mobility for their children through higher education.

There are good reasons for this phenomenon: schools are the most egalitarian of this society's inegalitarian institutions. It is probable that schools do prefer and better serve upper class and white students than working class and nonwhite students. But, it is also true that schools are more hospitable to working class youngsters than any other institution.

Secondly, college education fits neatly into our social ethic that individuals should be judged on merit; that they should be allowed to rise as far as their talents will take them. The ranking of individual life chances based on schooling is considered both more humane and more legitimate than a ranking based on birth. If grades in school have to be fairly earned, then, by extension, they signify a student's just deserts.

Finally, publically supported education seems to provide benefits to the poor without taking from the rich. So long as schooling is available to the poor and appears to compensate them for their lack of family resources, privileged parents can continue to bestow upon their children all the advantages of inherited position.

These factors, added to the unquestioned belief in the equalizing potential of schooling, help account for the growth seen in educational services. But the ACE data and other studies suggest that pursuing equality of opportunity through education is a mirage: educational services have grown and become less egalitarian at the same time. Many more students are going to college—yet, college enrollment is becoming less democratic. The existence of publicly funded services therefore is no guarantee of redress for heriditary inequalities or of redistribution of opportunity.

If education, the last best hope for achieving equality of opportunity, fails in its goal, perhaps the goal itself is not really viable. Any program whose benefits go principally to the least powerful members of society and whose costs are borne by the most powerful is unlikely to be implemented. Equality of opportunity conflicts directly with another, more commanding value: the desire to protect and to pass on advantages to one's children. Few privileged families would be willing to see their own children consistently passed over in favor of more promising youngsters from "the wrong side of the tracks," whatever this program's long-run benefits to society may be. Most people in privileged positions would like more security for their sons and daughters, not more competition. Equality of opportunity, were it to be realized, would increase the number of effective competitors upper middle class children face. That is precisely why it is resisted or, rather, subverted.

It has been the purpose of this essay to show that equality of opportunity is a goal not attainable for the working class simply by broadening their access to higher education. Both longitudinal and experimental studies have been examined to show that although more students go to college, the result is not more democracy but less—because of social, academic and, frankly, unknown reasons.

This study has also examined some of the reasons for our social belief in the efficacy of education as a democratic and egalitarian influence. It is important to note the extreme durability of this belief in the face of evidence to the contrary. Nearly ten years have passed since the ACE study was completed. The intervening years have seen declining economic returns to the educated but no corresponding decline in commitment to schooling on the part of the general public. The durability of this belief attests to the truth of the maxim that debunking ideas is not enough, that ideas are not replaced by criticism but only by other ideas— equally powerful and cohesive. American political discourse which has concentrated on individualism, meritocracy and capitalism is poor in alternative idea systems. It is not within the scope of this essay to provide or examine such alternative systems, but it is possible to hazard a guess that if the working class gives up on equality of opportunity as a viable goal, it may look to equality of condition as it has in other societies.

FOOTNOTES

1. The research reported in this article is based on data provided by the American Council on Education through its Division of Educational Statistics. I am also indebted to a number of people whose substantive suggestions, quantitative expertise and editorial skills have greatly improved the quality of the present paper. They are: Marsha Gordon, Michael Lewis, Cherry Michelman, Charles Page, Ronald M. Pipkin, Gerald M. Platt, Dee Weber-Burdin and James D. Wright. Needless to say, the errors in the paper are entirely my own.

2. Readers will notice that the works of Martin Trow and other exponents of the liberal theory of education are now nearly twenty years old. Use of such relatively old sources raises the question whether a straw man is being created only to be knocked down. This is not the case. All the authors whose earlier works are cited still maintain that education equalizes opportunity. The data used to refute this position have also been available to sociologists for some time. The persistence of a theory in the face of inconvenient facts can best be understood in Thomas Kuhn's terms (1962): disconfirming information by itself is not sufficient to dislodge an existing theoretical framework. Theories cannot be displaced by piecemeal critiques, only by other, equally cohesive theories. Thus, in all disciplines, transitional periods exist in which old paradigms, inadequate for explaining newly discovered facts, are patched and amended before they are replaced by new paradigms which offer

better explanations for the new observations. Such a transitional phase seems to be characteristic of sociology of education at present.

3. A further critique of Trow's enrollment figures is provided by Richard Hamilton and James Wright (1975, p. 304). They point out that in computing the percentage of the population enrolled in college, Trow used the total number of students as his numerator, and the total number of all persons aged eighteen to twenty-one as his denominator. To the extent that college students do not fall into this age bracket, Trow's statistics are misleading.

4. A recent commentary concludes that the prospects for mobility are far from bright in the coming decades. Hauser et al. (1975a, p. 597) write: "Despite the many social changes in the United States in the last two decades, it is a more favorable occupational structure, and only that, which has sustained or improved the mobility opportunities of American men. In light of this finding, it may be discomforting to ponder the social consequences of economic, technological or demographic impediments to further upgrading of the occupational structure."

5. The ratio of public to private enrollment in post-secondary education was 1.4:1.0 in 1960; 1.9:1.0 in 1965; 2.7:1.0 in 1970; 3.1:1.0 in 1974; and is projected at 3.8:1.0 in 1984 (U.S. Department of Commerce; Bureau of the Census; Statistical Abstracts of the United States, 1976, Table 233, p. 141).

6. The variables used in Tables 7–9 are defined as follows: *Social Class:* for purposes of the present study a combination of two factors, income and occupational prestige, is used to describe class origins. Six social classes are identified: low income farm, affluent farm, low income blue collar, affluent blue collar, low income white collar, affluent white collar. The national median income of 1969 was used as the dividing line between low income and affluent groups. Respondents were assigned a class value based on their report of father's occupation and family income. The use of categorical concepts (in place of a single factor occupational prestige score) to describe class structure follows the recent work of Hamilton (1972); Vanneman (1977); Wright and Perrone (1977).

School Type: Colleges and universities were ranked on the Scale of Institutional Differentiation (SID) developed by Talcott Parsons and Gerald M. Platt in their work on the American professoriat. For a more detailed description of scale construction, see Parsons and Platt (1969). The SID measures the degree to which a university or college conform to a highly differentiated full university model. A fully differentiated university is characterized by a large faculty, most of whom hold doctorates, a sizable graduate student enrollment, a large number of research journals in the library, a low student-faculty ratio, high per pupil expenditures and substantial income from faculty research grants. The least differentiated colleges are small in size, have relatively high student-faculty ratios, few Ph.D.s on the faculty, little income from research grants, no graduate students and few journals. Roughly speaking, then, the SID is a measure of institutional prestige. The most prestigious schools are assigned the highest numbers and the least prestigious the lowest.

Educational Aspiration: In 1961 respondents indicated their educational plans among four options: 1) none or associate degree; 2) bachelor's degree; 3) master's degree; 4) doctorate or professional degree.

Teacher Contact: Faculty contact is measured on a three-point scale (not enough, just about right, too much) in reply to the question: "All in all, in terms of your own needs, how much personal contact with the faculty did you receive in the past year?"

Work History: Work history, with values of 0 to 4, measures the number of undergraduate years for which the respondent reports that he or she worked during the academic year and while enrolled as a full-time student.

Peer Integration: Peer integration is a simple additive scale based on the number of undergraduate years the student lived on campus (dormitory, fraternity/sorority), the number of voluntary associations joined (e.g., intramural teams, fraternities), the number of people on campus the respondent regarded as close friends, and the number of dates the respondent had in an average period of time. The number of undergraduate years the respondent lived with parents was deducted from the total score.

Degree Completion, 1965: Educational attainment as reported in 1965 was coded into two categories: 0—had not completed a bachelor's degree; 1—had completed a bachelor's degree or more.

Educational Attainment, 1971: Educational attainment as reported in 1971 was coded into four categories: 1) less than a bachelor's degree; 2) bachelor's degree; 3) master's degree; 4) doctorate or professional degree.

Job Search Methods: A series of dummy variables was constructed from the question: "How did you obtain your current position?" Individuals were assigned scores (0 = no; 1 = yes) for the following options: referral by friends or relatives, direct application, referral by professor, teacher.

Occupational Attainment: Two dummy variables were constructed from the data on 1971 occupations. Respondents were coded as being teachers or business persons (in both cases, 0 = no; 1 = yes).

7. Although ability and peer integration appear to be correlated ($r = .13$), this relationship is an artifact, produced by the operational definitions of both variables. Ability is measured by grades. Peer integration is influenced by items such as club and team membership which require students to be in good standing—i.e., to have relatively high grades. In this way a correlation between ability and peer integration is produced which is not sensitive to the ways in which academically marginal students find friends on campus.

8. Again, the equation of ability with grades obscures an important relationship. Ordinarily, we would expect to find that school quality/prestige is highly related to ability. However, the observed correlation in this data is only .01. This low correlation occurs because the distribution of grades ($\frac{2}{3}$ Bs; $\frac{1}{6}$ each of As and Cs; a smattering of Ds and Fs) is approximately the same at every shool. Thus an individual's grades reflect his or her standing at one particular school, rather than in the national ability spectrum.

9. Table 8 is derived from a discriminant function analysis in which degree completion four years after college entry (0 = no; 1 = yes) is used as the (dummy) dependent variable. Discriminant function analysis is a statistical technique which provides information analogous to regression analysis (a prediction equation, standardized and unstandardized "regression" coefficients) for nominal level or dummy dependent variables. The standardized discriminant function coefficients in Table 8 can be interpreted in the same way as the standardized regression coefficients in a multiple regression table.

10. Table 9 is based on two discriminant function analyses using careers in business and public school teaching as dummy-dependent variables.

REFERENCES

Albertson, Dean, ed. (1963), *Eisenhower as President*. New York: Hill and Wang.

Aronowitz, Stanley (1973), *False Promises*. New York: McGraw-Hill.

Astin, Alexander (1965), *Who Goes Where to College?* Chicago: Science Research Associates.

_____ and Robert Panos (1969), *The Educational and Vocational Development of College Students*. Washington, D.C.: American Council on Education.

Becker, Howard et al. (1961), *Boys in White*. Chicago: University of Chicago Press.

_____ (1968), *Making the Grade*. New York: Wiley.

Berger, Peter L., and Thomas Luckmann (1966), *The Social Construction of Reality*. New York: Doubleday.

Blau, Peter M., and Otis Dudley Duncan (1967), *The American Occupational Structure*. New York: Wiley.

Bowles, Sam (1971), "Unequal Education and the Reproduction of the Social Division of Labor," *Review of Radical Political Economics* 3(Fall).

————, and Herbert Gintis (1976), *Schooling in Capitalist America*. New York: Basic Books.

Bravermann, Harry (1974), *Labor and Monopoly Capital: The Degradation of Work in the Twentieth Century*. New York: Monthly Review Press.

Bucher, Rue, and Joan Stelling (1977), *Becoming Professional*. Beverly Hills: Sage.

Cicourel, Aaron, and John M. Kitsuse (1963), *The Educational Decision Makers*. Indianapolis: Bobbs-Merrill.

Clark, Burton (1960a), *The Open Door College*. New York: McGraw-Hill.

———— (1960b), "The Colling Out Function of Higher Education," *American Journal of Sociology* 65 (May) 6:569–576.

———— (1962), *Educating the Expert Society*. San Francisco: Chandler.

Coleman, James et al. (1966), *Equality of Educational Opportunity*. Washington, D.C.: U.S. Office of Education.

Collins, Randall (1971), "Functional and Conflict Theories of Educational Stratification," *American Sociological Review* 36(December)6:1002–1019.

———— (1974), "Where are Educational Requirements for Employment Highest? *Sociology of Education* 47(4):419–442.

———— (1975), *Conflict Sociology*. New York: Academic Press.

Ellis, Robert A., and W. Clayton Lane (1967) "Social Mobility and Social Isolation: A Test of Sorokin's Dissociative Hypothesis," *American Sociological Review* 32(April)237–253.

Folger, John K., and Charles B. Nam (1964), "Trends in Education in Relation to the Occupational Structure," *Sociology of Education* 38(Fall)1:19–33.

Freeman, Richard B. (1976), *The Over-Educated American*. New York: Academic Press.

Furniss, Norman, and Timothy Tilton (1977), *The Case for the Welfare State*. Bloomington: Indiana University Press.

Gordon, Milton M. (1964), *Assimilation in American Life*. New York: Oxford University Press.

———— (1975), "Toward a General Theory of Racial and Ethnic Group Relations," in Nathan Glazer and Daniel P. Moynihan (eds.), *Ethnicity: Theories and Experience*. Cambridge, Mass.: Harvard University Press.

Granovetter, Mark S. (1974), *Getting a Job*. Cambridge, Mass.: Harvard University Press.

Hamilton, Richard (1972) *Class and Politics in the United States*. New York: Wiley.

————, and James Wright (1975) "From College to Factory Work: Backgrounds, Outlooks and Politics of College Educated Manual Workers in the United States," *Zeitschrift für Soziologie* 4(October):335–349.

Hansen, W. Lee, and Burton A. Weisbrod (1969), *Benefits, Costs and Finance of Public Higher Education*. Chicago: Markham.

Hauser, Robert M. et al. (1975a), "Structural Changes in Occupational Mobility Among Men in the United States," *American Sociological Review* 40(October)5:585–598.

Hauser, Robert M. et al. (1975b), "Temporal Change in Occupational Mobility: Evidence for Men in the United States," *American Sociological Review* 40(June)3:279–297.

————, and David L. Featherman (1973), "Trends of Occupational Mibility of U.S. Men, 1962–1970," *American Sociological Review* 38(June)3:302–310.

Jencks, Christopher et al. (1972), *Inequality: A Reassessment of the Effect of Family and Schooling in America*. New York: Basic Books.

Karabel, Jerome, and A.H. Halsey (1977), *Power and Ideology in Education*. London: Oxford University Press.

Katz, Michael (1971), *Class, Bureaucracy and the Schools*. New York: Praeger.

Kuhn, Thomas (1962), *The Structure of Scientific Revolutions* Chicago: University of Chicago Press.

Leik, Robert K. et al. (1975), "The Emergence and Change of Stratification in Social Exchange Systems," *Social Science Research* 4:17–40.

Miller, Herman (1964), *Rich Man, Poor Man*. New York: Thomas Y. Crowell.

Mills, C. Wright (1951), *White Collar*. New York: Oxford University Press.

Parsons, Talcott, and Gerald M. Platt (1969), Research Proposal Submitted to the National Science Foundation for "The Academic Profession."

Riesman, David; Joseph Gusfield; and Zelda Gamson (1970), *Academic Values and Mass Education*. New York: Doubleday.

_____, and Christopher Jencks (1962), *The Academic Revolution* (2nd ed.). New York: Doubleday.

Olesen, Virginia, and Elvi W. Whittaker (1968) *The Silent Dialogue*. San Francisco: Jossey-Bass.

Spady, William (1967), "Educations Mobility and Access: Growth and Paradoxes," *American Journal of Sociology* 73(November)3:273–286.

Tawney, R.H. (1961), *Equality* (4th ed.). New York: Capricorn.

Trow, Martin (1961), "The Second Transformation of American Secondary Education," *International Journal of Comparative Sociology* 2(September)2:144–166.

_____ (1962), "The Democratization of Higher Education in America," *European Journal of Sociology* 3(2):231–262.

_____ (1972), "The Expansion of Transformation of Higher Education," *International Review of Education:* 61–82.

Vanneman, Reeve (1977), "The Occupational Composition of American Classes; Results from Cluster Analysis," *American Journal of Sociology* 82(January)4:783–807.

Wallace, Walter L. (1966), *Student Culture*. Chicago: Aldine.

Wright, Erik Olin, and Luca Perrone (1977) "Marxist Class Categories and Income Inequality," *American Sociological Review* 42(February)1:32–55.

CONTROLLING OURSELVES: DEVIANT BEHAVIOR IN SOCIAL SCIENCE RESEARCH

Myron Glazer, SMITH COLLEGE

with the assistance of Magdalene Dufresne

In an ironic turn of events some social science research has itself become recognized as constituting a social problem. Since such research often exposes those studied to a variety of personal risks there is an increasing awareness, among social scientists, of the fact that scholarship in their disciplines can be socially as well as intellectually problematic. In the following paper Myron Glazer uses a deviance framework to good effect in analyzing what is socially problematic about social research. Not content with analysis alone, Glazer also risks proposing actions which might be taken to deal with deviance in the research process. Both his analysis and his proposals will no doubt spark considerable debate among social scientists.

The Committee was concerned that the term "informed consent" was open to a wide range of interpretation and potential abuse as documented to the Committee during the course of its extensive series of hearings on the

Research in Social Problems and Public Policy—Vol. 1, 1979, pages 43–64

"Quality of Health Care–Human Experimentation." Accordingly, the Committee defined *"informed consent"* to mean the consent of a person so situated as to be able to exercise free power of choice without the intervention of any element of force, fraud, deceit, duress, or other form of constraining or coercion, and set forth certain basic elements for informed consent in all but exceptional cases, defined as aforesaid in the bill.

The Committee was so impressed by the testimony regarding potential abuse of *"informed consent"* that the Committee amended that provision in S. 2072 which addressed itself to informed consent, to require written evidence of informed consent.

The written evidence of informed consent, in great measure, modeled upon the NIH guidelines, required the following basic elements:

1. A fair explanation of the procedures to be followed, including an identification of any which are experimental;

2. A description of any attendant discomforts and risks reasonably to be expected;

3. A fair explanation of the likely results should the experimental procedure fail;

4. A description of any benefits reasonably to be expected;

5. A disclosure of any appropriate alternative procedures that might be advantageous for the subject;

6. An offer to answer any inquiries concerning the procedures; and

7. An instruction that the subject is free to either decline entrance into a project or to withdraw his consent and to discontinue participation in the project or activity at any time without prejudicing his future care.

In addition, the agreement entered into by the subject shall include no exculpatory language through which the subject is made to waive, or to appear to waive, any of his legal rights, or to release the institution or its agents from liability for negligence.

National Research Service Award
Act of 1974 P. 3657

In the light of recently passed federal legislation governing social science research, a new debate has been generated among social scientists concerning the appropriate amount and type of regulation of research. Contributors to this dialogue include well-known social scientists whose research is located in the field distant from these shores as well as in laboratories in major university settings. Irrespective of the location and type of investigation, some of these researchers reject the intrusion of federal legislation into the research relationship. They maintain that it is too complex and fragile to be governed by the rulings of insensitive bureaucrats. Stanley Milgram, for example, argues that the best person to ask about possible harm accruing from participation in research is the subject himself. Where this has been done, Milgram reports, the majority of subjects have agreed that the research is beneficial (Milgram, 1977). Any inconvenience is more than outweighed by the benefit of the research findings. Murray Wax takes on federal regulation in a frontal assault (Wax, 1977a, 1977b). He rejects the model of the research relationship implied by Federal regulations in which an all-powerful researcher is presumed to control the very destiny of the vulnerable subject. Fieldwork, argues Wax, is far more complex. The researcher seldom has a monopoly on power and indeed is often a vulnerable and an ignorant traveler in other people's territory. Occasionally not even knowing the language and often untutored in the ways of the local population, the researcher, whether working in a far-off island or among urban poor in his own city, is often dependent on the guidance and good will of others for his very survival.[1]

Wax is not content to rest his case on this one argument alone. How can researchers be required to explain precisely what they're about, he asks, when they themselves are often unaware of the precise focus of their study? Wax ultimately comes down to his most telling point. Unlike some notorious cases conducted in medical research, social science research often accrues to either the advantage of the people being studied or to scientific knowledge in general. Wax throws down the gauntlet to potential critics by asserting that these advocates are required to show evidence of harm.

In the early part of his paper, Wax cites three cases which he considers to be "prototypical of the ethical problems generated by research activities" for members of this generation. Among this select group he includes "Springdale," "Tearooms," and Project Camelot (Vidich and Bensman, 1968; Humphreys, 1975; Horowitz, 1967). He writes:

> Yet, so far as is apparent, the body of federal regulations noted above were imposed and instituted in disregard of the rich and complex professional discussions of these troublesome cases (Wax, 1977, p. 332).

What does a careful analysis of these controversial cases reveal? In this paper I argue that the three cases provide telling evidence that abuses exist in all aspects of the research relationship. Serious and as yet unresolved questions of research sponsorship, informed consent, and reciprocity for acceptance of the researcher into a community have been raised as a result of the three studies. In no instance were any of these issues dealt with in a satisfactory manner. Indeed, each case documented the inability and unwillingness of social scientists to control their own members. The new regulations are an outgrowth, at least in part, of our own dereliction of duty.

An analysis of the three cases finds, moreover, that researchers often benefit directly even after their studies become the object of public debate. Those who complete research reports, despite their methods of data collection, reap the rewards. This lesson is not lost on neophyte researchers and raises serious issues about the direction of professional socialization.

A careful reading of some of the major methodological statements available in the literature indicates that the issue of informed consent has been present for a very long time but seldom sufficiently underscored by the writers themselves. William Whyte's study, *Street Corner Society,* begun during the late 1930s, has long been a classic among American social scientists (Whyte, 1955). Those of us who read it in graduate or undergraduate school admired Whyte's substantial contribution and his ability to overcome the challenges inherent in doing research in an Italian slum community. We seldom looked seriously at the ethical issues involved in the various kinds of deceptions utilized to win the confidence of local people and to gather the information which he desired. In another example, Melville Dalton, author of *Men Who Manage,* stated that he manipulated secretaries to obtain confidential corporate files. (Hammond, 1964). In an unusually honest statement, anthropologist Gerald Hyman related in detail how he used a family that had befriended him in order to observe a Potlatch ceremony (Glazer, 1972, pp. 88–95).

These few examples, which can be readily expanded, provide evidence that manipulation and deception have been an integral part of each stage of the research project. In some, it occurs during the early aspects when the field worker is attempting to gain acceptance by self-consciously promising potential respondents that they will receive far more than the researcher knows is possible. In other situations researchers have not even informed those under study that they are serving as subjects in a research project. The Laud Humphreys case, which we will be discussing below, is one of the best-known examples. Ethical issues and the use of deception can also occur after acceptance is gained and data are collected. In writing the report the researcher can break agreements with those studied and present them in a way that can cause pain and upset social relationships. We will see this clearly demonstrated in the discussion of Springdale.

Examples of problematic research relationships should be borne in mind as we analyze the three major cases suggested by Wax. An examination of these cases and others can help us evaluate federal legislation by focusing on the points of tension which exist in social research.

What other material in our own literature can we draw upon which may help us understand and correct abuses wherever they may exist? Since researchers have been accused of deviation from the norms standard in the profession, it appears appropriate to draw upon the literature in deviance in attempting to evaluate the claims and counterclaims. Where deviance seems to have occurred, some of the insights from this field may also enable us to understand the pressures which generate this behavior and mediate toward its continuance.

Merton's classic statement on social structure and anomie provides a useful starting point (Merton, 1957, Ch. 4). As all sociology majors know, Merton maintains that one form of deviance occurs when individuals are cut off from using legitimate means by which to achieve their goals. As a result, they "innovate'' or substitute other less legitimate means. Merton asserts that this type of behavior most clearly characterizes those lower down on the socioeconomic scale. His reasoning is simple. In a society in which material goals are stressed, and where cultural definitions emphasize the possibility and desirability of achievement, the use of legitimate means is likely to become defined as far less significant. A reading of the daily newspaper reveals that well-placed individuals, whether in government, industry or the professions, are not immune from engaging in such deviant behavior. The Watergate affair involved this country's most powerful and respectable individuals who had access to legitimate means to achieve their goals. To understand their behavior a slight modification of Merton may be useful. Deviance from adherence to legitimate means may occur when the use of such means limits (*Note:* limits not precludes) ability to achieve goals.

CASE I—TEAROOM TRADE

The Laud Humphreys case provides an appropriate example of this tendency. Humphreys had previously been both a working journalist and clergyman. In his career change he enrolled as a graduate student at Washington University in St. Louis, where he worked under the supervision of well-known sociologists. His very position there mediated toward a doctoral study which would result in a contribution to the field. This study, conducted in the mid-1960s, focused on those engaged in impersonal oral sex in park restrooms. These encounters were conducted in secret and every effort was made by those involved to camouflage their involvement. Through meetings in public toilets, Humphreys was able to make contact with a dozen of these men. They willingly agreed to participate in his research and to answer questions about their sexual outlets. As Humphreys later indicated, he could have pursued the study with willing informants. He wanted, however, a less biased sample. Humphreys decided to innovate by disguising his identity. Posing as a watch queen, he carefully placed himself in the position to observe interactions of oral sex in the public restrooms.

Later he made the momentous decision to copy down the men's license numbers, to trace their addresses, and to actually visit them in their homes. Accepting him as a researcher engaged in a health survey, they provided him with an abundance of information about their marital lives and the nature of their relationships to job, family, and spouse. They were even open in their discussion of their sexual activities in the marriage relationship although only a small percentage revealed anything about their tearoom visits.

When Humphreys' activities became public, the funding agency, HEW, demanded an investigation into whether the rights of respondents had been abused. In the subsequent investigation Humphreys and his supporters in the Sociology Department were able to convince the University against taking any action against Humphreys and his newly awarded Ph.D. Despite serious accusations that Humphreys had acted in an unethical manner, his defenders rejected the label of deviant for their protégé. They argued that while Humphreys had innovated in his research methods, his actions were defensible according to the values of the scientific community. They made no explicit statement that their numbers included one who had actually urged Humphreys to pursue his research strategy and others who knew of this decision and promised support. Humphreys' research was ultimately given a major stamp of legitimacy when his book won the C. Wright Mills award of the Society for the Study of Social Problems.

The controversy over Laud Humphreys' research might have ended there had the Vietnam war not intervened. As a faculty member active in a demonstration opposing the invasion of Cambodia, Humphreys led protesters off the university campus and through the doors of a local draft board. He stated that in an effort to minimize violence and cool tempers, he performed the symbolic act of tearing a picture of then President Richard M. Nixon. He was arrested, tried, and convicted of destroying government property.

His incarceration experience deeply affected Humphreys and provided a crucial epilogue to the debate. In the second edition to his book he recounts how two events led him to reconsider his position. The first mail he received during his imprisonment was a volume dealing with ethical and political issues in field research. Humphreys reports that he had abundant time to read and reflect upon the arguments in that volume. A second event proved to be even more telling. He was visited by state police investigators who questioned him about the activities one of his students. The student had been engaged in research in certain bars where "Albany's drug and prostitute traffic" was believed to be centered. The police investigators asked for the name of the student and for Humphreys' recollections of the student's precise work. In a moment of confrontation with the authorities, when he found himself under their control, Humphreys did not refuse to provide the student's name. Fortunately, he remembered little of the student's findings.

The confrontation and his reaction to the demand for information had a sobering effect. In his tearoom research, Humphreys had carefully guarded the names of his respondents. He had taken complex precautions to make sure the lists did not fall into the hands of the police or would-be blackmailers. Humphreys pronounced that he would go to jail rather than identify any of the men who had voluntarily or unwittingly served as his respondents. He was fully aware of the irreparable damage that could have come to these men had their activities been exposed.

The encounter in the Albany jail had undermined Humphreys' resolve. He could no longer maintain that the men's secret life was secure with him. He had to accept his own vulnerability and willingness to relent. The incident transformed his orientation toward any kind of disguised research.

Since then although I remain convinced that it is ethical to observe interaction in public places and to interview willing and informed respondents, I direct my students to inform research subjects before interviewing them. Were I to repeat the tearoom study, I would spend another year or so in cultivating and expanding the category of willing respondents into which the "intensive dozen" fall. Perhaps the sample of participants would not be as representative as in the original study, if I were limited to these methods, but the richness of data gained would certainly surpass those obtained from the interview schedules (Humphreys, 1975, p. 231).

An analysis of Humphreys' actions can only begin with Merton's deviance paradigm. A vital consideration goes beyond the motivation for such innovation and focuses on the opportunity to act it out. Here the work of Clifton D. Bryant provides an additional analytical structure to help explain Humphreys' actions. Focusing on deviance in organizational settings Bryant writes:

For ongoing commissionof deviant behavior, the individual must be able to acquire the necessary expertise, be strategically located to indulge in the behavior, be able to successfully disguise his actions and evade detection and sanction, encounter sympathetic and tolerant agents of social control, identify willing clients, victims, or co-perpetrators, and even if exposed, be able to enjoy a cushion for the resultant stigma and sanction. He must, in short, have an opportunity structure for deviant behavior, such as that often offered by his occupational specialty or the organizational work system in which he operates (Bryant, 1974, pp. 11–12).

The opportunity structure described by Bryant was available to Laud Humphreys. It enabled him to skirt the issues of informed consent. When challenged, his defenders characterized him as a researcher worthy of public praise. Their arguments and positions at the university provided the necessary "cushion" to ward off critics. Humphrey's turnabout occurred when his own experience supported his critics' charges that he could not protect his respondents. Without that firm belief he could no longer reject the arguments about the significance of informed consent.

CASE II—SPRINGDALE

An analysis of the Humphreys case shows the applicability of Merton's paradigm and Bryant's discussion of opportunity structures to ethical issues arising out of social science research. A second major controversial case concerns the work of another researcher who had access to legitimate means and innovated in a direct effort to achieve his own personal and professional goals. During the mid-50s Arthur Vidich was employed as a field director of a study of a community near Cornell University. The large-scale study involved the efforts of a number of Cornell professors and research assistants concerned with the nature of social relationships in a small town. To gain the cooperation of the residents, the research director and his staff had assured the townspeople that the study was an effort to highlight the positive factors which made Springdale a good community in which to live. Any anxiety about the impact of the research was further allayed when the researchers clearly stated that only statistical material would be published. No resident would be identified in the report.

To gather behind the scenes material, Vidich was assigned the task of living in Springdale, of meeting informally with many of its residents, and of observing them when they were not alert to the presence of a researcher. This exposure gave him valuable insights into the life of the community and led him to plan his own volume after he left the Cornell field staff. In association with Joseph Bensman, he wrote an analytical and critical account of the impact of the outer society on the life of the Springdalers. He emphasized the extent to which their presumably home-grown values were a direct reflection of the much maligned urban mass society. In addition, he cast away many of their illusions about the nature of community power. Influential individuals were discussed in detail. Despite the changing of names it was easy to identify the town's major figures.

The initial report came under heavy fire from local residents who read it and from administrators at Cornell itself. Vidich was charged with having broken the rules of the game by agreeing to the original definition of the research relationship and then by writing a report which markedly diverged from that understanding. Some of the townspeople were particularly irate because they felt that they had welcomed Vidich, had provided hospitality, and had been repaid by a document which held them up to public criticism. The university was concerned by the possible negative impact which the report could have on its relationship to nearby communities. The research director questioned Vidich's right to use study materials without his expressed approval. He also suggested that Vidich submit his report to the research team for its comments and modifications.

Vidich strongly rejected the various claims and charges. While he admitted being a party to the early agreement concerning the nature of the report, he felt it was appropriate for a researcher examining his field notes to write an analysis which accurately reflected the data. He admitted that it had been impossible to totally camouflage the identity of all the major figures. Yet he believed the cost to them was little in comparison to the overall contribution to knowledge which the study could make. He rejected the request of the research director, charging it derived from political rather than scholarly considerations. Any changes in the report made by the research team, he maintained, would be based upon Cornell's desire to smooth the feathers of disgruntled townspeople.

Vidich's major defense focused on the belief that the achievement of scholarly goals is far more important than other competing values. By going back on his agreements with the townspeople, he modified the agreed-upon means and instituted his own definition of appropriate behavior. He did not seek to have a new agreement but unilaterally decided that his definition could be defended in light of his ultimate aims. Unlike Humphreys, Vidich had to face the ire of many of his subjects. While he claims that some were sympathetic to this efforts, he is hard-pressed to provide evidence that they were vocal in their support of him. When he and his co-author Bensman were burned in effigy (probably a first in social science field research) there were no public counterdemonstrations mounted by his supporters. Unlike Humphreys, Vidich did not have the solid and public support of his superiors and co-workers. On the contrary, many of these people broke with him and charged him with questionable ethical behavior.

The opportunity structure which Humphreys so effectively used was severed in Vidich's case. Nonetheless, like Humphreys, Vidich survived the storm. He was outside of the geographical and influence sphere of the townspeople and of the Cornell researchers. Although condemned in personal correspondence and later in public communication, the publication of *Small Town and Mass Society* helped secure Vidich's name in the larger community of social scientists. His disapproving colleagues did not seek sanctions which might have undermined his reputation. During the time of the controversy there was no established forum to hear such complaints, and such sanctions were rare. It was only in the court of public opinion where Vidich might have been vulnerable. The ethical debate not only did not harm Vidich, it also provided an added luster when various communications were published in the second edition of his book (Vidich and Bensman, 1968). As with Humphreys, Vidich was able to reject the most scathing criticism by steadfastly maintaining his allegiance to the values of science. Since no formal inquiry was mounted, it was never necessary for him to defend his values and actions in a direct confrontation.

The Springdale case is another instance where a social scientist is severely criticized for his action and yet escapes with his publication in hand and his reputation intact. The critics in Springdale had to lick their wounds and no doubt promised that they would never cooperate with a researcher again. Yet they had little recourse beyond vocal protestations. Vidich rejected their charges and characterization of him as an ingrate. He did, years later, write that he had reciprocated by helping to educate many people to the realities of community power and thus force the political leaders to be more responsible. In addition, several young people taught by Vidich in Sunday school kept in contact with him over the years and used his book to evaluate their own lives. By providing these examples, he did implicitly admit that he recognized the legitimacy of some form of reciprocity in research relationships.[2]

CASE III—CAMELOT

Perhaps of all the controversial cases which generated discussion within the social science community during the past twenty years, the Camelot case is best known. The issues stemming from the case were debated in the highest councils of government, on college campuses both here and abroad, and within the media.

The international component generated far more concern than is normal in social science research. Unlike the Springdale situation, the funding for Project Camelot came not from a major university but rather from a branch of the United States Department of Defense. The $6 million provided by the Army is a massive amount of support, by social science standards.

The project focused on the nature of social discontent in developing countries and would have attempted to isolate the factors causing that discontent and how national governments might best deal with it. In addition, the lengthy proposal made explicit reference to the role which the United States military could play in alleviating conditions which lead to social upheaval.

The Project statement was distributed throughout the United States and the directors traveled from campus to campus eliciting comments and suggestions. In the process numerous consultants were added to the Project's staff. While some were concerned about the source of the funding and the direct references to United States military involvement in the solutions of social problems in developing nations, no one publicly condemned the Project or raised any ethical concerns in any professional forum.

Camelot ran into its major challenge when, in 1965, a part-time consultant attempted to seek the cooperation of Chilean social scientists in implementing the Project in that country. These men, together with the Norwegian social scientist, Johan Galtung, confronted the Camelot representative with the military implications of the Project. Initially, he denied the Project's sponsorship, claiming that well-known private foundations had provided the funds. This clumsy and foolish attempt was quickly exposed when the actual documents were produced with pointed reference to the clear-cut specification of military involvement.

The case was immediately brought to the attention of the left wing press in Chile which identified it with other U.S. efforts to intervene in internal affairs of Latin American countries. The American ambassador requested further information from the State Department, which brought the matter to the authorities in the Defense Department. As a result of the international notoriety, the Project was canceled. Its demise, however, did not end the controversy in the social science community. Lengthy debates were held in the corridors of convention halls, articles were written criticizing and defending the Project, and a full-length book was published, collecting the statements of a wide variety of contributors to the debate. Although the Project raised troubling issues about the significance of sponsorship in directing the nature of social science studies, no official professional forum was established by which these issues could be aired and recommendations forwarded to appropriate professional bodies. As in the Tearoom or Springdale cases, the Project participants did not directly confront their critics before any jury of their peers. While reputations were hurt and one of the major figures, Rex Hopper, died shortly afterwards, no definitive conclusions were drawn about the acceptability of the Project or the advisability of other social scientists pursuing similar paths. As in the past, each researcher had to decide what funding was appropriate and in what manner a funding agency could influence the nature of a project's development.

Had the formulators of Project Camelot been guilty of innovation in accepting military funds for a project focusing on social change in developing nations? Were these funds illegitimate, as the critics charged? Were they rather as acceptable as any other forms of sponsorship, as the defenders reiterated? These and other questions were given no definitive answer.

It became clear with the demise of the Project that the opportunity structure akin to the one used so effectively by Humphreys had quickly collapsed because of the decision of the Department of Defense. Camelot had found no local Chilean social scientists who would identify with its cause. American government authorities labeled the Project as too hot to handle. Unlike the Springdale controversy, the Camelot researchers were dependent on the good will of their sponsors. They had no independent source of funds and could not turn their back when their bureaucratic superiors rejected their explanations about the nature of Chilean hostility.[3]

IMPLICATIONS OF THE THREE STUDIES

A. The Attraction of "Innovations"

Where does a careful reading of these cases lead us as we evaluate the current federal regulations? As in other kinds of professional and white-collar work there are many pressures to modify or stretch the available means. The challenge in collecting research data often results in a series of decisions about appropriate paths to follow. In these decisions researchers are constantly aware of the rewards accruing to those who make significant research contributions. Merton's excellent statement on the importance of recognition in scientific research serves as a constant reminder about the social scientists' eagerness for professional rewards (Merton, 1957).

To date there has been little empirical research on the motivations of social scientists engaged in research. While we have been busy over the years studying the work lives of others, we have paid little attention to what drives us, the stresses and strains we feel, the pleasure and pains of our own efforts. Social scientists emphasize the ideal norms of contributing to knowledge by making major breakthroughs, It is not infrequent that a researcher's entire career may be secured by the publication of one well received work. Young researchers are aware of this at an early stage of their careers and often appear willing to stretch the appropriate means to achieve this goal.

That decision may be also influenced by the excitement factor attendant in many social science projects. Most of our research hours are spent in the humdrum of planning and executing a particular project. The excitement factor is heightened, however, and a sense of adventure is increased when the research experience takes on an element of intrigue.[4] Humphreys worked on the margin not only of social science ethics but also of the law itself. He was exposed to danger as he frequented the various "tearooms" and was almost arrested when accosted by plainclothes police. As a sympathizer of the underdog and a critic of the establishment, he would have faced the sort of danger that might have been highly attractive. Vidich was not threatened by arrest but did stand up to the authorities both in his own research team at Cornell University and in Springdale itself. He defined himself as one of a few people totally committed to advancing science despite the opposition and threats of a wide array of opponents. The Camelot researchers were raised up from their local college and university affiliations to the level of associates of those engaged in a well-financed and nationally based study. This effort necessitated travel beyond the borders of this country to the capital cities and backwater regions of many distant lands.

While each of the researchers was at a different stage of his career—Humphreys was a graduate student, Vidich a young professional, the Camelot researchers well along in their careers—almost all were part of the American university syndrome emphasizing the importance of continued productivity. All these researchers held appointments or were studying at major universities. Their teachers and role models were successful professionals. The norms of their departments clearly spelled out the significance of continued involvement in research and ongoing publication in major journals. Failure to produce in this way would lead to the loss of possible positions in prestigious educational establishments and exile to smaller schools where research funds were rare and teaching schedules made field work ever more difficult. In the 1960s in particular, the expanding market for well-trained social scientists made such an event unlikely for the successful researcher. But the successful researcher needed access to desired data and opportunity to publish that material in a way which would have the greatest impact on the field. The temptation to innovate in those circumstances is great.

Our evidence also indicates that this innovation can occur at various points in the research process. In the case of Project Camelot the innovation occurred in accepting military sponsorship and involvement in a comparative study of social change in developing nations. Knowledgeble Americans in the mid-1960s, such as those who were involved in Project Camelot, were aware of the suspicions generated by past United States military involvement in crushing rather than in understanding and supporting revolutionary movements.

The Humphreys case shows the temptation to innovate not in the stage of sponsorship but in the early design of the research. While Humphreys disguised himself in order to observe the men in the "tearooms," he and his adviser determined that the research would be far more substantive if he were able to gather background information on the men and their way of life. The research payoff seemed so profound that Humphreys and his adviser pursued a policy of deception seldom undertaken in social science history.

The Springdale case reveals that innovations can occur after issues of sponsorship and data collection have been handled to the apparent satisfaction of all concerned parties. Vidich reneged on early agreements made between the research directors and the community. He calculated successfully that his own study would be far more important if it were a critical account of Springdale's relationship to the rest of American society and if the field work data were utilized even if it meant certain of the actors could easily be identified.

B. The Risks of "Innovation"

In each of the studies the involved researchers knew that their decision to innovate incurred certain risks to respondents and researchers. In each instance the researchers seem to have concluded that the risks would be far outweighed by the potential gains. The Camelot researchers knew that their identification with military funding might impair their own reputations. They also knew that data gathered on the processes and people involved in social change could very well be misused by the American military. The researchers seem to have balanced out all these risks against the possible personal, scientific, and policy rewards. With $6 million to work with, they no doubt agreed among themselves that data gathered from six countries could be transformed into an impressive volume on social change. That effort would make a major contribution to social science literature and would enhance their own careers. In addition, some believed that the empirical and theoretical contribution could directly influence military and other government policy toward the problems of developing nations. Informed policy would be a fitting testament to the ability of social science to contribute to a more humane world.

In this case, and in the others as well, the major risks were not to the researchers but to those under scrutiny. The researchers put time, energy, and ultimately their professional reputations on the line. The subjects were called upon to risk the future of their nation and their very lives. The history of United States military intervention in Latin America was particularly well known. Subsequent events in Chile provide evidence for the view that data collected by projects like Camelot could very well have been used by the Chilean military, in cooperation with their American counterparts, to ferret out and "neutralize" actual or suspected opponents of the Junta which ultimately overthrew the constitutional Allende government. While this result probably would not have been desired by any of the social scientists involved, the research data could easily have contributed to such an outcome.

In the Humphreys research the risks to the unwitting participants were far more immediate. Each of them was engaged in an activity defined as deviant according to the norms of the larger society. Exposure of their activities would have resulted in devastating damage to their reputations, their familial relationships, their ability to hold jobs, and to their self-images as men able to carry on a variety of acceptable roles. These men, once they became part of Humphreys' sample, had their lives placed in his hands.

Unlike the Camelot and Humphreys cases, the risks incurred by Vidich's decision to write his account of Springdale were relatively minor. While many members of the community did not like the way they were portrayed, they did not stand to lose in any immediate way. They faced no repression from hostile authorities. They could not be blackmailed by readers of Vidich's report or even by those who might have gained access to his notes. The public definition of the nature of community relationships had been challenged and this may have provided some dislocation to their interactions.

REDUCING "INNOVATION"

The Committee's bill would authorize medical schools to seek Federal funding support and establish programs which would provide increased emphasis on the ethical, social, legal and moral implications of advances in biomedical research and technology with respect to the effects of such advances on individuals and society.

National Research Service Award
Act of 1974, p. 3659

How can the likelihood of innovation, risk-taking and potential harm be reduced? How can we constrict the opportunity structure which facilitates such a process? To answer effectively these queries and at the same time provide a supportive environment for legitimate social science research takes imagination and the courage to face ourselves and our work lives.

A. The Importance of Socialization

Undergraduates, particularly those who major in our disciplines, should be carefully exposed to the variety of ethical and political debates which serve as a constant background to social science research. These students should be forced to confront their own values. In this early stage teachers of undergraduates can publicly identify their belief in the union of intellectual and technical skills with sensitivity to the way in which these are applied to those people who serve as the sources of our research data. Professional associations should examine ways in which they might encourage college and university departments in these important tasks.

In my own teaching at Smith College I discuss such ethical issues in the introductory sociology course as well as in a course focusing on Ethical Issues in Social Organizations. In the introductory course the experiences of researchers are presented and the ethical dilemmas which they confronted are discussed in detail. This effort includes an analysis of research, for example, on prisoners, urban blacks, and a coal-mining community caught in a flood disaster (Gaylin, 1970; Liebow, 1967; Erikson, 1976). In another couse I spent the fall 1977 semester videotaping the presentations of twelve researchers who reported on the ethical as well as the substantive aspects of their investigations. This material includes research on Palestinians living on the West Bank, Caribbean women, violence in Ireland, and the Right-to-Life movement here in the United States. These tapes are now being edited for use here in a variety of courses as well as for presentation at a regional meeting of the ASA's Committee on the Teaching of Sociology. In the coming months I also hope to prepare a video film which focuses specifically on ethical issues in research. We believe that film can be an additional vehicle by which students can be introduced to the controversial and complex aspects of research ethics.

The graduate school has a vital part to play. As students enter an intensive period of learning, they can be informed that proper research behavior as provided in professional codes will be an integral part of their work lives. The conveying of this message cannot be left to informal contact or peer group socialization. Courses in research methods which include this material can be supplemented by colloquia emphasizing ethical problems facing the profession. Debates on significant ethical issues can be presented for students' consideration. As advanced graduate students prepare their own research statements, committees staffed by faculty and students should raise ethical as well as methodological and substantive questions. Available evidence indicates beginnings have been made in all of these areas.

A recent statement by Donald Warwick summarizes the current situation in graduate school training (Warwick, 1977). According to Warwick's reading of graduate school catalogs in the social sciences there are relatively few courses directly related to research ethics. Available offerings are found primarily in courses dealing with "methodology and professional practice." Issues raised by the Watergate scandal, exposure of corruption in other aspects of American life, and increased government regulation of research have led graduate departments to provide more emphasis on training in ethical issues. Despite these gains Warwick sees continued evidence for strong resistance against an emphasis upon training for ethical concerns. The reasons are varied. The strength of positivism and its emphasis on research findings emphasizes the importance of gathering data with far less concern to ethical issues involved in this process. Similarly the reward structure in the social science professions is clearly bent toward those who collect and publish empirical data. An emphasis upon ethical concerns can reduce a scholar's rate of productivity. On the more political plane, Warwick notes that a young researcher who openly challenged his senior colleagues' ethical stance would be in danger of having cut the ground out from underneath future professional advancement in that department.

Warwick completes his presentation by spelling out the questions confronted in a seminar jointly taught by him and Herbert Kelman at Harvard. These include the nature of "value-free social science," the impact of social science on the creation of norms concerning deviant behavior, social research and its contribution to power relations and, finally, issues of deception, informed consent, and privacy in social research.

All of these issues become increasingly pertinent during a period of job scarcity. The pressure for greater research productivity by graduate students involved in dissertation research or young faculty members striving for tenure can result in an actual lowering of ethical standards. Merton's anomie model and his emphasis upon the scarcity of means in innovative behavior may now become more applicable in the academic community. One way to reduce the possibility of deviant conduct is through ongoing processes of socialization which make all members acutely aware of appropriate behavior and the risks to ourselves and others of employing illegitimate means. Students would benefit from a careful analysis of the recent literature dealing with field work which often presents in honest detail accounts of specific encounters with respondents or informants. For example, both Jack Douglas and John Johnson have written with impressive and disturbing candor how they have manipulated and deceived respondents (Douglass, 1976; Johnson, 1975, 95–97). Johnson writes about "biographical reconstruction" whereby the researcher fabricates part of his personal history to ingratiate himself with those who have desired information. A crucial component in this effort is the knowledge that respondents will not be able to verify the researcher's statements. Students reading this account are instructed in the process and the rationale of blatant lying. The lesson is clear. The success of the research project justifies any and all procedures.

While the "reconstruction" of one's biography may help bridge the gap between the researcher and respondents as Johnson argues, is this appropriate behavior? Under what circumstances can a field worker mislead those with whom he desires to develop a relationship? Are such activities acceptable if one is to maintain the definition of being an ethical researcher. Aren't there more appropriate ways to win the trust of others? How can a graduate department indicate its own position regarding the use of such mechanisms? Can students be directed through a role-play situation in which the same goals can be achieved by using honest means? Programs to approach these and many other questions need to be developed. Federal funds should be sought to underwrite such efforts. Medical schools are not the only ones which have neglected their responsibilities and which need to re-think their curricula.

B. The Necissity of Social Control

> The Committee requires that the Commission develop and recommend to the Congress implementation of an appropriate range of sanctions (beyond those authorized by the legislation) to be applied if certified institu-

tional review boards fail to respond to Commission rules, regulations and procedures. The Committee also requires that the Commission develop and recommend to the Congress a mechanism to compensate individuals and their families for injuries or death that may have been directly caused by the participation of such individuals in the biomedical and behavioral research program under the Commissions' jurisdiction. Finally, with respect to the overall jurisdiction of the Commission, the Committee has asked that the Commission itself develop and recommend to the Congress within one year an appropriate mechanism to broaden the scope of its authority. It is the Committee's intent to work towards a day when all human subjects of biomedical or behavioral research programs, demonstrations and activities biomedical or behavioral research programs, demonstrations and activities are protected by the policies and procedures established by the Commission.

> *National Research Service Award*
> *Act of 1974, p. 3655.*

The emphasis upon socialization may only partially alleviate the problematic nature of social science ethics. The application of mechanisms of social control is also necessary. These controls will become increasingly derived from outside pressures. Federal legislation is an important impetus. The appointment of a national commission and institutional review boards will force us to respond to demands for more carefully conceived and executed studies. We can seek to resist or subvert such procedures by maintaining the right to do our thing. Such actions can be successful although costly. Or we can examine whether external regulation can facilitate more careful procedures on our part to protect those who provide us with the information necessary for our research reports.

Many of those we want to study have already indicated that they are suspicious of our efforts and may occasionally close the door and deny us access (Sagarin, 1973). We may be forced to learn to repect their decisions. This is easier to do when the research is focused on such groups as American deserters in Sweden who are suspicious of and reject the overtures of the researcher. It is harder to accept when the research subjects are defined by us as holding powerful positions. The challenge to study such a group confronted Bernard Barber and his associates in their investigation of medical researchers' using human subjects. After exploring the several paths used to gain cooperation with their study Barber makes an observation which should give us pause.

The research experience we have just reported, and, of course, the research experience of many of our sociologist colleagues, shows that we sociologists are not without considerable power to gain access to social situations where deep values and interests are involved. By our research in such situations, we may have the power to do considerable good or considerable harm. Such power, though probably less, is not unlike the power that the biomedical research profession has in its area, or that other professions have in theirs. In short, we have to be aware that we can no longer consider ourselves powerless or be unaware that, whatever our own view of ourselves, others may consider us powerful (Barber, 1973).

Barber's point is simple. We cannot define others as so powerful that they are not worthy of our active ethical consideration as we design our research. Such assumptions, which have held sway in our profession for many years, must now receive careful scrutiny. We should be able to defend our actions toward all research subjects.

C. The Reviewing Procedure

The Committee believes that the work of the Commission can best be carried out through institutional review boards, to be established wherever biomedical or behavioral research involving human subjects is undertaken. The Committee believes that the basic elements necessary for the proper functioning of institutional review boards should be standardized so that subjects in any given institution are protected to the same extent as subjects in any other institution.

National Research Service Award
Act of 1974, p. 3656

Experiences with peer review in other fields shows the difficulties in the system. In medicine, where there is a long history of questionable use of human subjects in research, Bernard Barber in one study and Bradford H. Gray in another both found marked deficiencies in the effectiveness of peer review studies. One of Barber's statements is particularly pertinent to the concerns of sociologists and bears repeating and careful consideration:

The major weakness in the system is the lack of key interest in and support of the review committees on the part of most working biomedical investigators. Research is their business; research is their mission and predominant interest, not applied ethics or active advocacy of patients' rights (Barber, 1976, p. 30).

Bradford Gray, who made a careful study of two research units, provides another observation that should give us pause:

A basic fact about institutional peer review committees is that many were established so that their institutions could remain eligible to receive research funds from the Public Health Service. When an organization adopts a procedure inorder to satisfy external requirements, one must be alert to the possibility that the procedure will be long on appearances and short on substance. Whether or not the procedure genuinely meets the official goal, it must *appear* to the outside audience to do so. Thus, we should carefully examine claims of successful self-regulation (Gray, 1974, p. 46).

The peer review procedure criticized by both Barber and Gray is founded on the basic assumption that professionals are in the best position to evaluate the work of their peers. Such an assumption has a long history and has been supported by the writings of many social scientists who define professionals as members of a unique community characterized by expertise, ethical standards, service orientation, and a reasonable but moderate financial return on their efforts.[5] Such a model has come under critical scrutiny in recent years. The traditional and most highly respected professions such as medicine and law have been reexamined and found to be far more self-serving than we had been led to believe. Law has been shown to have systematically excluded certain ethnic groups (Auerbach, 1976), while medicine, it is now documented, has a long and unenviable record of discriminating against women and minority groups (Walsh, 1977). Among these and other professions the granting of the exclusive license to practice has often provided for high rates of financial return and, at times, a protectionist cover for low levels of competence.

The social scientists ensconced in university settings have sought the professional respect and rewards accorded to their better-established peers. As a result they have attempted to project an idealized image of researchers requiring complete control over the nature and direction of their own investigations. Such a definition is challenged by the often expressed willingness to tailor-make research proposals according to the desires of private and government granting agencies. The time seems near at hand when the involvement of non-professionals may help us control our own orientations toward giving less than full consideration to ethical concerns in the designing of research proposals. Their participation can be less intrusive if it is part of a long-term process of ethical concern initiated in the undergraduate curriculum, solidified in graduate training, and integrated into the research strategies propounded by social scientists. In addition, review boards of whatever composition, will be effective only when they represent the views of the gatekeepers to professional success. We must ask continually the extent to which funding agencies, journal editors, and senior faculty and administrators are committed to higher standards of professional ethics. The issue is one not only of socialization and values but also of power.

WHERE WE STAND

In summary, a review of Camelot, Tearoom Trade, and Springdale highlights the tendencies toward innovation among researchers, the willingness to take risks, and the protections afforded by the opportunity structure to social scientists. Social scientists, when exposed and confronted, ultimately rely upon the argument of the primacy of their value system. That argument has consistently been abused in the past. Humphreys' change of heart should be heralded as a major instance of a researcher's coming to terms with the consequences of his own decisions. His experiences should be carefully studied by undergraduates, graduates, and professionals who too readily accept the propriety of deception in research.

An excerpt from a letter received from an old friend provides a fitting closing to this discussion. We had corresponded over many months about research ethics. He had consistently taken a hard line against arguments which defended deception in research relationships. He condemned me every time I seemed to waiver from this position. Finally, in a moment of pique, I wrote asking him about the kind of research he was involved in and how he handled his own ethical challenges:

> As for what I'm doing now, I'm writing up a book on a whole raft of empirical work and theoretical development that I've compiled over the last four years. Most of the empirical work was done under conditions of more or less serious unethical research, and I knew it to be such at the time, and I said, do it and be damned. . . . Yes, I sent students into hundreds of church services to behave like true believers when they were not—who knows what that did to the atmosphere and the experience of the real true believers? Yes, I wandered around an art gallery for a month with a hidden tape recorder in my jacket, and recorded and transcribed remarks made by people whose permission I didn't even ask, nor do I give them any credit or reciprocity in the use I make of what they said. Yes, I had students do biographies of living local artists for class assignments, and I'm using that data for my own work without paying or crediting either the students or the artists. Yes, I even had students take home tape recorders and secretly record their extended families at big dinner parties like Christmas and Thanksgiving, and I am using the transcripts of those tapes as "data" without anyone's permission except the student who spied on his folks for me. You see I've got a little demon of my own. He forces me to want to know how everyday occasions of social life are structured in North American culture, and he doesn't give a damn who gets hurt in the finding out. And I can't altogether resist his demands, but at least I can acknowledge that he puts me in a moral dilemma, and that as a result of his urgings I go around breaking eggs without even knowing whether there will be an omelet or not. That's bad enough, but I think it's even worse if most of us assume and assure others that he's a god to be praised, instead of a demon to be cursed and obeyed under protest.

There must be alternatives to either cursing or obeying that demon. As we want others to keep their demons under sway, so we must understand and control our own. Many of us will remember the exposure in mid-1977 of hidden CIA sponsorship of certain social science projects. Professor Richard Stephenson of Douglass College, Rutgers University, was shocked to learn that a study of Hungarian refugees which he and associates conducted after the 1956 uprising was sponsored by the Agency. Stephenson felt compromised and charged that the university and his profession had both been used by the CIA. He was more concerned, however, by the apparent access which the CIA had to his confidential data. He worried that that material might very well have been used to harm or embarrass those who had been active in the uprising and who had fled to this country. His words merit thoughtful deliberation by all concerned with the ethics of our own field and of others.

> Deliberate deception and misrepresentation are legally proscribed and morally condemned in most civilized human relationships. Where they are not, only overriding concern or urgent necessity may permit them, and provisions are made to give some assurance that such is the case. None of these conditions obtained in the situation described here and very likely in most others. One can only hope that Congressional investigations now under way will result in legislative or other controls that will give assurance that this does not happen again (*New York Times,* Op-Ed page, November 1, 1977).

Beyond being concerned with and condemning the uses perpetuated by others, we are responsible to monitor our own actions. As a result of federal legislation we now have another opportunity to carefully review our own procedures. The recently established Project on Ethical Problems of Fieldwork chaired by Joan Cassell and Murray L. Wax will be a significant effort toward this end. The result can be an active social science which continually strives to protect the rights of others while seeking achievement of its own legitimate goals.

FOOTNOTES

1. See the contrasting views presented by Pierre L. van den Berghe and Jerry Hyman in Myron Glazer (1972), pp. 88–96.
2. Personal correspondence with the author.
3. Much of the documentation on the Camelot Case can be found in Horowitz (1967).
4. Jack D. Douglas' discussion of "setting up" informants smacks of the challenge and excitement of outsmarting the reluctant person who has information but won't give it. It captures the essence of that sense of excitement and intrigue that is often part of social science research. See his *Investigative Social Research* (1976), especially pp. 174–175.
5. There is a rich literature on the professions, including Wilbert E. Moore (1970); Vollmer and Mills (1966); Carr-Saunders (1928); Hughes (1958); and Goode (1957), pp. 192–200.

REFERENCES

Auerbach, Jerold S. (1976), *Unequal Justice: Lawyers and Social Change in Modern America*. New York: Oxford University Press.

Barber, Bernard (1973), "Research on Research on Human Subjects: Problems of Access to a Powerful Profession," *Social Problems* 21, no. 1 (Summer):103–112.

Barber, Bernard. 1976. "The Ethics of Experimentation with Human Subjects," *Scientific American* 234, No. 2 (February):20, 25–31.

Berreman, Gerald D. (1962), *Behind Many Masks*. Ithaca, N.Y.: The Society for Applied Anthropology.

Bryant, Clifton D. (1974), *Deviant Behavior, Occupational and Organizational* Bases. Chicago: Rand McNally, pp. 11–12.

Carr-Saunders, A. M. (1928), *Professions: Their Organization and Place in Society*. Oxford: Clarendon Press.

Douglas, Jack D. (1976), *Investigative Social Research*. Beverly Hills, Calif.: Sage, pp. 174–175.

Erikson, Kai T. (1976), *Everything in Its Path*. New York: Simon and Schuster.

Gaylin, Willard (1970), *In the Service of Their Country: War Resisters in Prison*. New York: Viking Press.

Glazer, Myron (1972), *The Research Adventure*. New York: Random House, pp. 88–95.

Goode, William J. (1957), "Community Within a Community: The Professions," *American Sociological Review* 22 (April):192–200.

Gray, Bradford H. (1975), *Human Subjects of Medical Experimentation*. New York: John Wiley, p. 46.

Hammond, Phillip E., Ed. (1964), *Sociologists at Work*. New York: Basic Books, Pp. 50–95.

Horowitz, Irving Louis, ed. (1967), *The Rise and Fall of Project Camelot*. Cambridge, Mass.: MIT Press.

Hughes, Everett C. (1958), *Men and Their Work*. Glencoe, Ill.: Free Press.

Humphreys, Laud (1975), *Tearoom Trade*. Chicago: Aldine.

Johnson, John M. (1975), *Doing Field Research*. New York: Free Press, pp. 95–97.

Liebow, Elliot (1967), *Tally's Corner*. Boston: Little, Brown.

Merton, Robert J. (1957), *Social Theory and Social Structure*. Glencoe, Ill.: Free Press, Ch. 4.

Merton, Robert K. (1957), "Priorities in Scientific Discovery: A Chapter in the Sociology of Science," *American Sociological Review* 22, No. 6 (December):635–663.

Milgram, Stanley (1977), "Subject Reaction in Social Psychology: The Neglected Ethical Factor," Hastings Center *Report* (October):19–23.

Moore, Wilbert E. (1970), *The Professions: Roles and Rules*. New York: Russell Sage Foundation.

Sagaran, Edward (1973), "The Research Setting and the Right Not to Be Researched," *Social Problems* 21, No. 1 (Summer):53–64.

Stephenson, Richard (1977), "Victim of the CIA," *The New York Times,* November 1, Op. Ed. p. 37.

Vidich, Arthur, and Joseph Bensman (1968), *Small Town in Mass Society*. Princeton, N.J.: Princiton University Press.

Vollmer, Howard M., and Donald L. Mills, eds. (1966), *Professionalization*. Englewood Cliffs, N.J.: Prentice-Hall.

Walsh, Mary Roth (1977), *Doctors Wanted: No Women Need Apply*. New Haven: Yale University Press.

Warwick, Donald P. (1977), "Social Sciences and Ethics," The Hastings Center *Report* (December):8–10.

Wax, Murray L. (1977a), "Fieldworkers and Research Subjects: Who Needs Protection," Hastings Center *Report* (August):29–32.

Wax, Murray L. (1977b), "On Fieldwork and Those Exposed to Fieldwork: Federal Regulations, Moral Issues, Rights of Inquiry," *Human Organization* (Fall):321–328.

Whyte, William Foote (1955), *Street Corner Society*. Chicago: University of Chicago Press.

MODELS OF THE DECISION TO CONSERVE

Robert K. Leik, UNIVERSITY OF MINNESOTA

Anita Sue Kolman, UNIVERSITY OF MINNESOTA

For the past several years energy policy under conditions of increasing scarcity has been a major issue in the United States. After countless hours of debate in Congress a federal energy policy seems about to emerge, but its impact upon the quality of life in American society is difficult to predict. Conservation in the face of scarcity is obviously a reasonable policy option. Reasonable or not, however, it appears to be an option which too many Americans find difficult to accept. In the following paper Robert Leik and Anita Kolman offer a systematic analysis of the decision to conserve and in so doing point to the profound difficulties in making conservation an important cornerstone of a policy intended to cope with conditions of resource scarcity. Their reading of future behavior with regard to the conservation option is hopeful but hardly sanguine, to say the least.

Few topics have generated such a flurry of research activity as has the energy problems faced by the United States. Over a very few years, surveys and consumption studies have helped establish some disturbing facts. 1) Up to half of the

Research in Social Problems and Public Policy—Vol. 1, 1979, pages 65–91
Copyright © 1979 by JAI Press, Inc.
All rights of reproduction in any form reserved.
ISBN 0-89232-068-0

people are still unaware or unconvinced of an energy shortage (Milstein, 1977a); 2) there is little relationship between belief in the energy problem and actual conservation (Olsen, 1977); 3) those who favor conservation prefer policies which affect someone else or which provide rewards rather than limitations or penalities (Milstein, 1977b). None of these facts should be surprising, although they certainly argue against any easy resolution of the country's difficulties.

We have argued elsewhere (Leik and Kolman, 1977), that it is more rational to be wasteful than to conserve. That argument is based on a consumer's rational choice model intended to demonstrate some of the problems inherent in inducing conservation behavior. A basic aspect of the model is what has been (somewhat facetiously) labeled "chronic imminence," a state of continually waiting awhile before taking action (Leik and Tallman, 1976). Under deducible conditions, an imminent choice remains chronically so, and no action occurs. Because chronic imminence enters into many decision points of the model of energy conservation which we wish to develop, a review of that formulation will be useful.

CHRONIC IMMINENCE

Most rational decision theory assumes a binary choice situation. That is, the actor may choose either act A1 or act A2. We will later include the passive choice "WAIT," but for now let us consider just the two active options. Assume that there are profits associated with each option: P1 if action A1 is taken, P2 if A2 is chosen. However, let those profits depend on whether the selected action was the better choice. For example, if we calculatedly invest in solar heating under the assumption of continual fuel cost escalation for the next X years, then we will achieve a profit only if that assumption is correct, other things being equal. Conversely, not investing will produce a profit only if fuel costs do not escalate.

There are also related costs, C1 and C2, which occur primarily if a "wrong" choice is made. Those costs may be psychological ("Boy, was I dumb to do that!"); social ("My credibility is down"); or even economic ("That bad choice constrained my other possible investments and profits").

Because profits and costs depend upon an unknown ("Will fuel costs continue to escalate?"), there is no objective basis for action. However, subjective utilities can be calculated using the subjective probability that Hypothesis 1 ("Fuel costs will escalate") or Hypothesis 2 ("They won't") will be correct. Let $p(H1)$ and $p(H2)$ represent those subjective probabilities.

Following usual subjective expected utility formulations, the expected gain, $E(G)$, where $G = P - C$, for choosing A1, and the expected gain for choosing A2, can be written as follows.

$$E(G/A1) = P1 \ p(H1) - C1 \ p(H2)$$
$$E(G/A2) = P2 \ p(H2) - C2 \ p(H1)$$

(1)

Because $p(H2) = 1 - p(H1)$ for a binary decision, equations (1) can be rewritten in terms of $p(H1)$.

$$E(G/A1) = (P1 + C1)\, p(H1) - C1$$
$$E(G/A2) = P2 - (P2 + C2)\, p(H1). \tag{2}$$

For convenience, later derivations will focus on A1 as the dominant choice when a decision is about to be made.

A Bayesian Process

Normally, people are not faced with "now or never" decisions. That is, there is usually a possibility of deciding that there is some time yet before action must be undertaken, and any new evidence will be evaluated before a choice is made. Such a process suggests something akin to sequential sampling in statistics.

Step 1: Establish decision criteria.

Step 2: Draw a new piece of information.

Step 3: Calculate a decision index based on all information thus far.

Step 4: If the index passes beyond decision boundaries, go to Step 5. If not, go to Step 2.

Step 5: Decide.

This routine, coupled with Bayes's theorem, provides for gradual increase or decrease in confidence in (i.e., subjective probability of) a given hypothesis until an action can be chosen with reasonable assurance. Discussions of Bayesian analysis can be found in Mosteller et al. (1961) or Bradley (1976). A short explanation follows.

Probability theory states that if two elements, A and B, are independent, then the probability of their joint occurrence is the product of their separate occurrence probabilities

$$p(AB) = p(A)\, p(B) \tag{3}$$

If they are not independent, then a conditional probability statement is needed.

$$p(AB) = p(A)\, p(B/A)$$
$$= p(B)\, p(A/B) \tag{4}$$

Suppose some datum, D, is assumed to be more likely under H1 than under H2. For example, the datum, "Our cost per gallon of oil just went up" is more likely under H1; "Fuel costs are going to escalate," than under H2: "No, they aren't." Then we will need to use conditional probability statements for the likelihood of observing both D and condition 1 (i.e., H1 is true) or both D and condition 2. Note from (4) that there are two ways of expressing the probability of joint occurrences.

$$p(H1,D) = p(H1/D)\, p(D) = p(D/H1)\, p(H1)$$
$$p(H2,D) = p(H2/D)\, p(D) = p(D/H2)\, p(H2) \tag{5}$$

A ratio of the two probabilities of joint occurrence gives

$$\frac{p(H1/D)\ p(D)}{p(H2/D)\ p(D)} = \frac{p(D/H1)\ \ p(H1)}{p(D/H2)\ \ p(H2)} \tag{6}$$

Canceling P(D) in the left-hand term provides the basic Bayesian equation

$$\frac{p(H1/D)}{p(H2/D)} = \frac{p(D/H1)}{p(D/H2)}\ \frac{p(H1)}{p(H2)} \tag{7}$$

To the left of the equals sign is a ratio of the probability that H1 is true, given that datum D has been observed, to the probability that H2 is true, given D. This ratio is an odds ratio, and is referred to as the posterior odds ratio. That is, after the fact of observing D, the odds of H1 being true to H2 being true are expressed by the ratio. This ratio can be called Ω_{t+1}.

The term at the far right of equation (7) is also an odds ratio. It expresses the odds of H1 vs. H2 without being conditioned on D (i.e., before D is known). Not surprisingly, that term is called a prior odds ratio, designated Ω_t. The other term on the right side of the equation is a ratio of the likelihood that D will occur if H1 is true to the likelihood that D will occur if H2 is true. The ratio is called the likelihood ratio and will be designated LR_t.

By using subscripts t and t + 1 to represent time, we can demonstrate temporal processing of data in the making of a decision.

$$\Omega_{t+1} = LR_t\ \Omega_t \tag{8}$$

Equation 8, Bayes's theorem, states that the prior odds ratio multipled by the likelihood ratio provides the posterior odds ratio. The confidence about H1 or H2 is continually revised overtime by assessing a series of data. D_t, in terms of how likely each datum would be under each of the hypotheses being entertained.

Clearly, Bayes's theorem is prescriptive. That is, it is devised formally from statistical theory, and specifies optimal revision of the odds ratio for a rational decision process. There is considerable evidence to show that actual decisions follow a similar process (Peterson and Beach, 1967), but human actors are normally more conservative than equation (8) in revising hypotheses.

Consideration of costs and payoffs leads to two threshholds, or decision points, such that the rational choice is A1 if Ω_t exceeds α_1 or A2 if Ω_t is less than α_2. The thresholds could be found by requiring that expected gain be positive. Because that criterion is simpler, it will be calculated first. However, a more complex criterion exists if an expected gain is calculated for waiting and compared to that for immediate action.

From equation (1), and a criterion that E(G) > O, we get the condition for posterior probabilities that

$$P1\ p(H1/D) - C1\ p(H2/D) > 0$$

$$p(H2/D)\left[P1\ \frac{p(H1/D)}{p(H2/D)} - C1 \right] > 0$$

Assuming $p(H2/D) \neq 0$.

$$P1 \; \Omega_t > C1$$

$$\Omega_t > \frac{C1}{P1} \tag{9}$$

Consequently, $\alpha_1 = C1/P1$ is a rational boundary for choosing A1. Similar calculations demonstrate that $\alpha_2 = P2/C2$ is a rational boundary for choosing A2. The criterion of $E(G) > 0$, then, leads to rules which can be expressed graphically.

	$\dfrac{P2}{C2}$			$\dfrac{C1}{P1}$	
Choose A2	$\downarrow$		Wait	$\downarrow$	Choose A1

$$\leftarrow \text{Values of } \Omega_t \rightarrow$$

If costs are dominant in trying to reach a decision, then $C1/P1 > P2/C2$ and there will be three distinct regions for decision, as shown. It can be argued that C1, at least, is dominant in a problem of whether to conserve, but that P2 is also sizable in terms of comfort and convenience. However calculated, if profits were equal to or greater than costs, the boundaries would invert and there would be no "WAIT" region. Instead, the middle area would represent indecision between two options both satisfying the criterion.

Expected Gain for Waiting

An expression for E(G/WAIT) is more complicated than that for either action. If one waits too long, and a severe crisis occurs, then the costs of inaction are incurred. If a crisis did not occur, then acting now would incur unneeded costs of conservation. Assume that the actor is hovering on the brink of deciding on action A1. The point of waiting is to get better evidence, one or more new pieces of data on which to base Ω (setting aside long-term questions such as lower future costs of alternative energy systems). Assuming that cost and profit values stay fixed, a reasonable short-run assumption, then the only change in E(G) which waiting can bring about is to alter $p(H1)$ and $p(H2)$ so as to make the actor more confident.

If there is no deadline by which action must take place, the chance of getting useful new information without jeopardizing action options is near certainty. On the other hand, if there is an unknown but relatively imminent deadline by which a decision must be made, and there is a relatively low probability of obtaining relevant new data before the deadline, then there is danger in waiting and little chance of increasing knowledge in time. In short, the rationality of waiting depends on the probability of obtaining new information in time, which depends on both the rate of information flow pertinent to the decision and the actor's access to that information.

Let R_t designate the probability of obtaining new data between time t and time $t + \Delta t$. Necessarily this is also a subjective probability. The expected gain for waiting can be expressed as the revised expected gain, times the probability of having gotten new data on which to revise E(G), plus the expected gain for doing nothing times the probability of not getting information in time to revise E(G).

Formally, the expected gain for waiting one time interval can be expressed as

$$E(G/WAIT_t) = R_t E(G/A1_{t+1}) + (1-r_t) E(G/A2_t) \qquad (10)$$

Again assuming that A1 is the dominant choice at time t. The term $E(G/A1_{t+1})$ can be re-expressed, using equation 2, as

$$(P1 + C1)[p(H1_t) + \Delta_t p(H1)] - C1 \qquad (11)$$

Because notation becomes increasingly cumbersome in longer expressions, let p stand for $p(H1_t)$. Then equation (10) becomes, with appropriate substitutions,

$$E(G/WAIT_t) = R_t[(P1 + C1)(p + \Delta p) - C1] + (1-R_t) E(G/A2_t). \qquad (12)$$

Rationally, the actor should choose to wait only if $E(G/WAIT) - E(G/A1_t) > 0$. Clearly, the boundaries obtained earlier for choosing A1 no longer apply. Examination of the new criterion provides the following basis for deciding to wait.

$$\begin{aligned}
& E(G/WAIT_t) - E(G/A1_t) \\
&= R_t \left[(P1 + C1)\Delta p + E(G/A1_t)\right] + (1-R_t) E(G/A2_t) \\
& \quad - E(G/A1_t) \\
&= (1-R_t) \left[E(G/A2_t) - E(G/A1_t)\right] + R_t(P1 + C1)\Delta p
\end{aligned} \qquad (13)$$

The quantity in equation (13) exceeds 0 if

$$\Delta p > \left[\frac{1 - R_t}{R_t} \right] \left[\frac{E(G/A1_t) - E(G/A2_t)}{P1 + C1} \right] \qquad (14)$$

There is no way for the actor to know Δp in advance. That term will have to be considered a subjective estimate of the utility of new data if such data become available. We can calculate the value of Δp if the diagnostic value of D_t is known via the likelihood ratio. That derivation will be pursued shortly. Note first, however, that equation (14) states, "If confidence in H1 (our assumed dominant hypotheses) will change sufficiently due to the next datum, then wait for that datum before deciding to act." The right-hand side of equation (14) provides what "sufficiently" means. In general, the right side of the equation will be small if 1) R_t is large, meaning a good chance of getting new data before having to decide; 2) current expected gains are about equal; or 3) there are large stakes involved in choosing A1.

To get some notion of Δp, it is necessary to return to Bayes' theorem, as expressed in equation (8).

$$\Omega_{t+1} = LR_t \Omega_t$$

$$\frac{p_{t+1}}{1 - p_{t+1}} = LR_t \Omega_t$$

$$p_{t+1} = (1 - p_{t+1}) \, LR_t \Omega_t$$

$$= \frac{LR_t \Omega_t}{1 + LR_t \Omega_t} \tag{15}$$

$$= \frac{LR_t \dfrac{p_t}{1 - p_t}}{1 + LR_t \dfrac{p_t}{1 - p_t}}$$

$$= \frac{LR_t \, p_t}{1 + p_t \, (LR_t - 1)}$$

Consequently, $\Delta p = p_{t+1} = p_t$, can be expressed as

$$\Delta p = \frac{LR_t \, p_t}{1 + p_t \, (LR_t - 1)} - p_t$$

$$= \frac{p_t \, [LR_t - 1 - p_t \, (LR_t - 1)]}{1 + p_t \, (LR_t - 1)} \tag{16}$$

$$= \frac{p_t \, (1 - p_t) \, (LR_t - 1)}{1 + p_t \, (LR_t - 1)}$$

Before returning to the decision to wait, it is worth noting that equation (16) represents a kind of modified logistic process. The rate of change of p is essentially $p(1-p)$ times a complex term which involves both p and the likelihood ratio determined by the new datum. The $p(1-p)$ term assures keeping Δp within necessary bounds so that $0 \leq p + \Delta p \leq 1$ for all t.

Because LR is a part of equation (16), hence Δp, and because the size of Δp determines (in part) the rationality of waiting rather than acting, a complete statement of when to wait would involve assumptions about the distribution of D under each of the competing hypotheses. That is, if the actor expects clearly diagnostic data in the near future, that amounts to expecting a large value of LR. When p is moderate, $LR - 1$ will be considerably larger than $1 + p(LR - 1)$, and Δp will tend to be large. Adding this condition to the three previous conditions favoring a decision to wait provides four alternative, interacting bases for deciding that it would be rational to wait rather than act now.

The preceding formulation depends throughout on the assumption that there is yet time before something *must* be done. Given that the actor feels that there is still time, that more data are probably going to be available in time, especially data with considerable diagnostic value, that a clear choice is not currently available and that stakes are large, action is simply not rational. We think that the current energy problems of the country provide *all* of these conditions. It is not surprising that most people show little if any conservation behavior.

Two final notes

Before the notion of chronic imminence is applied to various stages in the decision to conserve energy, two further aspects of the formulation deserve attention. The first is a generalization of equation (14) to include the possibility of waiting an unknown number of discrete time intervals. Formal derivation is somewhat tedious and will be omitted. The derivation rests on an infinite series of future time intervals. If action is delayed from the present, time t, to some future period, time t + u, and each time a new datum, D_{t+i}, i = 1, u, is examined, then all those data must have become available without a deadline occurring. Assuming that R remains fixed (constant flow of data and no apparent "moving up" of the deadline for action), the probability of i successful waiting periods is R^i.

At each successive time period, a new Δ p is also relevant, which in turn depends on the diagnostic value of each new datum. It can be shown that the following conditions satisfies the criterion that E(G/WAIT) > E(G/A1).

$$\sum_{i=1}^{\infty} R^{i-1} \Delta^{(i)}p > \frac{1}{R} \frac{(1 - \frac{R}{1-R}) E(G/A1_t) - E(G/A2_t)}{P1 + C1 + (1 - R)(P2 + C2)} \tag{17}$$

where $\Delta^{(i)}$ p refers to the total change in p from time t to time t + i. Compared to equation (14), equation (17) clearly favors waiting. First, the numerator of the right side is smaller than that of equation (16), while the denominator is larger, for all values of R such that $0 < R \leq 1$. In fact, if R > .5, the right-hand term become negative unless the costs of a wrong decision to choose A2 are very large. We doubt that most people are as yet convinced that the costs of ignoring conservation are very sizeable. With reasonable expectancy of timely technological advancement or other resolution of the energy shortage, the value of the right hand term in equation (17) becomes quite small.

The left-hand term represents a weighted average of anticipated changes in p over future time periods, where weighting is by the probability of having that many new data available before a deadline has occurred. Since Δ p depends on the LR_i values, if each new fact favors A1, then Δ p will increase asymptotically over successive times. Let Δ *p represent an appropriate value of Δ p such that

$$\Delta^*p \sum_{i=1}^{\infty} R^{i-1} = \sum_{i=1}^{\infty} R^{i-1} \Delta^{(i)}p \tag{18}$$

It can be shown that, for 0 < R < 1, the infinite series R^{i-1} sums to 1/(1−R). Consequently the left side of equation 17 is Δ *p/(1 − R). The value of Δ *p is not readily obtained, but again assuming a preponderance of data favoring A1, hence an expected asymptotic increase in p over time, it is clear that Δ *p will not be less than Δ p nor greater than 1 − p. Even letting Δ *p = Δ p, the left-hand term in equation (17) exceeds that of equation (14). In short, longer-term considerations of waiting show that it is increasingly rational as the flow of new information seems to assure a number of future opportunities to recalculate Ω before having to act.

The other aspect of a complete discussion of whether it is rational to wait is how Δ p depends on the relationship between D and the alternate hypotheses, H1 and H2. An expected value of Δ p requires an expected value of LR, which depends upon the conditional probability of H1/D and of H2/D. Assume that D is a continuous variable which has been standardized on a 0 − 1 range so that D = 0 is the strongest evidence in favor of H1 and D = 1 is the strongest evidence of H2. For convenience, let p(H1/D) = 0 and p(H2/D) = 1 when D = 1, and p(H2/D) = 0 and p(H1/D) = 1 when D = 0. That is, the limiting values of D imply certainty about the hypotheses.

The problem of interest is the diagnostic utility of intermediate values of D. Two very different conditions are represented in Figure 1. The curves in the upper portion indicate difficulty in discerning the true hypothesis except for very extreme values of D. By contrast, the lower curves provide quite strong evidence when D departs moderately from .5. The former case is most likely when evidence has multiple interpretations, when "experts" debate the true state of affairs using the same data for opposed arguments. The latter case is more in keeping with a classical critical experiment.

The point of the comparison in Figure 1 is that, under present circumstances, most evidence regarding a need to conserve is apparently treated by the public as if it came from Figure 1a. Data which appear to be clear indicators of a serious problem seem to evoke only modest departures from unity in the likelihood ratio. As shown in Figure 2a there are markedly different likelihood ratios for the two curves. To maintain reasonable scale, the logarithms of the likelihood ratios are displayed (use of ln LR is quite common). The flat central portion of the curve for the distribution in Figure 1a implies little shift in Δ p for intermediate values of D, as is borne out in Figure 2b. By contrast, moderate departure of D from .5 implies sizable ln LR, hence Δ p, for the distribution in Figure 1b.

It should be recalled that it is more rational to wait when Δ p, or an expected indefinite future Δ p, exceeds a rather complex function of rate of information flow, current expected gains, and profit and cost considerations [equations (14) or (17)]. If data are not very diagnostic, as in Figure 1a, then Δ p shows small probable changes. Does that mean waiting is nonrational? In general, the answer is "no." Unless the costs of inaction are too severe, and most people seem to think that there is no drastic future consequence of continuing as usual, if the rate of flow of new data is adequate, the right-hand side of equation (17) can readily be negative. All that is needed for an actor to find waiting rational is that the

Figure 1.

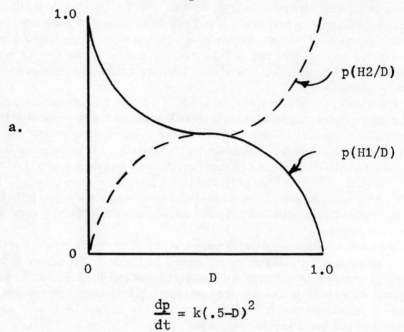

$$\frac{dp}{dt} = k(.5-D)^2$$

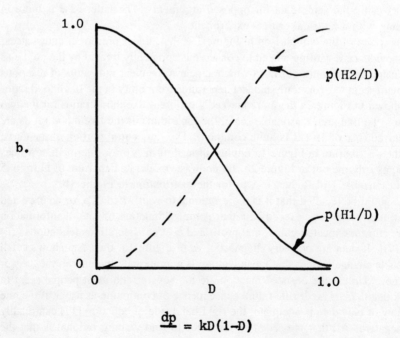

$$\frac{dp}{dt} = kD(1-D)$$

Figure 2.

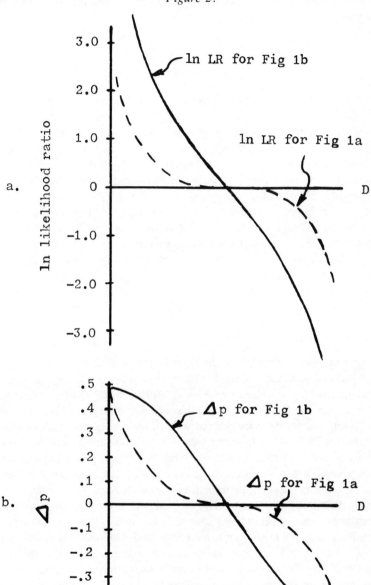

deadline is vaguely in the future and the prospect of new evidence flowing in is good. That seems to sum up much of the people's reaction to the country's energy problem.

A CHAIN OF DECISIONS

The discussion of chronic imminence sounded as if only one decision was under consideration. There are several steps involved before someone initiates serious conservation measures, however. Throughout this chain of steps, the actor is making decisions, and each decision has its own aspects of chronic imminence. Figure 3 is a simplified flow diagram of some of the major behavior and decision processes relevant to conservation. We will address various portions of the figure in subsequent sections of this discussion.

Boxes 1–3 in Figure 3 represent a simple cybernetic system without external system constraint. Something is wanted; that want leads to consumption, which in turn satisfies the want (perhaps only momentarily or inadequately) and the degree of satisfaction in turn affects the want. For either home heating or automobile driving, for example, there have been at most minor or irrelevant constraints on this cycle in the past. Basically the cycle has been equilibrated entirely internally, based on desired levels of heating or driving.

Attributing cause

The first external constraint (to the right of the vertical dash line) shown in Figure 3 is costs, which are currently being affected by the shortage and will no doubt be increasingly so. The arrow from EXPERIENCED COSTS leads to one of the boxes labeled C.I., indicating a decision point subject to chronic imminence. To some extent there are costs associated with any action, but many costs are so minor or so removed from the behavior which incurred them that they do not enter into the cybernetic system of boxes 1–3. Specifying a chronic imminence step implies that, when costs are experienced and cognitively connected with the behavior in question, there is still no necessary impact on behavior. The actor must deliberate, however briefly, illogically or even "unconsciously," on whether the evidence necessitates a change in behavior.

A common first conclusion, on being confronted with undesirable cost levels for one's behavior, is to attribute those costs to a source other than one's self [whereas profits are readily attributed to one's own efforts (cf. Kelley, 1971)]. Indeed, throughout the processes suggested by Figure 3, whenever a chronic imminence box is encountered, there is a question of how the actor attributes cause for the data which are forcing his/her attention to a possible need to alter behavior. Much work has been done on attribution theory [for a brief overview, see Shaver (1975)]; it would be too much to review that work here. However, an

Figure 3.   A Chain of Decisions.

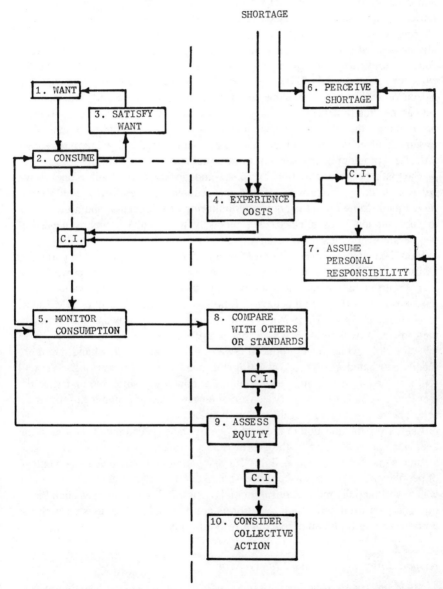

excellent paper by Ajzen and Fishbein (1975) demonstrated that attributions themselves seem to follow a Bayesian decision model.

The implications of incorporating attribution processes into the chronic imminence boxes of Figure 3 is that facts have multiple possible interpretations. Different attributions about the cause of the fact lead to different implications for altering one's own behavior. This process of observing, attributing and eventually arriving at some confidence about reality can be very quick or very slow. Actions implied by a possible conclusion can be put off indefinitely while the evidence is being weighed. Because even the attributions about the data on which a decision will be based are subject to a Bayesian serial processing, a decision to act can be greatly delayed. So long as attributions are to others (e.g., "There's no shortage—the oil companies are just trying to rip off the public,") rather than to self, the decision may well be that the problem is artificial, temporary, someone else's problem or perhaps not even a problem.

The path between experiencing costs and deciding to monitor one's own behavior to determine how to effect a cost reduction is therefore a readily interrupted path. More often than not, no monitoring of self occurs, and no feedback to consumption is established. Yet precisely this feedback link is needed if people are ever to learn to conserve.

From behavior theory in general to energy conservation research in particular (Milstein, 1977a), the evidence is clear that feedback is crucial and powerful. In fact, experiments indicate, not surprisingly, that rewarding conservation is the most powerful influence on behavior, followed by providing feedback (Milstein, 1977; Kohlenberg et al., 1976). Recall, though, that rewards are readily attributed to one's own actions, which makes self-monitoring desirable in order to have the skills which have produced reward. Costs, on the other hand, are more readily attributed elsewhere, negating the need for self-monitoring. We will return to the question of monitoring later. For now it will suffice to underline the fact that all roads to voluntary conservation pass through monitoring of one's self. The rest of Figure 3 is useless without box 5.

Aside from the question of costs, the energy shortage can induce conservation behavior via recognition of the shortage as a problem, per se, and deciding to assume some personal responsibility for alleviating it. An increasing percentage of people apparently are aware of the shortage, but relatively few are acting in a way to substantially reduce consumption [Olsen, (1977), and sources cited therein]. The path from perception to action is not often taken. Let us start with the portion leading to assuming personal responsibility.

Responsibility and Bystander Intervention

Since the 1964 murder of Kitty Genovese, there has been a large number of studies and a good deal of theoretical effort devoted to the question of when someone will assume personal responsibility for taking a needed course of action. In the Genovese case, many people watched the assault for a long time but made no effort to stop it. On the other hand, instances are readily found of one or more persons quickly entering such a situation and acting. What can be said about responsibility in the energy shortage based on the bystander intervention work?

Darley and Latané (1968) suggested that responsibility can diffuse among those present at an emergency such that each feels only a small share of responsibility, hence tends not to act. Someone else will do it instead. Of course, the theory pertained to emergency situations where one or more onlookers were present and only one needed to act. Nevertheless, the notion of diffused responsibility is useful for our purpose here.

To incorporate and make compatible a diverse set of results on bystander intervention, Morgan and Leik (1978) developed a mathematical and computer simulation model based on a simple expression and four assumptions. The model has subsequently been successfully tested by Morgan (1978). The assumptions, which need to be reconsidered in the energy conservation case, are that 1) each bystander has a response threshhold such that intervention occurs if felt responsibility exceeds that threshold, 2) thresholds are normally distributed in the population, 3) bystanders present in any emergency are a random sample from that population and 4) each bystander feels increased personal responsibility the longer no one intervenes in the emergency.

The amount of responsibility felt by each bystander was then expressed as

$$R = \frac{G}{N} + I \qquad (19)$$

where R is felt responsibility, G is the costs or benefits accruing to the group of bystanders (or the population in general) if intervention occurs, N is the number of bystanders and I is nondiffusible person obligation felt by the individual bystander without reference to collective costs or benefits. The latter could derive purely from personal interests, from commitment to values being threatened by the emergency, or from other idiosyncratic reasons to intervene. G, then, is a diffusible source of responsibility; if everyone, collectively, gains, then everyone shares responsibility. I is not diffusible.

The model works well in explaining apparent contradictions in bystander intervention data. Specifically, some evidence has indicated that a larger number of bystanders increases the likelihood and speed of intervention, whereas other evidence indicates the contrary. The Morgan–Leik model demonstrates that response latencies (and intervention probabilities) can show a nonlinear nonmonotonic pattern. A single bystander is likely to intervene sooner than two or three bystanders, because the diffusion of responsibility among so few people makes large changes in how much responsibility each bystander feels. As the number of bystanders increases, however, diffusion becomes decreasingly relevant (adding one person to a sizable group hardly alters the value of G/N) while there is increasing likelihood of the group's including someone with a low response threshold. The resulting curve looks like Figure 4. Note that a small number of bystanders, around three to six, produces the greatest response latency for all curves except $I = 0$. This fact will be returned to when we consider household fuel consumption.

What relevance has this work for energy conservation models? First, as is shown in Figure 3, feeling a personal responsibility to conserve is essential unless sheer costs (fuel bills, fines or ostracism) force conservation. Felt personal responsibility is no guarantee of conservation behavior, but it at least is a stimulus in the decision to monitor one's own actions and to consider revising one's patterns of consumption. The C.I. box between "consume" and "monitor consumption" has only two inputs: costs and personal responsibility. If collective costs are personally experienced, that fact may, via a chronic imminence process, lead to taking responsibility oneself.

Second, although the problem of an impending energy shortage is quite different from that of an emergency such as the Genovese murder, it is instructive to compare the two. Some contrasts are readily evident. The bystander work pertains to a sudden, immediate need for action; the energy shortage is more likely to be seen as a possible need for future action. A bystander is one of the people on the spot who might step in to help, so potential bystanders constitute a relatively small, usually mutually observable group. For the energy problem, everyone is a bystander and most are not mutually observable. In the bystander problem, a single intervention is assumed sufficient; it only takes one call to the police, or one person to administer emergency first aid. The energy problem requires majority "intervention" on a continuing basis.

Some similarities are also evident. One hypothesis offered to account for inaction by bystanders has been the inhibiting effect of seeing other bystanders doing nothing. In like manner, we anticipate that apparent lack of conserving by others will deter conservation behavior. This point will be discussed later regarding feelings of equity. The strongest parallel, however, is the fact that in each case the individual actor is faced with a decision to act, recognizing that such action carries possible costs, versus not to act while allowing a serious problem to go uncorrected or hoping that someone else will take responsibility. To the extent that a problem is perceived, a decision to take personal responsibility is essential before action occurs. That decision involves a chronic imminence process.

The assumptions of the Morgan-Leik model imply quite different concerns if we are analyzing how people drive (gasoline consumption or conservation) or how people heat their residences (oil, coal, electricity or natural gas consumption or conservation). Since these two areas of domestic consumption account for about 80 percent of all domestic use of fuels (Carter, 1977), they provide the major areas of potential saving.

Figure 4. Expected Response Latencies in Bystander Intervention.

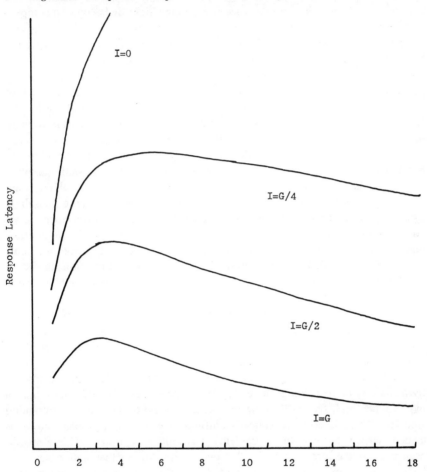

The first assumption, that each bystander has a response threshold, poses no problem in either instance. The second and third assumptions, that bystander thresholds are randomly drawn from a normally distributed population, makes sense only when the number of potential bystanders can be assumed to come from a population at large. For driving, that assumption may be reasonable. Some few drivers will have low enough thresholds to adhere carefully to driving 55 miles per hour or less on highways, to making slow, easy starts, to having frequent routine maintenance and even to buying low-consumption vehicles. Most people will presumably cluster somewhat beyond the most concerned group, showing moderate to small accommodations to an awareness of a shortage. A few, of course, will drive gas guzzlers as if they were at Daytona or Indianapolis. Unfortunately, not conserving on the highway becomes a competitive stimulus for other drivers. Single instances of conservation-oriented driving do not even have much potential for generating a diffusion of conserving behavior because of the offsetting diffusion of competitive driving.

For household consumption, however, the relevant population is the set of persons living in a particular residence. No one else is going to come in and turn down the thermostat or extinguish unneeded lights. Clearly, a normal distribution assumption is not appropriate. Note, though, that households seldom have more than four or five residents, which is the size of group producing the greatest response latencies according to the model. The implication of a small set of bystanders is that diffusion of responsibility is dominating the threshold sampling process. It is easy for each member to let someone else do it. If there are agreements regarding who is specifically responsible for overseeing household conservation, the problem of personal responsibility does not arise. Such a division of labor is certainly uncommon at this time, and may have negative implications for other family relationships if it is too clearly a police-type role. In short, the model predicts that typical households will show slowest reactions to energy problems unless some procedures are devised to aid the household decision process.

Assumption 4 of the Morgan-Leik model is most pertinent at this point. When people are observing an emergency and seeing no one else reacting, the assumption specifies that each bystander will feel increased pressure to take personal responsibility. In the case of driving, there is no evident emergency and, as noted above, there is an offsetting competitive urge to keep up with the faster drivers. In the case of home heating, there may be a mild sense of ''emergency'' once a month when high fuel bills come in, but that single event is not a continuing stimulus. There is no increasing discomfiture over seeing a problem go unattended, largely because the ''problem'' has only an episodic, widely spaced occurrence in the form of a fuel bill. Consequently, rather than anticipate eventual response in most instances, as predicted for the bystander intervention problem, it is likely that the household will show little or no response.

If personal responsibility is to be felt by one or more household members, it would seem necessary either to initiate a very large-scale campaign to create high individual (I) rather than collective (G) values for equation (19), or to provide continual or frequently recurring stimuli regarding home fuel consumption. Based on results of current efforts to convince people they need to conserve, the first alternative seems doomed to little or no success. The second alternative is feasible. We will address that approach next. Thus far, though, there is reason to believe that necessary feelings of personal responsibility will not develop on a wide enough basis to materially reduce gasoline consumption for private transportation. Other solutions, such as federal miles-per-gallon standards or the development of alternative fuels, appear necessary.

Monitoring consumption

When costs were discussed, it was stated that a decision to monitor one's own consumption is the result of a chronic imminence process. It is typically easier to put off such deliberate, and sometimes embarrassing, examination of one's own behavior. That is true whether the impetus is costs (box 4) or feelings of personal responsibility for a collective problem (box 7). It is also true that intentions to monitor consumption may not be readily fulfilled. Determining daily or hourly fuel consumption is difficult or impossible for most people. Measuring the actual consumption impact of using, say, a self-cleaning oven or an electric dryer, is not possible in most households. Consequently, even if someone were to develop feelings of personal responsibility, those feelings are likely to be defeated in the decision process by inadequate means by which to monitor consumption.

As currently arranged, most drivers confront evidence of fuel consumption whenever refueling or being billed for charge account purchases of fuel. That is, consumption is apparent at, say, weekly or perhaps monthly intervals only. Household fuel consumption is, similarly, confronted only on a monthly billing basis. When more than one person contributes to the costs, but only one experiences those costs via paying accumulated bills, it is virtually impossible to develop effective knowledge of how specific behaviors effect consumption rates. There is no direct, immediate feedback.

Both cybernetic and behavioral theory make clear that feedback is essential for self-correction and for learning. Experiments show the utility of feedback in inducing conservation (Seligman and Darley, 1976; Milstein, 1977b). Perhaps the simplest expression of a cybernetic feedback mechanism is as follows.

$$\frac{dC}{dt} = k(S - C) \qquad (20)$$

The term C, for our purposes, is consumption, S is some standard and k is positive. The equation indicates that, if consumption falls below the standard, the rate of change of consumption will increase. If C exceeds the standard, the rate of change will decrease. Such a mechanism produces monotonic approach to S, with the rate of approach depending on k, which is a parameter indicating responsiveness of the system to divergence of S from C. In integrated form the equation is

$$C_t = S - (S - C_o) e^{-kt}$$
$$\text{As } t \to \infty, e^{-kt} \to 0 \text{ and } C \to S \qquad (21)$$

Two questions are worth pursuing regarding equations (20) and (21) and our concern with conservation of fuel. First, where does S come from? Second, is it likely that, if adequate time series data were available on daily fuel consumption, they would show a simple trend to a stable standard? The answer to the second question is surely "no," but why that is so depends upon the origin of S. For convenience, let us emphasize home heating rather than driving automobiles, since the earlier discussion implied that home heating is more amenable to developing feelings of personal responsibility if adequate feedback is provided.

As used in equations (20) and (21), S is constant. In fact, the desirable amount of consumption of heating fuel depends upon a set of factors: 1) what is a comfortable temperature for the residents, 2) what is the temperature outside, 3) how efficient are heating and insulating systems, 4) what is the relationship between comfort and cost utilities, 5) how are these utilities affected by a decision to conserve for reasons other than cost. The least interesting of these questions for our purposes (though possibly the strongest influences on heating fuel consumption) are the second and third. It is readily demonstrable that fuel consumption follows temperature fluctuations and that it varies by amount of insulation in a residence. It is also demonstrable that, after statistically controlling for such sources of variation, there is a great deal of unexplained variance in household usage. Let us assume that temperature changes and heating/cooling/ insulation variations have been extracted from the consumption data being analyzed. We are left with comfort, cost and conservation as our major inputs to replace S in the previous equations.

From Figure 3 it is apparent that, without concern over cost or conservation, consumption would rapidly and monotonically approach that needed for comfort. Only boxes 1–3 of the figure would be involved. With either box 4 or box 7 becoming salient, some monitoring (box 5) is likely, with input to the consumption box. Adjustments in consumption will still be monotonic if cost problems and conservation concerns remain fixed. To consider changes in those inputs, it may help to re-express equation (20) in discrete time form.

$$\Delta C = k(S - C) \tag{22}$$

The right side of equation (22) will need separate terms for comfort, cost and conservation.

For simplicity, let τ be the consumption level associated with desired comfort. It is possible to find τ by determining the necessary amount of fuel for a (standardized) day in order to keep residents comfortable, or at least to achieve a compromise temperature for households in which residents disagree about what is comfortable. If a more complete model were desired, outside temperature could become a leading indicator and insulation quality a scalar adjustment. Presumably τ would be a negative function of daily outside temperature; the insulation term would depend upon a residential construction factor.

Let $K_1 (\tau - C_t)$ express the contribution to ΔC_t due to the extent to which current consumption level departs from that needed for comfort (outside temperature not included, but statistically removed from the time series). Similarly, let δ indicate the amount of fuel consumption associated with an amount of acceptable level of expenditure for fuel. Then $K_2 (\delta - C_t)$ expresses the contribution of direct fuel costs to ΔC_t. Presumably, this expression is overly simplified, in that if $S > 0$, a period of no fuel use would generate consumption up to S. We can either assume that S = 0 or recognize that the results to be obtained do not apply completely for periods of no fuel consumption.

Finally, let γ represent an acceptable level of fuel consumption from the point of view of a commitment to conserve out of felt personal responsibility. Then K_3 $(\gamma - C_t)$ expresses the impact of such a commitment on ΔC_t. Again, low consumption periods will produce anomalies with this very simple expression.

Combining the above inputs produces equation 23.

$$\Delta C_t = k_1 (\tau - C_t) + k_2 (\delta - C_t) + k_3 (\gamma - C_t)$$
$$= (k_1 \tau + k_2 \delta + k_3 \gamma) - (k_1 + k_2 + k_3) C_t \tag{23}$$

If that equation is re-expressed using $Z_t = C_t - E(C)$ and incorporating a random error term, the resulting expression is that of a simple auto regressive, or AR(1), process (Box and Jenkins, 1976).

$$z_{t+1} = \phi z_t + e_t \tag{24}$$

Equation (24) assumes that the parameters of equation (23) are constant. Some of the earlier discussion suggests, to the contrary, that at least cost and conservation terms can be expected to vary. Let us consider only comfort and cost at first.

If the cost of heating is a continuous input for equation (23), then whatever interval is represented by Δt will be irrelevant. In fact, heating costs are typically confronted once per month, whereas comfort is confronted daily. For $\Delta t = 1$ day, there will always be the $K_1 (\tau - C_t)$ term, but $K_2 (\delta - C_t)$ will appear only every thirty days. Setting conservation aside, equation (23) will be

$$\Delta C_t = k_1 (\tau - C_t) + k_{2t} (\delta - \overline{C}_t) \tag{25}$$

$$\text{where } \overline{C} = \frac{1}{30} \sum_{t-30}^{t-1} C_i \text{ and } k_{2t} = \begin{cases} 1 \text{ every 30th day} \\ 0 \text{ otherwise} \end{cases}$$

The nature of $\overline{C}$ means that, in effect, there are thirty more autoregression terms in equation (25), each with the same coefficient and each appearing only on billing day. Consider what the time series will look like.

When costs are not present, the terms will be

$$\Delta C_t = k_1 (\tau - C_t) \tag{26}$$

and it can be readily shown that

$$\lim_{t \to \infty} C_t = \tau \tag{27}$$

For practical purposes we can assume that C_t adjusts fast enough that, by the end of 30 days with no fuel bill, it will approximate its limiting valued of τ, and ΔC will go to zero.

Now let us introduce a fuel bill. We have

$$\Delta C_t \cong k_1 (\tau - \tau) + k_2 (\delta - \overline{C}) = k_2 (\delta - \overline{C}) \qquad (28)$$

Suppose C adjusted fast enough that $\overline{C} \cong \tau$. Consequently, assuming that $\delta < \tau$ because acceptable cost level of consumption is lower than acceptable comfort level of consumption, ΔC_t will be negative. Let $k_2 (\delta - \overline{C}) = -a$, where $a < o$. Then the days from the fuel bill onward will show:

$$
\begin{aligned}
C_{t+1} &= C_t - \Delta C_t = \tau - a \\
C_{t+2} &= C_{t+1} - \Delta C_{t+1} = \tau - a + k_1 [\tau - (\tau - a)] \\
&= \tau - a (1 - k_1) \\
C_{t+3} &= C_{t+2} + \Delta C_{t+2} = \tau - a (1 - k_1) + k_1 [\tau - \tau - a(1-k_1)] \\
&= \tau - a (1 - k_1)^2
\end{aligned}
$$

or in general,

$$C_{t+j} = \tau - a (1 - k_1)^{j-1} \qquad (29)$$

Clearly, as j gets large, assuming $0 \leq k_1 \leq 1$, C_{t+j} again approaches τ asymptotically. The time series would look like that shown in Figure 5. The overall consumption level will be somewhere between τ and $\tau - a$, and closer to the former to the extent that the monthly shock was brief and comfort was a continuing concern. Of course, the shock may be remembered longer, such that return to a pure comfort model is slower. Nevertheless, without continual cost input to the adjustment of consumption, a time series similar to Figure 5 should obtain. There is in limited use at this time a continuous readout consumption indicator which can be installed in private homes. We are attempting to develop a device which also provides daily recording of fuel consumption so as to test models such as that just discussed and to determine the conservation utility of continuous feedback on costs.

The presence of a concern over reducing consumption due to feelings of personal responsibility in the energy shortage will have a different effect on the time series of daily fuel use. Prior to such a concern, only comfort and cost will be involved. After a decision is made (subject to the delays of chronic immi-

Figure 5. Adjusted Daily Consumption; Monthly Billing.

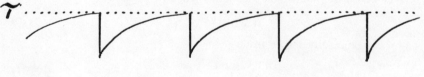

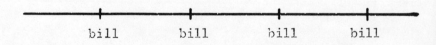

nence), that a reduction is necessary, Δ C will include the $k_3(\gamma - C_t)$ term. To the extent that γ is a constant, there will be a monotonic decrease in C to a level between comfort on the one hand and acceptable cost and conservation levels on the other.

Is γ, or a comsumption level appropriate to a felt need to conserve, likely to be constant? Probably not. There are two main influences on γ, one tending to lower it, the other to increase it. That which will lower it is further evidence of fuel difficulties, resulting in a revision of what is an appropriate level of consumption. It may be assumed that each downward revision will occur only after longer and longer chronic imminence processes. A two-degree adjustment of a thermometer is easy; a five-degree adjustment may take some deliberation, and so forth.

The major source of an increase in γ is, necessarily, a loss of feeling personally responsible for conserving. That loss may be due to either of the following: new data on the shortage or reinterpretation of data which previously led to the decision to conserve. New data may be in the form of evidence that the shortage is over (such as following the summer shortage of 1974, when filling stations lines disappeared). It may also be indicative of current or impending alternatives which will alleviate the long term need for a fuel in short supply.

Revising or reinterpreting old data is likely to be a consequence of developing new attributions regarding those data. If, for example, one's friends all insist that there is no real shortage, but only a conspiracy of oil companies, then the earlier Bayesian process will be revised and γ allowed to ''float'' closer to comfort level, τ. A more subtle influence, though, in the long run just as pervasive, is for the actor to observe that others do not seem to be doing their share, hence that adhering to γ is not equitable. We turn next to this problem.

Equity

Numerous reports have indicated a concern for equity in responding to the energy shortage (Gottlieb, 1977; Morrison, 1977; Milstein, 1977b). Not surprisingly, it is often assumed that one's own share of the burden of the shortage is greater than that others are bearing. As shown in Figure 3, monitoring consumption can lead to comparison with others as well as to some general standard. The comparison with others is most likely when feelings of personal responsibility are the source of the monitoring.

Assessing equity, according to Adams (1965), amounts to a comparison of input-output ratios. That is, equity obtains between actors A and B if

$$\frac{I_A}{O_A} = \frac{I_B}{O_B} \tag{30}$$

where I and O are inputs and outputs, respectively. (The Adams expression uses O/I, but the I/O version will prove more convenient below.) The major problem with assessing equity is the difficulty of measuring I and O, especially in terms of energy consumption. We can make a convenient translation from the comfort and conservation parameters previously used, however.

Given an assumption that γ is a "proper" or "fair" level of consumption under conditions of collective shortage, the input one makes to solving the shortage can be considered the proportion of one's total obligation that one has fulfilled. That is, remembering that τ is the desired level of consumption, actor's input is

$$I_A = \frac{\tau - C}{\tau - \gamma} \tag{31}$$

Output, on the other hand, could be simply relative comfort.

$$O_A = \frac{C}{\tau} \tag{32}$$

Some algebraic manipulation provides

$$\frac{I_A}{O_A} = \frac{\dfrac{\tau}{C} - 1}{1 - \dfrac{\gamma}{\tau}} \tag{33}$$

Since $C \leq \tau$ according to earlier derivations, and $\gamma > \tau$ by assumption, equation (33) will be positive. Its precise value is less important than how it compares with O/I values for others. Determining conservation equity seems less a person-by-person comparison process than a comparison of self with an imputed generalized other. In part, such an other derives from cultural assumptions such as "nobody is going to conserve unless forced to—you take what you can get" (i.e., others will take what they can get). If it were assumed that others did not conserve at all, $C = \tau$ for them, and their input, hence their I/O ratio, becomes zero.

It would be easy under such an assumption to conclude that to conserve fuel oneself would lead to inequity. There would even be very little delay in reaching such a conclusion. In consequence, the inequity would feed back to reduce personal responsibility, increase τ, hence increase C. By way of avoiding indeterminant I values, it should be noted that $\tau - C$ should be less than $\tau - \gamma$, hence the limit of I as γ approaches τ should be zero. Multiplying equation (30) by O_A provides what A's equitable input (or conservation effort) should be. If I_B is zero and O_B is unity, then O_A should also be unity and conservation ignored.

Even without a general assumption that others will not conserve, it is difficult to observe whether "they" really are doing their part. A quick glance at highway speeds leads to the conclusion that "they" are ignoring conservation. If, for home heating purposes, the salient others could be defined as other household members, though, it would be evident that all were sharing equally in the effort to conserve. In fact, if recurring feedback and emphasis on household wide collective conservation efforts were combined, both cost constraints and equitable returns from conserving would operate to maintain the conservation effort.

The importance of equity should not be underestimated. Gottlieb (1977) found that "Texans endorse vigorous police enforcement of the 55 mph speed limit . . . " among other indications of willingness to conserve. Enforced speed limits are, we suspect, more a symbol of equity than of absolute saving. I'll do it if everyone else has to.

Note on Figure 3 that not only does inequity lead to altered responsibility, but it also has possible consequences for belief in the shortage (if I'm getting an unfair deal, they've probably just made up the shortage to rip me off) and for willingness to monitor own consumption. Thus, feelings of inequity can wipe out what impetus to conservation might have existed.

Implications for a Dynamic System

No attempt will be made to create the type of societal or even community level dynamic model implied by the foregoing sections. To do so would require adjusting each actor's behavior according to: 1) decisions made as facts flow in about the shortage (subject, of course, to attributional biases and other distortions), 2) experienced cost escalations, 3) personal responsibility thresholds for converting collective need to personal action, 4) ability to monitor own consumption, 5) ability to compare with others consumption and assess equity, 6) feedback from relative equity to prior aspects of the system. In a sense the model becomes an imperfect dynamic input-output system, where each actor's resolution of the problem depends on other actors' resolutions as well as on exogenous factors. Such a model would imply a complex, network based social diffusion process.

To add further complexity, recall that there is a box number 10 in Figure 3, labeled CONSIDER COLLECTIVE ACTION. In the event that inequity is evident and that it seems widespread (the poor are hurt most, or fuel producing states aren't getting a fair share, etc.), it is likely that some attempts at collective action will develop. That is, individuals will try to consolidate interests in some way calculated to effect change in the inequitable system. Regional efforts to benefit from local resources are one example. Enforced standards, such as speed limits, are another.

The problem of collective action in the fuel shortage is that it is hard to create the resource base needed for bargaining. As Coleman (1973) has demonstrated, control of something not particularly important to self can be exchanged for control of something more important, but no exchange will occur unless something others value is controlled to begin with.

How can ordinary people exert influence over supplies of fuel, development of alternate systems, distribution of existing supplies, enforcement of standards, and so forth? In part, influence is being exerted currently by political processes and also by economic pressures. Those influences are mostly fragmentary and sporadic. When most people confront real shortages, the extent to which inequities are perceived will govern the extent to which extensive and potentially devisive collective action can be anticipated. If the overall system is kept in reasonable balance, though, such actions can materially reduce inequities and possibly generate solutions.

At the current rate of chronic imminence re either costs or personal responsibility, it is unlikely that enough people care one way or the other. Our extended commentary on models of conservation is an attempt to explain why there is so little conservation at this time, to sort out what might produce conservation in the future, and to indicate how data over time are likely to look if our assumptions are correct. We continue to hope that rational assuming of personal responsibility and voluntary conservation will gain popularity, but our models do not make that eventuality seem near. The beginning of this modeling effort was a seminar (Leik and Lewis, 1974) focused on various areas of social science model building which could help policy makers in responding to the impending shortage. Perhaps that conference plan was too optimistic regarding both the feasibility of combining models and the utility of such an effort for shaping policy. This paper has advanced the modelling effort, but finds little prospect of large scale changes in public response. At least we may have located some areas more amenable to change, and helped explain why others are not so changeable.

REFERENCES

Adams, J.S. (1965), "Inequity in Social Exchange," in L. Berkowitz ed., *Advances in Experimental Social Psychology, Vol. II.* New York: Academic Press, pp. 267–299.

Ajzen, Icek, and Martin Fishbein (1975), "A Bayesian Analysis of Attribution Processes," *Psychological Bulletin* 42:261–277.

Box, George E., and Gwilynn M. Jenkins (1976), *Time Series Analysis: Forecasting and Control.* (San Francisco: Holden-Day.

Bradley, James V. (1976), *Probability; Decision; Statistics.* Englewood Cliffs, N.J.: Prentice-Hall.

Carter, L.F. (1977), "On the Public 'Need to Know' Concerning Energy Policy Alternatives," unpublished manuscript.

Coleman, J.S. (1973), *The Mathematics of Collective Action.* Chicago: Aldine.

Darley, J.M., and B. Latané (1968), "Bystander Intervention in Emergencies," *Journal of Personality and Social Psychology* 3:377–383.

Gold, Raymond L. (1978), "Toward Social Policy on Regionalizing Energy Production and Consumption," paper presented at Social and Behavioral Implications of the Energy Crisis: A Symposium, Houston, Texas, June 27–28, 1977, and printed in S. Warkov, ed., *Energy Policy in the Unites States: Social and Behavioral Dimensions.* New York: Praeger.

Gottlieb, David (1977), "Texans' Responses to President Carter's Energy Proposals," unpublished manuscript.

Kelley, H.H. (1971), *Attribution in Social Interaction.* Morristown, N.J.: General Learning Press.

Klausner, Samuel Z. (1978), "Household Organization and Use of Electricity," paper presented at

Social and Behavioral Implications of the Energy Crisis: A Symposium, Houston, Texas, June 27–28, 1977, and printed in S. Warkov ed., op. cit.

Kohlenberg, Robert; Thomas Phillips; and William Proctor (1976), "A Behavioral Analysis of Peaking in Residential Electrical-Energy Consumers," *Journal of Applied Behavior Analysis* 1(Spring):13–18.

Leik, Robert K., and Anita Sue Kolman (1978), "Isn't It More Rational to Be Wasteful?" paper presented at Social and Behavioral Implications of the Energy Crisis: A Symposium, Houston, Texas, June 27–28, 1977, and printed in S. Warkov ed., op. cit.

————, and Michael Lewis (1974), *Energy Scarcity: Sociological Models of Resource Allocations,* report on NSF sponsored conference. Amherst, Mass.: University of Massachusetts.

————, and Irving Tallman (1976), "Chronic Imminence: For Some People It Is More Rational to Wait," paper presented at Pacific Sociological Association, San Diego (Spring).

Milstein, Jeffrey S. (1978), "How Consumers Feel About Energy: Attitudes and Behavior During the Winter and Spring of 1976–77," paper presented at Social and Behavioral Implications of the Energy Crisis: A Symposium, Houston, Texas, June 27–28, 1977, and printed in S. Warkov, ed., op. cit.

———— (1976), "Attitudes, Knowledge and Behavior of American Consumers Regarding Energy Conservation with Some Implications for Governmental Action," paper presented at the 1976 National Meeting of the Association for Consumer Research.

Morgan, Charles J. (1978), "Bystander Intervention: Experimental Test of a Formal Model," *Journal of Personality and Social Psychology* 36:43–54.

————, and Robert K. Leik (1978), "Computer Simulation and Theory Development: The Bystander Intervention Case," in R.B. Smith, ed., *Social Science Methods,* Vol. IV. (New York: Holstead Press.

Morrison, Denton E. (1978), "Equity Impacts of Some Major Energy Alternatives," paper presented at Social and Behavioral Implications of the Energy Crisis: A Symposium, Houston, Texas, June 27–28, 1977, and printed in S. Warkov, ed., op. cit.

Mosteller, F.; R. Rourke; and G. Thomas, Jr. (1961), *Probability with Statistical Applications.* Reading, Mass.: Addison-Wesley.

Mulligan, Linda W. (1978), "Energy Regionalism in the U.S.: The Decline of the National Energy Commons," paper presented at Social and Behavioral Implications of the Energy Crisis: A Symposium, Houston, Texas, June 27–28, 1977, and printed in S. Warkov, ed., op. cit.

Olsen, Marvin E. (1978), "Public Acceptance of Energy Conservation," paper presented at Social and Behavioral Implications of the Energy Crisis, etc., ibid.

Peterson, C.R., and L. R. Beach (1967), "Man as an Intuitive Statistician," *Psychological Bulletin* 68:29–46.

Seligman, C., and J. M. Darley (1976), "Feedback as a Means of Decreasing Residential Energy Consumption," paper presented at American Sociological Association, New York (August).

Shaver, Kelly G. (1975), *An Introduction to Attribution Processes.* Cambridge, Mass.: Winthrop Publishers.

ADOPTION IN AMERICA:
AN EXAMINATION OF TRADITIONAL
AND INNOVATIVE SCHEMES

Howard Altstein, UNIVERSITY OF MARYLAND

AT BALTIMORE

Rita J. Simon, UNIVERSITY OF ILLINOIS

One of the major dilemmas faced by those who attempt to develop public policy centers on the fact that what is often the most rational course to follow can turn out to be politically unfeasible. The rational and potentially most effective solutions to many problems are frequently rendered impossible to execute because of conditions which, although exogenous to the problems, and nevertheless constraining in their impact upon response options. Nowhere has this circumstance been more apparent than in the area of adoption. Rationality would dictate that a policy which maximizes the pool of potential adoptive parents should be instituted. If it is assumed—as it is in American society—that child-rearing is best accomplished in a family setting, then it follows that making willing and able adoptive parents available to children who are presently growing up in custodial institutions is a course that should be maximally embarked upon. In fact, however, such a course has been impossible to pursue. In the following

Research in Social Problems and Public Policy—Vol. 1, 1979, pages 93–111

paper Howard Altstein and Rita Simon undertake a systematic analysis of rational adoption
policies and the impediments to their execution. Aside from its important substantive focus,
this paper can be understood as presenting a heuristic paradigm of interest constraints as they
impinge on the policy process in general.

Children are a society's most valuable resource. They represent its future. The
treatment and care that a society or a community gives to its children are part of
the insurance it buys for its own future. In American society today, there are, as
there have been in societies all over the world throughout history, thousands of
children for whom there are no parents or "next of kin" who are willing to
assume responsibility for rearing them. These children are totally dependent on
the impersonal resources and institutions of the community and the society for
their survival and development.

Different societies, at different periods in time, have adopted different
strategies for responding to the needs of such children. Some communities have
assumed their responsibilities with a sense of gratitude—somehow the children
have survived, and therefore they themselves have a future. Such was certainly
the view of the international Jewish community following the Second World War
when that community helped to relocate the thousands of Jewish children who
miraculously survived the concentration camps.

The primary response that American society has made to children without
"next of kin" has been to designate them as wards of the state and to maintain
them in public institutions. A secondary response has been to allow the "best" or
"most desirable" of them to be adopted in infancy by married adults unable to
bear children. Still another group has been temporarily housed in nuclear families
willing to assume the role and responsibilities of foster parents. But consistently
the largest number have spent all their childhood and adolescence in public
institutions.

At different times, alternative schemes have been proposed by adoption agencies and professionals for altering this pattern so as to radically increase the
number of infants and young children who are removed from institutions and
placed in family settings. During the 1960s, one such scheme, transracial adoption, allowed for the adoption of children whose racial and ethnic characteristics
differed from those of the prospective parents. In practice, it resulted in the
adoption of thousands of American black and Indian children by white parents.
Since black children represent the largest group of children in public institutions,
the willingness of professional agencies to broaden the population from which
prospective parents might be selected represented an important opportunity for
placing homeless children in nuclear family settings.

The practice of transracial adoption gained in popularity and notoriety through
the sixties and into the seventies, until it came to an abrupt halt a few years ago.
The practice abated not because the institutions had been emptied, nor because
the availability of potential parents was exhausted, but because leaders of black
and Indian communities saw in it a threat to the future of their communities.

They viewed adoption of black and Indian children by white parents as acts of cultural genocide. Through the organized efforts of black social workers and Indian tribal council members, pressure was brought to bear on family and child care agencies in many states, and transracial adoptions were either severely curtailed or, in some states, eliminated.

This article reviews traditional inracial adoptions and nontraditional schemes such as transracial, subsidized, and single-parent adoptions. It presents arguments for and against each of these alternatives and summarizes the data that are available for evaluating the effectiveness of each. The most common standard used in deciding how successful a scheme has been is the adoption rate, a figure representing the number of homeless children moved from institutions and temporary placements into permanent families. The first section of this article provides data on rates of adoption between 1971 and 1975. The next section reviews the reactions and experiences of white parents who have adopted transracially and describes the racial attitudes and self-perceptions of transracially adopted children and their white siblings. The third section reports black attitudes toward both inracial and transracial adoption. The last two sections examine subsidized and single-parent adoptions.

Trend data indicate that by 1975, the most recent year for which data are available, black and white Americans were inracially adopting fewer children than at any other time. After a steady increase starting in the fifties, inracial adoption rates reached its peak of 175,000 per year by 1970. Table 1 shows that by 1971 adoption rates began to decline, dropping to 169,000 in 1971; 99,552 in 1972; 113,042 in 1973; 107,874 in 1974; and 104,188 in 1975.

Nonwhite adoption rates reflect the overall downward trend. In 1971, nonwhite adoptions accounted for 22,000 of the 169,000 total adoptions. In 1975, 7,285 of the 104,188 adoptions were between nonwhite parents and children: a drop from 9 to 7 percent.[1]

During the same period, the decline in transracial adoption suffered even

Table 1. Total Number and Types of Adoptions in the United States: 1971–1975.

Adoptions	Year—Estimated Total*				
	1971	1972	1973	1974	1975
Total number of white adoptions	147,000	59,158	71,940	54,095	56,977
Total number of nonwhite adoptions	22,000	9,902	12,953	11,364	15,167
Total number of black adoptions	15,100	No data	No data	6,331	7,285
Total number of adoptions	169,000	99,552	113,042	107,874	104,188

Source: HEW Publication No. (SRS) 76-03259, NCSS Report E-10 (1971, 1972, 1973, 1974, 1975).

Table 2.   Number of Black Children Adopted by
White Families: 1971–1975.*

Year	Number of Black Children	Number of Agencies Reported
1971	2,574	468
1972	1,569	461
1973	1,091	434
1974	747	458
1975	831	565

Source: Opportunity: a Division of the Boys and Girls Aid Society of Oregon,
December 30, 1976.

more, falling from 2,574 adoptions in 1971 to 831 by 1975. The decline is even
more dramatic than it appears because from 1971 to 1975, the number of reporting agencies increased by 97 from 468 to 565.[2] (Table 2 above.)

Although transracial adoption has waned significantly in the past six years, the
explanations for its curtailment are different from those underlying the reduction
in inracial adoption. Inracial adoption diminished essentially for demographic
reasons. Simply, a sharp reduction in the number of available white and black
"blue ribbon" children (e.g., less than twelve months old and in good physical
and psychological health) resulted from an increased knowledge of contraceptive
practices. In addition, an across social class awareness of the abortion option,
particularly as it impacted upon the Medicaid eligible population, that traditional
group usually surrendering their infants for adoption, and a willingness on the
other hand of some females to keep their children, all contributed to the curtailment of adoptable children. Transracial adoption declined, and in some states
disappeared, because of political and cultural opposition. The alternatives to
transracial adoption, institutionalization or foster care, have been historic failures
and have been recognized as failures by both whites and nonwhites. Both types
of placements tend to make permanent what was originally conceived of as
temporary measures. In other words, children placed in these settings many times
spend most if not all of their childhood years in either of these "temporary"
facilities. Other than transracial adoption, one possible solution to the problem of
parentless nonwhite children is the widespread acceptance of a uniform national
standard for subsidized adoption. This concept, which will be discussed in section 4, has only begun to be implemented.

1. TRANSRACIAL ADOPTION: PARENT AND CHILDREN PERCEPTIONS

The discussion in this section is based on our recent study of 204 families who
adopted transracially. We include it in order to describe the characteristics,

experiences, and attitudes of families who have adopted transracially. Most of the parents we interviewed were college-educated. A majority of the fathers held degrees past the bachelor's and most were professionals or engaged in technical positions. Most of the parents were also regular churchgoers and told us that they could trace their motivation for adopting nonwhite children to their religious beliefs and church affiliations.

Unlike the traditional image of couples who adopt because they cannot bear children, 81 percent of these parents had biological as well as adopted children. Almost all had borne their first child before they adopted one. Fifty-six percent of the families adopted more than one child. About 70 percent adopted their child before he or she was a year old. Only a minority of the parents (about 30 percent) wanted, as their first choice, to adopt a nonwhite baby; the majority wanted a baby who was physically and mentally healthy and normal. Only after they had contacted an adoption agency and become aware of the difficulties and the waiting time involved if they insisted upon adopting a white, healthy baby, did they become interested in adopting a black or American Indian child. The sex of the child was much less important than its mental or physical health or age.

Many of the parents who adopted a child after they had had children claimed that their children participated in the discussion and in the final decision about whether to adopt and what type of child to adopt. They used the phrase, "Adoption is a family affair." In discussing relations between the adopted children and the children born to the parents, almost all of the parents characterized those relations as good. What conflict existed they credited to "normal sibling rivalry."

About a third of the parents reported initial as well as long-time and continuing hostility on the part of grandparents, aunts and uncles, and other relatives to the adopted child. But none of the parents reported accepting a compromise which would have allowed the grandparents to relate to the natural grandchildren but not to the adopted children. Nor did the parents indicate that they had included their parents in the preadoption decision-making process.

When the topic shifted to the future and we asked the parents to anticipate how their adopted child (especially if he or she was black) would cope during adolescence, 70 percent said that they had given this question considerable thought before adopting and had decided to adopt even though they recognized that their family and their child would be confronted with serious problems. About 12 percent expressed the hope that American society would change significantly so that prejudice and discrimination would be diminished to the extent that their child would not suffer from it. To support this hope, they pointed to the changes that had occurred institutionally in the United States (largely as a result of the Supreme Court decision in *Brown v. Board of Education*) and in the informed attitudes and feelings they had seen manifested since the end of World War II. One family said simply, "We're betting on a good world."

But the great majority expected that their adopted child would experience rejection by many of the groups that comprise white society, and that rejection would be especially strong on the part of the parents of their white friends. They also expected that adolescence would be the first time their child would undergo a crisis about his or her identity. Overwhelmingly, however, the parents believe that the type of home they provide for their children before they reach adolescence, and the emotional security with which they endow them, will see them through the crisis.

Most of the parents believed that by the time their adopted children became adults they will have worked out their relations with the larger society such that they will feel secure and well adjusted. Twenty-five percent believed that their children will be able to marry anyone they choose, and that color will not present exclusive barriers. The others would not commit themselves and claimed only that their child would find his or her place and would make a workable adjustment. How many of these statements were wishful thinking on the parents' part, and how many of them were deliberate convictions was hard to determine.

The last formal question of the interview asked:

> If a family like your own, in terms of religion, income, and education living in the community asked you to advise them about whether they ought to adopt a nonwhite child, what would your advice be?

Save for 7 percent who answered that as a matter of principle, they would not advise anyone on such an important personal decision, all but 3 percent said they would urge the family to go ahead and adopt.

Forty percent warned that the family should be very clear in their own minds that they are not making their decision because of their belief in "some social cause," "civil rights," or "racial equality" issue. The parent's decision must be made on the basis of how much they wanted a child and because they believed they could offer the child a good home. Slogans, causes, and political ideology should have no place in their decision. Most of the parents gave as examples of bad motives "proving you are liberal," "wanting to do something noble," "taking a stand against the population explosion." The good motives were the "selfish ones, including wanting a child very badly."

The major purpose of our study was to find out how racial attitudes, racial awareness, and racial identity were likely to be affected by the merging of different races within a nuclear family. The focus was on the children, not the parents. Our target population was young children whose opinions, attitudes, and perceptions on these matters were still in the formative stage. The procedures we used for assessing the children's attitudes were projective devices (involving dolls, puzzles, and pictures) similar to those that have been employed by social scientists over the past three and a half decades.

The most important finding of our study was that black children who are reared in the special setting of multiracial families do not acquire the ambivalence toward their own race reported in all other studies involving young black children. Our results also show that white children do not consistently prefer white to other groups, and that there are no significant differences in the racial attitudes of any of the categories of children. Our findings do not offer any evidence that black children reared by white parents acquire a preference for black over white. They show only that black children perceive themselves as black as accurately as white children perceive themselves as white. It is still too early to say whether this sense of black identity will persist, and what effect will be attached to it as these children grow up.

There was only one instance in which the black children showed less awareness, or perhaps ambivalence, regarding their identity than did the white children, and that was in the matter of selecting puzzle figures with skin shades that matched those of their own parents. The blacks, as well as the Indian or Asian children, erred more than the white children in selecting figures whose skin shades matched their own rather than the figures whose skin shades more closely resembled those of their parents. They did not make this error in selecting figures that represented either themselves or their siblings.

Most previous studies of young children's racial preferences have reported pro-white attitudes on the part of white, black, and Indian or Oriental children living in the United States (Clark, 1958, p. 171; Horowitz, 1939, p. 91; Greenwald, et al., 1968, p. 49; Goodman, 1964, p. 256; Porter, 1971, p. 22; Morland, 1976; Williams, et al., 1967, p. 671; Hraba, et al., 1970, p. 398). Other studies have suggested that black children acquired an awareness of race earlier than white children but were less likely to identify themselves accurately as black. In other words, while black children were able to discriminate between racial categories at an earlier age than white children, because the concept of identity involves feelings or affect about race, black children's responses are likely to be less accurate than white children's. The less accurate scores for identity measures are consistent then with the greater ambivalence black children manifest in their attitudes toward race. While some of the studies referred to go back two or three decades, even those made in the 1960s, the era when slogans such as "black power" and "black is beautiful" became popular, young black children continued to exhibit pro-white attitudes.

We concluded our analysis of the children's responses with the belief that the practice of transracial adoption had a significant and perhaps even a revolutionary impact on the racial identity and attitudes of young black and white children. But we also recognize that it is too early to predict with any degree of accuracy what is likely to happen to these children in later years, during their adolescence and adulthood. It may be that the attitudes and prevailing tones of the larger society will have sufficient impact so as to alter or confuse the identity and attitudes formed within the relatively unique setting of these multiracial families.

2. BLACK ATTITUDES TOWARD INRACIAL AND TRANSRACIAL ADOPTION

Contrary to popular impressions, black couples adopt at a higher rate than white couples in similar financial circumstances. Using 1967 adoption figures, the pool of potential adoptive parents can be defined as married couples between the ages of 25 and 44 earning at least $5,000 per year. The ratio of prospective nonwhite adopters to available nonwhite children was then 15.3 per thousand whereas the ratio for inracial white adoptions was 9.2 per thousand (DHEW, 1967). Nevertheless, because most of the children in need of adoptive parents in this country are black, ways of enlarging the pool of potential black parents must be found.

Most studies of nonwhite adoption report that a major barrier to enlisting potential minority group adopters is their discomfort with large-scale bureaucracies. These institutions are perceived by nonwhites as extensions of white culture with its racial overtones. Such studies suggest that adoption agencies that will be most successful in finding nonwhite parents will be those that are able to (1) present a black image and stress black control, (2) engage in grass-roots community education programs that explain the adoption process and describe the number and types of available children, and (3) simplify the forms and procedures for establishing eligibility criteria and requirements for adoption. Two programs, in New York (Khiss, 1977, p. 39) and Michigan, (Jones, 1976, p. 53) have recently demonstrated that successful placement of black children with black adopters can be achieved by using any or all of the above mentioned policies.

In New York state, a program was recently introduced to find homes for 4,000 children available for adoption, 60 percent of whom were nonwhite. Seeking adoptive parents from a pool composed of black couples who previously applied to be adoptive parents but never completed the process, The Citizens Coalition for Children in cooperation with the New York State Board of Social Welfare introduced the "Black Parents of Black Children" project. In four months, 150 black couples were recruited, of which three have adopted and 40 are in various stages of the adoption process. Modest as these initial figures are, they represent a trend toward increasing the number of inracial black adoptions.

In Detroit, Michigan, "Homes for Black Children," an eight-year-old program, has achieved remarkable success in finding permanent black placements for black children, placing 600 children in adoptive homes. Although 60 percent of Detroit's unwed mothers were black, a 1967 study demonstrated that the city's thirteen adoption agencies had managed to place only 93 black children for adoption during the same period in which 1,300 whites were placed.

Minimizing printed forms (relying instead upon individual home interviews) while maximizing exposure of their program in the black press, Homes for Black Children was able not only to establish a pool of potential black adoptive parents, but to exhaust their supply of healthy infants and move toward placing multiple handicapped nonwhite children. In 1976, their ratio of approved black homes to available children was 35 to 1. Only four years earlier, the national ratio, reflecting the findings of traditional adoption agencies, was 51 approved nonwhite homes per 100 nonwhite children.

Using conventional techniques and traditional indices, adoption agencies were never able to develop a substantial pool of "qualified" black adopters. According to Alfred B. Herbert, Director of H.E.W.'s The Black Child Development Institute:

> Agencies traditionally tested the motivation of applicant families by sending out long complicated questionnaires that asked about age, family stability, religious affiliation, income and even fertility tests. . . . Lots of black families took one look at that form, assumed they wouldn't qualify, and forgot the whole idea (Jones, 1976, p. 56).

The idea that grass-roots community organization and educational programs will increase the number of potential black adopters by projecting an image of black control over agency policies warrants further examination. Joyce Ladner urges intensive recruitment of black adopters within black communities as a means of reaching potential adoptive families and thereby reducing agency reliance upon transracial adoption (Ladner, 1977). Ladner's idea has been suggested by earlier investigators and has an interesting history.

Some have argued that the ratio between adoptable black children and available black homes is deflated as a result of a conscious effort by white-controlled agencies not to involve the black community more fully in attempting to reach black adoptive parents. A 1972 study has shown that there is an inverse relationship between the number of adoptable black children on an agency's caseload and the frequency of transracial adoption (Billingsley et al., 1972, p. 198). An agency that has many available black children is less likely to look for white adoptive parents than an agency that has only a few black children. The implication is that adoption agencies located in black communities with large constituencies of adoptable black children have more contacts and programs within the black community and are therefore in a better position to locate black adoptive couples.

Wachtel's (1972, p. 84) examination of the relationship between an adoption agency's practices and the placement of black children supported earlier results which indicated that the use of mass media to attract potential adoptive black couples is not an altogether effective method of recruitment (Bradley, 1966, p. 433; Fanshel, 1957). In examining the dropout rate of black couples attracted to the adoption agencies by the media, the study noted that there was a lower rate of application completion among these individuals than among black applicants who were informally referred. The latter are defined as successful black adopters who have positive experiences with (black) friends who are themselves adoptive parents. The study concluded that the informal system (i.e., word-of-mouth communication) was the best method by which to insure eventual black inracial adoption. The difficulty lay in the ability of white-administered adoption agencies to attract enough black adopters into the "system" in order to establish credibility.

It should also be noted that adoption agencies serving predominately black children tend to have a higher portion of black social workers on their staffs than agencies with small populations of black children. Two recent studies revealed that a social worker's race appeared to be one of the strongest factors affecting attitudes toward transracial adoption, with black social workers disapproving more often than white social workers (Ferber, 1972; Wachtel, 1973). One study found a correlation of $-.85$ between the number of white social workers employed and the frequency of inracial adoption (black–black) (Wachtel, 1973).

Not only was there a negative correlation between the presence of white social workers on agency staffs and the number of black children adopted by black families (conversely, the more black social workers, the greater the number of inracial black adoptions), but there also appeared to be a negative association between a white social worker's professional contacts (National Association of Social Work membership) and his or her agency's involvement with inracial black adoption (Wachtel, 1973). This, too, lends support to the hypothesis that agencies with large black clienteles employing black social workers make fewer transracial placements.

Aside from the rhetoric of the National Association of Black Social Workers condemning transracial adoption for being a form of cultural genocide, there is little empirical evidence about black attitudes toward transracial adoption. But at least two studies have been done. In the first, one member of each of 150 black families who live in nine census tracts in Dayton, Ohio, which contain high black populations, was interviewed concerning his or her attitudes toward transracial adoption (Howard et al., 1977, p. 184). Approximately three-fourths of the respondents were female and 25 percent of them referred to themselves as housewives. Howard et al. examined attitudes toward transracial adoption by asking about preference for transracial adoption over other placement alternatives. They reported that slightly more than one-half (56.7 percent) of the population had an "open" attitude toward transracial adoption and only 6.7 percent were "most favorable." Three-fourths thought a white home might be better for a black child if no black home was available, and 81 percent felt that transracial adoption would be more beneficial than either foster care (with black foster parents) or institutionalization. Paradoxically, although 80 percent felt that "liberal white parents would be qualified to raise a black child if they gave up some of their white culture in order to give the child a chance to develop some black identity," more than one-half felt that black children, ". . . have special problems that white parents cannot understand or cope with."

In a 1973 survey of a black community in a medium-sized Midwest community, Simon asked a sample of 324 respondents whether they approved of a practice whereby white couples adopt black children. Forty-five percent said that they approved of the practice.

When asked to explain why they felt as they did, responses fell into two major categories. Those who said they approved of the practice did so primarily out of concern for the children. Put simply, adoption was better than having children remain in institutions. A second reason was that the practice of transracial adoption would help to integrate the races. Twenty-six percent cited the first as their reason, and 23 percent the second.

Among those who said they disapproved of the practice, the major reasons were that "Black children would lose their identity" (26 percent); and "Whites do not understand black culture" (16 percent). Fifteen percent said they do not believe in "mixing the races."

Simon also turned the question around and asked:

Do you approve of black families adopting white children?

Thirty-nine percent said they approved of this practice. Over 90 percent of those who approved of white families adopting black children also approved of the reverse practice; and for the same reasons.

When asked,

In your opinion, do white parents know how to raise black children; and
Will black children adopted by white families grow up belonging to a black community?

39 percent answered "yes" to the first item and 31 percent "yes" to the second item.

Both of these percentages are lower than the proportion who said they favored the practice of white couples adopting black children. Cross tabulations showed that a small proportion of those who favored the practice believed that the child would be lost to the black community. But all things considered, they felt that living with a white family was better than having the child remain in an institution.

The results of this survey, unlike the one cited prior, suggest that it is not only black leaders who attack and object to the practice of transracial adoption, but rank-and-file, middle-class blacks as well. Between 60 and 70 percent believe that white parents do not know how to rear black children and that those black children who are adopted by whites will be lost to the black community. As adults they will either not perceive themselves as "black" and therefore have no desire to identify with the black community, or they will not be accepted by the black community.

3. SUBSIDIZED ADOPTION

Subsidized adoption may be the most practical alternative to both inracial and transracial adoption for moving large numbers of parentless children out of institutions and into homes. Although not a new development, it signifies a fundamental shift in adoption ideology. The major difference between nonsubsidized and subsidized adoptions is that in the former, after the adoption is final, there is no further official agency involvement with the adoptive parents. In subsidized adoption the agency continues to maintain an ongoing financial relationship with the adoptive parents, although the adoptive parents have full legal responsibility for the child.

As an alternative to any other type of adoption, subsidized adoption has been endorsed by the Child Welfare League of America. In their Standards for Adoption Service, the League states:

> Provision should be made for supplementing the income of families that have the essential qualifications required to meet the needs of adopted children but that are unable to assume financial responsibility for the full cost of the child's care. Subsidies that would make it possible for a child to have both a permanent home and continuity of care and affection are clearly a more beneficial arrangement for a child. . . . A more positive use of subsidy is expected to result in the adoption of more nonwhite children who might not otherwise be placed.

The National Association of Social Workers (NASW) recently stated:

> The often limited resources in adoptive placements for minority and minority mixed children must be recognized. Social efforts should be made to place children in need of permanent homes in homes of like racial background to that of the child's biological parents; and subsidized adoption should be extended to all adoptive children in need, in order to extend the benefits of subsidized adoptions to low income families of minority groups.

As of August 1975, 41 states had statutes pertaining to subsidized adoption, a number almost double that of ten years before. Although there are some differences among the states regarding subsidized adoption legislation, each state has recognized that the subsidies are intended to be supplemental in nature. In none of the states are the subsidies designed to provide for a child's total financial support. In a majority of statutes, subsidized adoption payments are specifically linked to the state's foster care scale. Although opinions differ as to whether adoption subsidies should be tied to the financial requirements of the adoptive families (e.g., a means test) or to the specific needs of a child (e.g., medical, education, etc.), the matter is usually resolved in favor of the child's needs.

Practically every statute has the proviso that subsidies are to be granted for the purpose of having a parentless child adopted by an otherwise eligible family only after nonsubsidized avenues have been exhausted. This condition appears to be the overriding one under which the majority of subsidies are granted. In effect then, subsidized adoption is viewed as a method of last resort, reserved specifically for the adoption of hard-to-place children who otherwise would not be placed in an adoptive home.

Although the regulations of individual states vary, most deal in some manner with issues such as: (1) the subsidy's duration (short or long periods), but usually not longer than the child's 18th or 21st birthday; (2) the amount of the subsidy (tied in some fashion to foster care payments); (3) the method of payment (categorical allocations marked for direct payments such as medical, special education, or direct grants, or when applicable, payments attached to public assistance); (4) income limitation of adoptive families; and (5) periodic reexamination of financial eligibility. The above requirements are incorporated in the 1975 Model State Subsidized Adoption Act developed by the Child Welfare League of America for the Children's Bureau of the Office of Child Development.

In most cases, the conditions under which eligibility for a subsidy is determined relate to whether a child falls into one of the hard-to-place categories. One of the characteristics of hard-to-place is nonwhite. Most subsidized adoption laws recognize race as a criterion determining whether a subsidy should be used in order to increase a child's eligibility for adoption. It may be argued that subsidized adoption is of particular benefit to nonwhite children since they constitute one of the largest blocks within the hard-to-place category (Jones, 1976, p. 56). The widespread use of subsidies to prospective nonwhite adopters of nonwhite children should then lead to a reduction in the number of nonwhite children available for adoption and consequently to a curtailment of transracial adoption.

An August 1975 Senate Subcommittee report investigating foster care and adoptions found that in 1971, of approximately 330,373 children in foster care, 21 percent were either in institutions or group homes and argued that institutional placement was the most expensive type of nonadoptive care, its cost more than double that of foster care. Approximately 100,000 of the children in foster care in 1971 were legally eligible for adoption, and 90 percent of these children were classified as children with special needs (i.e., hard to place). The report clearly argued for the merits of adoption over nonadoptive placements when it said: the cost for a single infant who entered the New York foster care system in 1971 will amount to $122,500 by the time the child reaches 18 years of age (U.S. Senate, Commission on Labor and Public Welfare, 1975, p. 18).

States that have begun to implement limited subsidized adoption programs report significant financial savings over other types of nonadoptive practices (i.e., foster care). For example, in 1975, Michigan reported that during the first half of 1974, 130 subsidized adoptions were made, costing the state $63,692.67. Were these children to have remained in foster care, the cost to the state for the same period would have been $150,115. Thus Michigan realized a savings of $86,422 or 57 percent (State of Michigan, DHEW, Children's Bureau, 1975).

Both Ohio and Illinois describe similar savings using subsidized adoption in lieu of foster care. Over a two-year period, Ohio reported a savings of $20,547 for 36 children (State of Ohio, DHEW, Children's Bureau, 1973). Illinois, projecting to the age of 18 the costs of 45 children adopted under subsidy who would have otherwise remained in foster care, realized a savings of $292,518 (State of Illinois, DHEW, Children's Bureau, 1970).

One of the operational weaknesses of the subsidized adoption concept is the lack of program uniformity among the various states. States have differing financial aid limits, different categories for which they allocate funds, and different age ceilings for children. What is a fundable category in one state—special education, for instance—may not be eligible for funding in another state and could prevent the relocation of an adoptive family.

In order to rectify the across state discrepancies in aid eligibility, Senator Alan Cranston of California has introduced a Senate bill to provide supplemental federal support through the Social Security Act for low and moderate income families who adopt children with special needs. The aid would be available until the child reached 18 and could total no more than $1,500 per year (*New York Times*, July 28, 1977, p. 14).

Not only would the Cranston proposal benefit parentless children and adoptive families, it is projected to cost substantially less than the annual $1.2 billion spent by federal and state agencies on "hard-to-place" children, $700 million of which is borne directly by the federal government for foster care (Wicker, 1977, p. E19; Swoboda, 1977, p. 1; McGrory, 1977, p. 21). In addition to offering federal subsidies to adoptive families, the Cranston bill calls for the establishment of a national information center which would collect and disseminate information on children available for adoption, and a nationwide adoption registry which would match available children with adoptive parents. The registry proposal is new only in the sense that it would be under the aegis of the federal government. A voluntary organization, The Adoptive Resource Exchange of North America (ARENA), has been in existence for a decade fulfilling the functions essential to the registry idea (Simon et al., 1977, p. 174).

Sufficient evidence exists to support the argument that many foster parents would adopt their foster children were it not for their own limited finances (Watson, 1972, p. 20). In fact, some state laws regarding adoption subsidies stipulate, and many imply, that payments should be awarded only to foster families who wish to adopt children originally placed in their care, where a relationship has already been demonstrated (Gentile, 1970, p. 576; Goldberg, 1969, p. 97; Lansberry, 1968, p. 499). Apparently, this is the assurance sought by many legislators that public money is being well spent (Gallagher, 1971, p. 50).

For nonwhite children and families, the passage of the Cranston bill would be significant. Clearly, many of the children with special needs and many of the low to moderate income families would be nonwhite. Enactment therefore should increase the pool of potentially adoptive parents and make some reduction in the estimated 100,000 to 300,000 hard-to-place but adoptable children presently in institutions and foster care.

The well-established negative relationship between the length of time a child remains in a nonfamilial environment and the chances of eventual adoption clearly indicates that for a majority of institutionalized children, adoption under conventional conditions would not be forthcoming (Maas, 1959). In those cases where financial circumstances prevent adoption, in states where subsidized adoption is allowable, it appears both desirable and logical to link hard-to-place children with potential adoptive parents willing to adopt but financially unable to do so. On the basis of 1975 data, it is estimated that approximately 15,100 nonwhite children (of which approximately 7,300 were black) have been adopted (DHEW, 1975). Although overall adoptions appear to have fallen in 1975, the number of nonwhite adoptions remains fairly stable. The number of actual nonwhite adoptions in all probability belies the more accurate figure of between 40,000 and 80,000 potentially adoptable nonwhite children (Herzog et al., 1971, p. 67). To what extent an offer of subsidy payments to prospective adotive black parents would increase the frequency of nonwhite adoptions is difficult to project. All that can be said on the basis of limited documentation is that the number would increase (Wicker, 1977, p. E19).

4. SINGLE-PARENT ADOPTION

The trend toward acceptance of single-parent adoption, another nontraditional method for dealing with parentless children, offers support for the contention that society's ideas toward marriage, divorce, and child-bearing are changing. The feminist movement has played a significant role in changing traditional patterns of thinking and the acceptance of single-parent adoption may be attributed in large measure to changes in conventional thinking about sex roles.

The basic question of single-parent adoption is whether one legal parent is better for a parentless child's development than any of the other options that do not involve parents.[3] Viscerally the answer appears to be positive. What happens, for example, when one of the parents of any young child dies, or divorce occurs? The child is reared by the one parent. The latter is a natural consequence. Adoption, however, is a planned event, still somehow not quite natural.

Consideration by adoption authorities of the 21 million "recently single" (11.7 million widowed, 5.9 million divorced, 3.3 million separated) adults would certainly help bolster the ranks of those individuals who could be used as resources for parentless children, without taking into account the 22 million who never married (Levine, 1975, p. 1). The popularity and acceptance of single-parent families, especially as they affect the aspirations of women, should make it easier for those involved in adoption to come to peace with the idea of defining single individuals other than natural parents as potential adopters. The fact that one-seventh of all children are being raised in approximately 4.2 million single-parent families, 35 percent by black women, should make the notion of single parents more palatable (Dullea, 1974, p. 46; *New York Times,* July 28, 1975, p. 9). Indeed, between 1960 and 1973, there has been an increase of 67 percent in father-headed single-parent families. Between 1973 and 1975, there was a 23 percent increase in the number of children residing in single-parent families. The increase for white children was more than double that for black children (16 percent and 7 percent, respectively) (Hill, 1976, p. 36).

As with any other new development, the prevalence of the single-parent concept (family or adoption) has effects on social policy. In 1975 the Senate Subcommittee on Children and Youth held sessions evaluating the effects of government-financed programs on single-parent adoptions (Johnson, 1975, p. 65). Testimony was heard on how to improve day care service and on the 9 A.M. to 5 P.M. workday, two issues of particular importance in maintaining the single parent idea.

There have been recent moves to combine programs of child care and parental employment. In 1976 Congress enacted the Tax Reduction Act which allows for a 20 percent tax credit covering job-connected child-care expenses up to $2,000 per child, to a ceiling of $4,000 for two or more children. The advent of the Tax Reduction Act, combined with the acceptance by child welfare agencies of single-parent adoption as an acceptable type of child placement, should make adoption much more attractive to fully employed single individuals.[4]

It is not clear, however, where in the hierarchy single-parent adoption should fall in relation to transracial adoption. If a white couple seeks to adopt a nonwhite child, they can expect to receive priority over a single individual wanting to adopt, even if the latter is racially similar to the child. Some observers, however, would seriously question the prevailing assumption that a two-parent family of a race different from the child's is better for the child's development in the long run than a single parent of the same race.

As with subsidized adoption and other variants of the historic two-parent inracial match adoption, the development of single-parent adoption increases the available pool from which potential adoptive parents can be drawn. If eligible black single individuals are included in this expansion, it would further reduce the need for transracial adoption as a method of obtaining homes for black children.

CONCLUDING REMARKS

For a variety of reasons, it is difficult to set a precise figure on the number of children available for adoption. One hundred thousand is the figure cited most recently. If we remember the number of adoptions that occurred between 1971 and 1975, it should be clear that traditional inracial adoptions—and for quite different reasons, transracial adoptions—cannot by themselves satisfy the need for placing parentless children in family settings. If there is consensus, and there seems to be, that a stable family setting is a healthier environment in which to rear a child than institutions or foster care, then support should be given toward expanding and publicizing the subsidized and single-parent adoption programs. There are already sufficient data to substantiate the belief that both of these schemes, in addition to providing healthier and more positive environments for the children, would cost less money than maintaining those children in institutions or in foster care.

On the basis of the results of our study we would also argue in favor of transracial adoption as still another alternative. The burden of supporting transracial adoption falls primarily on the adoption agencies, the most often used organization for obtaining a bona fide adoption, and on the field of social work, the profession that legitimizes these agencies' functions. The basis for any type of adoption is the union of a homeless child with a family desiring a child. In terms of adoption practice, an improvement in each of the participants' quality of life should be achieved by the successful completion of this process. The information summarized in this article indicates that the transracial adoption of nonwhite children by white families does not jeopardize the nonwhite child's racial awareness, identity or attitude. It achieves the positive result of reducing the number of children in temporary placements. To accept the politically motivated argument against transracial adoption, that it is a nefarious device conceived by whites to rob nonwhites of their children, and that these children will eventually be lost to their respective racial groups, calls into question one of social work's overriding principles, that a multiracial society is not only possible but desirable.

This paper recognizes that it is too early to say with whom these transracially adopted children will identify, how they will characterize themselves, with which community their ties will be closest, and how they will relate to their white parents and siblings. However, if the hopes and expectations of the parents involved in transracial adoption are realized and their children are emotionally whole, well-adjusted, and able to move easily within and between black and white communities, society's failure to maintain the program will be remembered with deep regret.

FOOTNOTES

1. Figures for nonwhite adoption, defined under the Department of Health, Education and Welfare, Definition of Terms category, Race/Ethnicity, can be at times misleading, given the following definition of race: Race and ethnicity, as used in this report, do not denote clear-cut definitions based on anthropological origins. For the purposes of this report, race or ethnicity of a person (child, petitioner) should be determined on the basis of the group to which the person *appears to belong,* with which the person *is identified,* or the group which the community *regards the person as belonging* . . . (italics are the authors') (HEW, 1975, p. 2). The adoption figures cited in Table 1 rest

on the number of states reporting to the Department of Health, Education and Welfare. As can be seen, the number varies by year, totaling no more than 43 during 1971–1975. However, several crucial states did not consistently report racial background data. For example, in 1971, when California did dichotomize their adoption rates by racial background, they had the largest number of nonwhite adoptions of any reporting state (HEW, 1971, p. 2). In 1975, California only indicated the total number of adoptions, eliminating any mention of race (HEW, 1975, p. 8). Alaska in 1971 had the second highest proportion of non-white adoptions (HEW, 1971, p. 2). In 1975, Alaska failed to report any adoption figures (HEW, 1975, p. 6).

2. The basis upon which transracial adoption statistics are accumulated are perhaps less reliable than the Department of Health, Education and Welfare figures. Transracial adoption statistics have only very recently been available from HEW. By 1975, *Opportunity* reported that of the 565 reporting agencies, only 319 had previously reported in 1974. In addition, 139 agencies who reported in 1974 (of 458) failed to do so in 1975. This lack of consistency in reporting tends to belie the accuracy of transracial adoption figures in that only certain agencies report from year to year.

3. Single-parent adoption should not be confused with single-parent family, a term used to describe a home where one of the natural parents is absent (once referred to as a "broken home").

4. Some major corporations have abandoned industrial-based child care schemes, supporting their arguments by citing an updated survey of the 1971 Ford Foundation Study which found that only 6,000 children were receiving care in the 150–200 employer-based centers, while 900,000 children were enrolled in nonemployer-supported centers, both private and public, near where they lived.

REFERENCES

Billingsley, Andrew, and Jeanne Giovannoni (1972), *Children of the Storm: Black Children and American Child Welfare*. New York: Harcourt Brace Jovanovich, p. 198.

Bradley, Trudy (1966), "An Exploration of Caseworkers' Perception of Adoptive Applicants," *Child Welfare* 45(October):433–443.

Bureau of the Census (1969), Current Population Reports, Series P-60, #59, (April).

Child Welfare League of America "Standards for Adoption Service," revised CWLA, 173, pp. 72–73, Sect. 7.5; p. 92, Sect. 0.8.

Clark, Kenneth, and Mamie Clark (1958), "Racial Identification and Preference in Negro Children," in E. Maccoby, T. Newcomb, and E. Hartley, eds., *Readings in Social Psychology*. New York: Holt.

Department of Health, Education and Welfare, Publication No. (SRS) 76-03259, NCSS Report E-10 (1971, 1972, 1973, 1974, 1975) USDHEW, Social and Rehabilitative Service, Office of Information Services, National Center for Social Statistics.

———— Adoptions in 1967, Supplement to Child Welfare Statistics—1967, Children's Bureau Statistical Series 92.

Dullea, Georgia (1974), "The Increasing Single Parent Families," *New York Times* (Dec. 3), p. 46.

Fanshel, David (1957), *A Study in Negro Adoption*. New York: Child Welfare League of America.

Ferber, Anne (1972), "Attitudes of Adoption Workers Toward Requests for Transracial Adoptions," unpublished research project, Baltimore: University of Maryland, School of Social Work.

Gallagher, Ursala (1971), "Adoption Resources for Black Children," *Children* 18(March-April):50.

Gentile, Angela (1970), "Subsidized Adoption in New York: How Law Works—and Some Problems," *Child Welfare* 49(December):576–580.

Goldberg, Harriet, and Llwellyn Linds (1969), The Case for Subsidized Adoptions," *Child Welfare* 48(February):97–99, 107.

Goodman, Mary Ellen (1964), *Race Awareness in Young Children*. New York: Collier.

Greenwald, H. J., and D. B. Oppenheim (1968), "Reported Magnitude of Self-Misidentification among Negro Children—Artifact?" *Journal of Personality and Social Psychology* 8:49–52.

Herzog, Elizabeth; Cecelia Sudia; Jane Harwood; and Carol Newcombe (1971), "Families for Black Children, the Search for Adoptive Parents: An Experience Survey. Washington, D.C.: Office of Child Development, Children's Bureau, Supt. of Documents, U.S. Government Printing Office, p. 67.

Hill, Herbert (1976), Letter to the Editor, *New York Times* (October 11):36.

Horowitz, Ruth (1939), "Racial Aspects of Self-Identification in Nursery School Children," *Journal of Psychology* (January): 91–99.

Howard, Alicia; David Royse; and John Skerl (1977), "Transracial Adoption: The Black Community Perspective," *Social Work* (May):184.

Hraba, Joseph, and Geoffrey Grant (1970), "Black Is Beautiful," *Journal of Personality and Social Psychology* 16:398–408.

Johnson, Sheila (1975), "The Business in Babies," *New York Times Magazine* (Aug. 17):65.

Jones, Iris (1976), "Private Agency in Detroit Eliminates Adoption Obstacles," *Ebony* (June):53.

Khiss, Peter (1977), "Drive Will Seek Adoptive Parents for Many Black Foster Children," *New York Times* (June 19):39.

Ladner, Joyce (1977), *Mixed Families: Adopting Across Racial Boundaries*. New York: Anchor/Doubleday.

Lansberry, Charles (1968), "A Major Question in Subsidized Adoption," *Child Welfare* 47(October):499–500.

Levine, JoAnn (1975), "Between Loneliness and Satisfaction," *Baltimore Sun* (March 2):1.

Maas, Henry, and Richard Engler (1959), *Children in Need of Parents*. New York: Columbia University Press.

McGrory, Mary (1977), "Adoption Sainthood Get a Cranston Push," *Boston Evening Globe* (April 6):21.

Morland, J. K. (1976), *Race, Color, and the Young Child*. Chapel Hill: University of North Carolina Press.

National Association of Social Workers (1977). *News* 22(March):19.

New York Times (1977), "Bill for Adoption Aid Introduced" (July 28):14.

——— (1975), "Census Cites Rise in Blacks' Status" (July 28):9.

Porter, Judith (1971), *Black Child, White Child: The Development of Racial Attitudes*. Cambridge, Mass.: Harvard University Press, p. 22.

Simon, R. J., and Howard Altstein (1977), *Transracial Adoption*. New York: Wiley-Interscience.

State of Illinois, Department of Health, Education and Welfare, Children's Bureau (1970).

State of Michigan, Department of Health, Education and Welfare, Children's Bureau (1975).

State of Ohio, Department of Health, Education and Welfare, Children's Bureau (1973).

Swoboda, Frank (1977), "Adoption Subsidy in Works as Carter Abortion Option," *Baltimore Sun* (July 1):1.

United States Senate (1975), Commission on Labor and Public Welfare, Subcommittee on Children and Youth, Foster-Care and Adoptions, "Some Key Policy Issues," Washington, D.C. (August):18.

Wachtel, D. D. (1972), "Adoption Agencies and the Adoption of Black Children: Social Change and Equal Opportunity in Adoption," dissertation, Ann Arbor: University of Michigan.

——— (1973), "White Social Workers and the Adoption of Black Children," paper presented at the August meetings of the ASA, New York.

Watson, K. W. (1972), "Subsidized Adoption: A Crucial Investment," *Child Welfare* 4:20–28.

Wicker, Tom (1977), "While Children Wait," *New York Times* (June 26):E19.

Williams, J. E., J. K. Roberson (1967), "A Method for Assessing Racial Attitudes in Preschool Children," *Education and Psychological Measurement* 27:671–689.

"THE RACE RELATIONS INDUSTRY" AS A SENSITIZING CONCEPT

Lewis M. Killian, UNIVERSITY OF MASSACHUSETTS

One of the major developments in contemporary society is the professionalization and, quite frequently, the bureaucratization of social reform. Where once the reform of social conditions was a matter of legislative and judicial determination spurred forward by intense political action, today it is frequently a matter of administrative edict and regulation developed by individuals who claim a special competence to deal with the conditions presumably in need of reform. Lewis Killian, a distinguished student of race relations, raises some hard questions about this development in the paper which follows. In his comparative analysis of race relations reform in the United Kingdom and the United States he draws our attention, in particular, to what may very well be counterproductive constraints upon such reform emanating from the organizational characteristics of the professionalized "race relations industry."

When Herbert Blumer proposed that sociological concepts were and should be "sensitizing" rather than "definitive" concepts he gave as examples weighty terms from the language of the discipline—assimilation, institution, anomie,

Research in Social Problems and Public Policy—Vol. 1, 1979, pages 113-137 stratification, and the like. The gist of his definition of a sensitizing concept is, of course, that whereas "definitive concepts provide prescriptions of what to see, sensitizing concepts merely suggest directions along which to look" (Blumer, 1969, p. 148). In another essay he observed that one function of the concept is that it "permits one to catch and hold some content of experience and make common property of it. Through abstraction one can isolate and arrest a certain experience which would never have emerged in mere perception" (ibid., 1969, p.158).

It seems obvious that sensitizing concepts might as well be drawn from the everyday language of the subjects of research as from the vocabulary of sociologists, even though the terms may appear imprecise, inelegant and even facetious. Invented and used by actors in what Blumer likes to refer to as the "natural social world of everyday experience" such concepts must direct our attention to some features of the empirical world which are real in the sense of being important to the actors.

Because such terms often appear facetious, they may be dismissed by social scientists as inconsequential. In American academia such a word, for example, is "grantsmanship." Following up its implications as a serious project could expose numerous unacknowledged realities about how we actually do research, in contrast to how we talk about doing it.

A term which is virtually unknown in the United States but is often used in England is "the race relations industry." What makes the concept even more startling to the American visitor is the recognition that it might easily be applicable in this country but is not used. Hence, exploration of the directions along which it guides our observation of the British situation may offer clues as to what might be found in the United States.

ENCOUNTERING THE CONCEPT

The expression "race relations industry" was first encountered by the author in the course of interviews exploring the possibility of studying a black power movement in Britain. At every turn all the indications were that the short-lived black power movement of the 1960s had long since dissipated. The concept of the "race-relations industry" was very much alive, however. Therefore uses of this term were followed in the daily press, in scholarly and political writings on race relations and in interviews with people who might be considered "members" of the "industry."

Such a person was a Community Relations officer who, in discussing black leaders in Britain, commented that there was a great deal of cooptation of them by the "race-relations industry." When asked what this term meant he indicated that it was a name coined by Peter Simple, a writer for the conservative *London*

Daily Telegraph. He also observed that although Simple used it derisively, it had been taken over and made a point of pride by some of the very people to whom it might apply and, also, that it was used pejoratively by some black power advocates. Both of the latter assertions later proved to be valid.

Shortly afterwards the director of an important foundation funding race relations research was asked, "What do you understand by 'the race relations industry'?" He, too, ascribed the term to Peter Simple who, he said, "writes scathing attacks on the race relations laws, the Race Relations Board, and the Community Relations Commission" and "tries to conjure up an image of a huge number of people drawing salaries." When asked if he thought his own foundation was included he said, "No, I think the term applies only to government agencies."

THE WORLD OF PETER SIMPLE

"Peter Simple," an anonymous writer or group of writers who compose a column called "Way of the World" for the *Daily Telegraph,* does indeed write scathing but highly humorous attacks on race-relations professionals; his regular readers would be quite familiar with the structure of the "race-relations industry" as he describes it. It is a part of the sinister social world of liberal do-gooders and bureaucrats which he has constructed and made so convincing that the editor of the *Daily Telegraph* believes that many people believe that it is real. But the editor asks, "*Is* it so odd that some simple souls should think these people real? In a certain sense they are! They live in our midst. They mirror our times" (Simple, 1975, p. 4). Thus, Peter Simple's readers are familiar with the mythical headquarters, "Ethnic House." He reports a real event but concludes with a jibe at the "race-relations industry" which it will affect:

> Lord Rothschild's Central Policy Review Staff—an important agency of the planning industry—has made a recommendation of great interest to another key British industry—race relations.
> It has suggested that the Community Relations Commission and the Race Relations Board should merge. This has naturally cuased concern at Ethnic House, the 45 million pound London headquarters of the industry (Simple, 1975, p. 48–49).

But there are also laborers in the industry, as the comment of the "managing director" of a small "family race relations business" (obviously Community Relations Council) indicated:

> "What will become of our workers if they are made redundant by amalgamation?" He gestured towards a shed where a group of ageing discrimination testers could be seen closely watching a Pakistani who was trying to order a pint of draught Guinness from a hard-faced White landlord in a cardboard "mock-up" saloon bar (ibid, 1975, p. 49).

Peter Simple, in November 1975, discovered "tokenism," described in what he called "one of the innumerable trade periodicals produced by the race relations industry." He went into raptures over the prospects it offered:

> Tokenism, though a product of American know-how, should have a great future in our own race relations industry. Anybody starting a career in race relations might be well-advised to specialize in this new field, in which the demand for experts is bound to grow with the general expansion of the industry (*Daily Telegraph,* November 19, 1975, p. 14).

While often describing the race relations industry as "Britain's Economic Growth-point No. 1," he also saw problems in it, as the following column shows:

> It looks like being a good year for the race relations industry as for the discrimination industry in general. . . . A new Race Relations Commission is being set up, while the humming factories of the Race Relations Board go on turning out their own range of race relations goods and accessories in ever increasing quantities to suit every pocket and handbag.
>
> So it is dismaying to find that some of the high-up in another sector of the industry, the local Community Relations Councils—there are 85 of them, each receiving up to 100,000 pounds a year from government and charitable funds—are complaining that they don't know quite what they are supposed to be doing (*Daily Telegraph,* January 23, 1976, p. 14).

His conception of what workers in the industry do is revealed in his description of their possible reaction to the discovery (reported in a social science survey) that there is prejudice and conflict between children of different minority groups, including Indians of higher and lower castes:

> What joy even to be the humblest assistant caste discrimination tester in race relations institutes vaster and more complex than any yet known! To observe with sociological eye these children of many races and castes who persist in the strange, wicked and ineradicable human tendency to be themselves: to question, test, tabulate, chide, lecture, warn, issue reports and more reports, research studies and more research studies . . . on, on to the end of time! (Simple, 1975, p. 6).

It is evident that this conservative British spokesman, like some American congressmen, regards social research as costly busy work done at the taxpayers' expense. But a final quotation from him shows that he also regards this busy work as having a pervasive and sinister effect:

> We cannot all be "career" discrimination experts, of course. But even if we are only amateurs, we can all make sure that the subject of discrimination—whether racist, sexist, heightist, weightist, ageist, brainist, beautyist or tokenist—is never absent from our waking thought. With a little practice we can even dream about it too (*Daily Telegraph,* November 19, 1975, p. 14).

Clearly, then in the right-wing perspective which Peter Simple reflects the "race relations industry," whatever it includes, is a fit subject for ridicule and for condemnation. It was, therefore, with some trepidation that I started asking people who worked in some clearly identified branches of the "industry," such as the Community Relations Commission and the Race Relations Board, what the term meant to them. Through queries addressed to a dozen such people located at various levels in the professional hierarchy I evoked no hostile responses but some very animated discourses on the significance of the term.

THE "INDUSTRY" AS SEEN BY THE WORKERS

Only one person I talked to, a white official of the Race Relations Board, even seemed offended by the term. He said, "It is a term of abuse, used by people who feel that a lot of people, many of them using public money, are living on the subject of race when really the whole topic is not worthy of so much time. There isn't any race relations industry. I don't think the Race Relations Board's budget is yet over a million pounds."

Much to my surprise, however, I found that the "laborers" in the so-called race relations industry saw the term not as offensive but as quite applicable. A West Indian CRO (Community Relations officer) said, "It's an industry. Between 1965 when the white paper called for sponsorship of liaison committees (there were only three at the time) and 1971 you've never seen a growth rate so large in an industry." (Peter Simple often referred to the high growth rate!)

Another West Indian made his lack of objection explicit:

> It refers to an industry that absorbs a fair proportion of articulate blacks who work at helping people to live together better—people like me! Why should it be a derogatory term? Many of us wouldn't be functioning if there weren't one!

An Indian Official of the Community Relations Commission felt it implied criticism with which he agreed:

> I use the term myself—except when I say "race industry." I take a very cynical view of the development of this kind of work. The whole structure started with a few scattered CRO's—I was one of them—each working in his own way. We developed a wide variety of techniques. But some people did nothing more than organize tea parties and that sort of thing. All sorts of things are going on that mean nothing. That's why I call it an industry. There is a lot of busy work without any impact.

THE SCOPE OF THE CONCEPT

In some instances the term was limited in its application to the governmental agencies explicitly concerned with race relations—the Race Relations Board, the Community Relations Commission, and the 85 Community Relations Councils and their employees. For some people the referent was broader, however. A West Indian official of CRC, the Community Relations Commission, declared:

> It is the biggest growth industry there is! The term is very often used in a semi-pejorative sense. You see, a lot of people have gotten into the race act who are not particularly committed to racial equality. It provides them with good jobs or good research opportunities. There is hardly an institution of higher learning now that isn't offering a race relations concentration or at least a race relations course.

Asked what the "race relations industry" meant to him, a white CRO replied emphatically and bluntly:

> It means me! It means all the people who get jobs from working in race relations. The Community Relations Commission, the Race Relations Board, the Runnymede Trust, research people in universities, *you!* I don't particularly like the term but it is a fair term.

Another CRO, a West Indian, was asked whether he would include university researchers in his conception of the "industry." He pulled no punches:

> Definitely. I'll be frank, when you called I knew you were an American and a sociologist and I almost refused to see you. We have been studied until I think black people are the most researched people in Britain. Students go to the universities and they all do their research on race relations. Some people even get jobs on the basis of being experts on black people!

The last quotation from a laborer in the industry reveals another theme suggested by the term. The speaker was a West Indian who was still in his probationary year as a Community Relations officer. Before taking the job he had been very active in a number of voluntary West Indian organizations and had some reputation as a militant. He said, "Yes, there is such a thing as a race relations industry. It's a cynical term, even though I'm in it. It's something of a racket. When I took the job a lot of my friends kidded me and said the poacher had turned gamekeeper!"

The notion that its professionals are the "gamekeepers" of Britain's black citizens makes the term "race relations industry" a bitter slur when uttered by militant minority spokesmen.

THE MILITANT PERSPECTIVE

One such spokesman was an Indian who heads an organization devoted to protecting people against abuses by the immigration authority, duplicating a government organization supposed to be doing the same thing. He said of the "race relations industry":

> I think it is a sort of sarcastic expression against most of the people involved in the race relations area. Let's face it, the Community Relations Commission is appointed by the government. Money is channeled from the Home Office to the Community Relations Commission

and from it to the various community relations councils and officers. It is natural that people who still suspect the establishment would use this kind of sarcastic expression for a place where people can get good jobs—why a CRO must make 4500 to 5000 pounds now—working in race relations.

Although he would not place himself in the ranks of the sarcastic critics of the establishment, the British sociologist Michael Banton himself used the concept of the race relations industry in a way suggestive of the militant critique. In his book, *Racial Minorities,* he suggests that an urban industrial social system can contain great tensions because its members see their interests in very varied ways. Thus, he suggests:

> It is a system which can assimilate anti-social forces and turn them to somebody's advantage. As crime increases so does employment and profit in the security industry. As citizens become concerned about polution so companies are formed to market anti-pollution measures. As racial tension is identified, a race-relations industry takes shape (Banton, 1972, p. 183).

The militant notion of the function of the race relations industry is made explicit in a little book by a young black sociologist, Robert Moore, *Racism and Black Resistance in Britain.* To the book he adds an appendix entitled, "Policies for Containment: The Race Relations Industry." He subsumes under the concept only the Race Relations Board, the Community Relations Commission, and its affiliates, the Community Relations Councils. Like a number of other critics, he finds sinister implications in the very term "community relations." Thus he says:

> In a way the whole concept of "community relations" is misleading. It is based on a theory that once we have dealt with the problem of immigration (by stopping it) it is only a problem of helping strangers to understand our ways, our language and customs and to understand one another. . . . The "problem" is one of systematic and deliberate domination and exploitation of a mass of immigrants—who occupy a special position within British society and the British economy. They are not separate communities in this sense. Nor do they need integrating—they are already integrated; into the lowest-paid and worst-unionized jobs in the service and high-risk sectors of the economy, in menial and unpleasant tasks that are needed to keep our affluence enjoyable. They are fully integrated *at the bottom.* The question is do we organize to keep them at the bottom, or do we organize for something else?" (Moore, 1975, pp. 109–110).

He ascribes an even broader political significance to the race relations industry when he says:

> British political parties and political activities are based on the conflict of social classes within an industrial society, and all our political institutions reflect this. "Race" is outside this set-up and confuses the issues for politicians and trade union officials. So they have "subcontracted" the race question to specialist organizations while they get on with what they regard as the *real* business of politics (ibid., 1975, p. 11).

MEANINGS OF THE CONCEPT

So, as we look at the uses of the term "race relations industry" from the "white right" to the "black left" we can discern at least three different meanings. The first, Peter Simple's view, is that the industry is a group of busybodies who gain a sense of self-righteousness out of creating racial problems where none exist and who make a very good living in the process. The second view, expressed by workers in the "industry," seemed to be that while they were not sure what good their work did, the industry did indeed provide good jobs for minority people. *Punch* picked up this theme in an article on the emergent black middle class. Discussing what avenues of mobility might be open to a young black man, the authors concluded, "If all else fails, he could join the payroll of one of the race relations organizations. They could hardly hold his colour against him" (*Punch*, December 10, 1975: 1085).

The third view, articulated most clearly by Robert Moore but also reflected in the writings of some other militant blacks, uses the concept to attack a structure believed to have been deliberately created by white liberals and the Labour government as a device to contain and divert effective minority protest. Moore and A. Sivanandan, a Sri Lankan who inherited all that remains of the Institute of Race Relations after a "Third World Revolt" decimated it, write as if the "industry" is the result of a conspiracy. They can identify villains—white liberals and black moderates—who had been volunteers in such nongovernmental organizations as the Campaign against Racial Discrimination and the Institute for Race Relations but were at the same time involved in government service. Sivanandan singles out for special attention a number of intellectuals, including several social scientists, who were associated with the "Survey of Race Relations in Britain," initiated in 1963, funded by a private foundation and deliberately designed to be "a Myrdal for Britain." Sivanandan says that "bringing together a variety of part-time "race professionals" the Survey "was the cornerstone of the race industry" (Sivanandan, 1974, p. 11).

It is not necessary to subscribe to a conspiracy theory, as Sivanandan does, to be alerted to important aspects of social action by the concept of the race relations industry. The term itself and its different usages reflect different perspectives on race relations. Of particular interest are the differences in the perspectives of militant minority members who criticize the "industry," and the perspectives of the workers whom they criticize.

First, let us consider those near the top of the "industry," full-time government officials and members of commissions. Their very position in the social structure suggests an approach to race relations as a subject for social engineering, or as a management problem. Sivanandan (1974, p. 7) calls it "managerial liberalism." It calls for expertise, and assumes that such expertise exists. Several of the top people in the British race relations constellation made one or more trips to the United States to confer with their American counterparts—"experts with experience''—before attempting to formulate British law. Two of these men, one of whom is still very high in the government, wrote an unofficial book called *Race and Law* (Lester and Bindman, 1972). While the book is mildly critical of British race relations law as it existed at the time, the managerial outlook is suggested in a statement in the introduction:

> And it is hoped that it will provide a much-needed practical handbook for the growing number of public officials, voluntary bodies and private citizens who sometimes refer to themselves ironically as the race relations industry (Lester and Bindman, 1972, p. 11).

The race relations laws which provide the material for this ''handbook'' reflect, of course, what the party in power was able to get through parliament. Neither that which was proposed nor that which was passed was the creature of the minorities for whose benefit they are allegedly intended. One of the most frequent criticisms of the ''community relations'' concept was that it emphasized peace and harmony for the Kingdom, not justice and equality for the oppressed.

By the same token, while laborers in the ''race relations industry'' may suggest changes in the laws or in the ways in which they are administered, the decision-making power remains with the government ministers and the majority in Parliament. In the meantime, the workers must operate within the framework established by these forces.

It was indeed true that, as Peter Simple gleefully reported, lower-level workers were confused as to their role. The few studies that have been made of Community Relations Councils and Community Relations officers showed a variety of styles. One of the most prevalent was described by a black journalist who did the most recent study as a ''Community development role.'' It is, in effect, a combination of the social worker's and the ombudsman's role. This journalist, Lionel Morrison, observes that as long as the CRO can deliver the goods it makes no difference whether he is black or white. He argues that, for blacks, ''What matters . . . is whether you can produce the 'goods' to their satisfaction. This new sophistication among blacks marks a departure from the 'black is at all cost beautiful' concept which so many blacks in the race relations industry still tenously hide behind'' (Morrison, 1976, p. 122).

The way in which Morrison uses ''race relations industry'' suggests that he is not really critical of it in the way that a militant black would be. His acceptance of what the ''industry'' is and the differentiation of his perspective from that of the militants is found in another statement, one to which they would not take exception but from which they might draw different conclusions. He writes, ''The community relations movement is on the whole a government-sponsored exercise and it would be ludicrous to expect a subsidised revolution, and a black one at that'' (Morrison, 1976, p. 120).

The perspective of the militants causes them to see race relations not as a matter of community development, nor of management, nor of expertise, but as first and last political. The race leader should be a fighter, not a manager; a strategist, not an expert. His goal should not be harmonious community relations and racial peace, but maximizing the power of the minority community. Hence the "race relations industry" is perceived as hostile to minority interests not simply because so many of its workers are indeed government employees but even more because of the definition of the problem of race relations implicit in their approach.

For this reason officials of private foundations, such as Runnymede, and university research personnel, particularly social scientists, were perceived by some people as part of the race relations industry. To the extent that race relations are perceived as a problem to be studied and, hopefully, solved through social engineering, the supposedly independent intellectual departs from the political frame of reference and approaches the industrial perspective. There is an important question of motivation here, also. Without imputing too much purity of heart to him, the "race leader" works first of all for the welfare of his group. For what does the community relations professional work? For an abstract ideal of "racial harmony" and "racial justice," plus a salary which is secured by Civil Service wage scales and the strength of his labor union. And for what does the social scientist in the academic department of the race relations industry work? In Britain, the ones who seem to come closest to the social engineering approach of the rest of the industry are those in the Research Unit on Ethnic Relations of the Social Science Research Council. The SSRC is a government-funded agency, unlike its American counterpart; and is thus likely to be suspect in the eyes of militant minority leaders. As for other social scientists, the great majority are in universities working out of intellectual and humanitarian interest in the problems of minorities but also working for the satisfaction of publication and the professional prestige and advancement which it brings. Race relations is not the "in" topic which it is in the United States but in comparison with the period before 1960 there has been a virtual "boom" in race relations research in England. Thus, as has been the case in the United States, the complaint was heard from some blacks in England that social scientists are making a living from studying them. Sivanandan voiced the classic criticism of detached, objective social science when he wrote of the Institute of Race Relations:

> But at its very inception the Institute had decided to forswear commitments to any particular race or group. In the event, therefore, the solutions that the Institute's research would throw up would address themselves not to the problems of black people but to black people as the problem (Sivanandan, 1974, pp. 3-4).

LOOKING AT THE UNITED STATES

Is there a "race relations industry"? In 1974 an official of the Runnymede Trust, which some people regard as part of the British race relations industry, visited the

United States to observe developments in equal employment opportunities in that country. He was impressed by "the existence of a large Government machine at Federal and State levels to deal with employment cases," the Equal Employment Opportunity Commission alone having more than 2,000 employees (Rees, 1974, p. 7). This figure dwarfs the number of people involved in the British "industry," no matter how broadly it is conceived. Yet the concept of a "race relations industry" does not have the currency in the United States which it has in Britain, if it is used at all. As has been suggested earlier, however, it is not difficult to envisage its application to the American scene. What would the American scene look like if viewed through the filter of the construct, "race relations industry?"

While not using the exact term, Benjamin Heineman, an American who did research on race relations in Britain, offers a suggestion as to why the concept emerged there:

> Because the racial problem came to Britain with relative swiftness, the number of people actively concerned about shaping public policy to aid immigrants was relatively small at the time. Those involved, whether academics, members of official or semi-official organizations, or activists in "immigrant groups," tended to know others with similar predilections and concerns. A "race relations constellation" developed, comprising a number of organizations linked informally by common concerns and common attitudes, and a group of "race relations professionals" who worked both within and outside the Government (Heineman, 1972, p. 126).

If there is a "race relations industry" in the United States, it has had a much longer period in which to develop than was the case in England. America's race problem did not come "with relative swiftness" but existed over a long time. That what might be viewed as the "race relations industry" did not flower correspondingly early inspires the first commentary on how this nation has dealt with its racial problems.

It might be said that our first body of "race relations professionals" working within the government were those men of diverse training and motivation who served in the Bureau of Indian Affairs from 1824 until even now, and in the Freedman's Bureau from 1865–1872. These were America's first "experts" on its two largest racial minorities. In the first case the body of professionals grew out of an earlier Indian service whose "location within the War Department implied that, in the last analysis, the relations were those of control and subjugation of peoples outside of the frame of the Union" (Wax, 1971, p. 47). The short-lived Freedman's Bureau was hastily thrown together by the Reconstruction Congress to deal with the problems of thousands of newly freed slaves recently made citizens. That this first bureaucratic structure devoted to the welfare of black Americans was dismantled within less than ten years reflects the turning away of the nation from the issue of racial justice.

In the decade of the 1870s all three branches of the federal government shifted to a hands-off policy toward the black minority and a laissez-faire policy vis-à-vis the state governments. Except for the Bureau of Indian Affairs, which persisted as an ever-expanding bureaucracy, there were no official race relations agencies. Indeed, just as the employment of blacks in the federal government went into a steady decline, the presence of whites who showed unusual interest in the plight of blacks became anomalous.

There did develop over the years, nevertheless, a constellation of race relations professionals, but it did not have even such an unofficial link to government as the early Institute of Race Relations had in England. It grew up, instead, in academic departments in a small number of universities. During the first half of the present century small clusters of scholars of different disciplines emerged and their work came to be known to each other. Thus at Columbia there was Franz Boas, in anthropology, and Otto Klineberg, in psychology, and their students. At the University of Chicago, Robert E. Park founded what came to be known as "the Chicago School" and subsequently was the subject of acrimonious debate. The training, research and writing that went on in these institutions served to establish race relations as a recognized field of study, with a cadre of scholars familiar with one another's work, and with a succession of apprentices coming in through graduate study. The Chicago School subsequently came in for criticism for its alleged assimilationist bias and lack of appreciation of the pluralistic viewpoint of the black minority. A product of the Chicago School, Everett C. Hughes makes a more general comment on the growth of the constellation of race relations experts which is suggestive of the "industrialization" of the field—although he speaks of "professionalization."

> Our problem is not that we are too deeply involved in human goings-on but that our involvement is so episodic and so bound to the wheel of particular projects with limited goals; in short, we are too professional. While professionalizing an activity may raise the competence of some who pursue it by standardizing methods and giving license only to those who meet the standard, it also may limit creative activity, by denying license to some who let their imagination and their observations run far afield, and by putting candidates for the license (Ph.D.) so long in a straitjacket that they never move freely again (Hughes, 1963, p. 890).

Here is an intimation of the often overlooked fact that "scholarly" or "professional" interest in a social problem is not the same as personal involvement as a victim. Furthermore, there may be incentives for the professional to study a topic which may operate independently of his concern for the problem. They may be neither political nor purely scholarly, but primarily financial, although the donors obviously hope that those who study race relations—or mental health or law enforcement or welfare policies—will do so out of motives that are at least mixed. The existence of the phenomenon of grantsmanship suggests, however, that it is indeed true that very often intellectual interests go where the money is.

THE BUYING OF RACE RELATIONS RESEARCH

The growth of a race relations industry in the United States was indeed stimulated from an early date by financial incentives. The encouragement started in a small way in 1911 at two segregated southern universities! In that year the Phelps-Stokes Fund established fellowships at the University of Georgia and the University of Virginia to reward graduate students who would do their master's research on the problems of the Negro. As late as 1940 the Phelps-Stokes Fellowship was the only fellowship available in the social sciences at the University of Georgia.

But six years after the Phelps-Stokes Fund originated, a much more munificent program of subsidizing students, black and southern white, for studies which might be related to race relations came into existence. This was the Julius Rosenwald fund, established in 1917. During the thirty-one years of its operation from 1917 through 1948 the fund awarded fellowships to over 290 scholars. The most frequently chosen field of study was sociology (Embree and Waxman, 1949, pp. 160–161). Among the Rosenwald Fellows who became well-known "race relations professionals" within the academic world were Brewton Berry, John Dollard, C. Wilson Record, C. Vann Woodward, W. O. Brown, Mildred Mell, Lewis C. Copeland and Donald Pierson. A few went outside of academia into an activist role, such as James Dombrowski, of the Southern Conference Educational Foundation, and John A. Griffin, one of the earliest officials of the U.S. Community Relations Service. While there is no basis for claiming that these fellowships were all that induced these scholars to specialize in the field of race relations, it is reasonable to assume that they did facilitate the pursuit of this interest.

The Rosenwald Fund engaged in another activity which was to grow increasingly characteristic of foundation involvement in the "race relations industry," first in the United States and later in England. Toward the close of its existence in 1947, it contributed $95,000 toward a study of "Segregation in the Nation's Capital." While this study employed a small number of social scientists, later studies subsidized by foundations demonstrated that race relations research could indeed be "big business." The classic venture of this sort was the comprehensive study of the Negro in the United States financed by the Carnegie Foundation and directed by Gunnar Myrdal. It provided employment and research opportunities for scores of social scientists, many of whom later became well known in their own right as experts in race relations. At the same time, we may wonder how the ideological leanings of the already existing constellation of race relations professionals shaped Myrdal's conclusions, for he drew heavily on members of the Chicago school for advice and assistance, particularly Louis Wirth and E. Franklin Frazier, while Arnold Rose did much of the writing of *An American Dilemma*.

The optimistic and assimilationist bias characteristic of this school is strongly evident in Myrdal's analysis, particularly in his theory of cumulation. The implications for intervention were for those of a social engineering type, designed to set in motion a spiral of improved race relations starting with either reduction of white prejudice or improvement of black standards of living. One of Myrdal's few but severest critics, Oliver C. Cox, called *An American Dilemma* "an apology for reformism" (Cox, 1947, p. 535). At the most, the work is a blueprint for "managerial liberalism"; it is not a handbook for revolution. As Cox charges, it nowhere calls for a rearrangement of power relations in the United States. This is characteristic of an "industrial" approach to race relations, for the "industry" is created and financed by the ruling class, or at least by its liberal segment.

Subsequently the massive Rockefeller Brothers Foundation and the Ford Foundation financed many research projects which helped sustain the interest of established scholars in race relations and financed the graduate training of new recruits to sociology and the other social and behavioral sciences. These and smaller foundations, such as the Field Foundation, played an important part in supplying "capital" for a healthy but still immature "race relations industry" during a long period, from the early thirties until the early sixties, when the government would support race relations research only when it was incidental to some other issue—such as rural poverty—and when too active an interest in "the Negro problem" could cause a white scholar to be suspected of subversive leanings.

The foundations have not only funded research; they have also contributed heavily to black or interracial protest and improvement associations, such as the NAACP, the National Urban League, the Southern Regional Council, Southern Christian Leadership Conference, and CORE. It is on account of this support that we find some black leaders decrying the conservative and restraining influence of a race relations "establishment" or "industry."

In 1964 the militant black editor, LeRone Bennett, Jr. wrote an essay denouncing "The Black Establishment" which, he charged, was distinguished by its reluctance to act boldly and its failure to organize the masses for social contention. His description of "The Black Establishment" showed that he saw it really as a *"race relations establishment"*:

> The Black Establishment, oddly enough, is not all-black. It a group of Negroes *and whites* who command the power lines *in* the Negro community: the executive secretaries, the board chairmen (often white), the presidents (often white), and board members (Negro and white), of protest and improvement associations; the bishops of Negro denominations and pastors of the largest and most influential churches (the two are not necessarily synonymous), the editors and publishers of major Negro newspapers and periodicals; the leading educators, business and professional men (Bennett, 1964, p. 52).

Then Bennett sketched the outline of an even broader "establishment" which included "liberal" organizations such as labor unions, the American Civil Liberties Union and a variety of religious organizations, plus the foundations. Of the latter he said:

> Another layer of hidden power on the fringes of the Establishment centers in philanthropic organizations and their representatives. The Rosenwald Foundation, the American Missionary Association of the Congregationalist Church, the Rockefeller Foundations and the Harmon Fund have played huge roles in shaping and breaking Negro policy. Of crucial importance in the context of current power realities are the Taconic Foundation and the Phelps-Stokes Fund (ibid., 1964, pp. 58–59).

Subsequent to the writing of Bennett's essay, there were drastic changes in the nature of black protest, with the eruption of black violence, the rise and decline of the Black Power movement, and the entry of blacks into a new kind of black politics. It would appear that the ''black establishment'' might have demanded and received more from this ''layer of hidden power.'' Yet ten years later another black leader, Vernon E. Jordan, Jr. was still critical of the foundations. First he charged that the major foundations had supported neither the early campaign of the NAACP against segregation nor the subsequent voter-registration campaign of the Southern Regional Council. After the passage of the 1969 Tax Reform Act which provided for extensive federal regulation of foundation activities, he feels there was a marked slowdown in ''the flow of grants to blacks and black-led programs.'' His summary judgment of the role of foundations in the area of race relations is harsh:

> In spite of individual instances of great generosity, an honest appraisal of foundation activities leads to the conclusion that foundations have placed black people and black agencies in the same ghettoized category that typifies their living arrangements in the cities. One need only look at the proportionately small funding made available to black causes to know that these areas represent the slum sector of foundation giving. Here, as elsewhere, black folk get the leftovers (Jordan, 1976, p. 488).

Jordan notes that the partial vacuum left by the inadequacy of foundation giving has led black agencies to turn more and more to Washington for assistance. He warns against the expansion of the race relations ''establishment'' in this direction:

> History has shown that dangerous or, at best, relatively unhealthy situations can be created when governments assume roles previously filled by the private sector. It should also be stressed that among the recipients of foundation moneys there is a preference for funding from a variety of sources, which decreases dependence upon any single source. If private and foundation giving does not increase to a reasonable level, black agencies are likely to find themselves seriously restricted in their movement potential and open to a buffeting by political winds (Jordan, 1976, p. 488).

Here again is the recognition of the restrictive nature of a race relations ''industry,'' particularly a government sponsored one. To repeat Lionel Morrison's observation, ''It would be ridiculous to expect a subsidized revolution, and a black one at that.''

THE FEDERAL GOVERNMENT AND THE ''RACE RELATIONS INDUSTRY''

But the threat that the federal government might bid to become a major partner in America's ''race relations industry'' is a recent one. It has been suggested that the earliest ventures into the field arose in connection with the subjugation of the

Indians and the war which resulted in freeing black slaves. Ironically, one of the next forays into subsidizing race relations research took place in the midst of battle. In 1945 the social scientists of the Research Branch of the Army Information and Education Division found themselves assigned the task of studying the reactions of white troops to the addition of black platoons to their companies during the Battle of the Bulge. Although this was only one small study done by this team, the Research Branch of I & E probably had the largest collection of social scientists ever gathered under one director—the sociologist Samuel Stouffer. It is a bitter commentary on the nature of the partnership between government and social science that while the experiment was pronounced a success by the officers in the field, the Chief of Staff decided that the findings should not be published, and as soon as the war was over the Army returned to its former policy of segregation. Not until a manpower crisis arose again, this time in Korea, was the policy of segregation by unit changed again. Once more social scientists were sent to study the new arrangement after it had been adopted as a "field expedient" but this time the policy became permanent.

It was still the case as the decade of the 1950s opened that "race relations professionals" in the United States had little influence on government policy or on the course of race relations generally. Such impetus for even moderate change came from the "Black Establishment," particularly the NAACP. In illustration, a Department of Justice attorney told the New York City Commission on Human Rights that all of the school desegregation cases brought between 1954 and 1965 came as the result of private litigation (Dunbaugh, 1975, p. 12).

In Britain it was the unprecedented influx of large numbers of dark-skinned immigrants which stimulated interest in race relations and the growth of a "race relations industry." Yet in the opinion of David Stephen, former director of the Runnymede Trust, the reforming impulse in that country came not from black demands or general public concern but "from a small band of parliamentary 'liberals,' in a sense as paternalist measures" (Stephen, 1975, p. 2). In the United States, in contrast, the termination of the laissez-faire, states-rights era which hung on even through the years of the Eisenhower administration resulted from the pressure of a revitalized black protest movement. It is clear in retrospect that the federal government, save for the judiciary branch, was essentially hostile to the Civil Rights movement until the dramatic "conversion" of Lyndon B. Johnson and the passage of the 1964 Civil Rights Act. With that law, the federal government entered the business of race relations on a large scale. Already, however, a small constellation of civil servants concerned with race relations had begun to arise within the bureaucracy which Arthur Schlesinger, Jr. has described as "the permanent government" (Schlesinger, 1965). Thus according to Rainwater and Yancey, in 1965, the first opposition to the Moynihan report came from inside the government from what they call the "civil rights network" (Rainwater and Yancey, 1967, p. 170). This was a small group of people, smaller than the already existing "welfare establishment," scattered amongst the

Department of Labor, the new Department of Health, Education and Welfare, and the Office of Economic Opportunity.

Although the controversy over Moynihan and the 1965 White House Conference "To Fulfill These Rights" created a conviction among blacks that Johnson's dedication to civil rights did not equal his rhetoric, the 1964 law nevertheless provided the foundation for an ever-expanding "race relations industry" within the federal government. It was to include the Equal Employment Opportunities Commission and the Office of Federal Contract Compliance, the Office for Civil Rights in the Department of Health, Education and Welfare, and compliance officers charged with monitoring race relations in almost every branch of government. In addition, hundreds of state, municipal and private bureaus and functionaries have been created to promote racial justice and, importantly, to keep their employers out of trouble with the "feds." Here, for example, is an excerpt from an academic job description:

> The Assistant to the President for Human Resources is an executive staff position reporting to the President of the University, with responsibility for serving as Affirmative Action Officer and for Coordinating University Programs for cultural, racial and ethnic diversity. The Assistant is responsible for institutional compliance with all relevant equal opportunity and affirmative action legislation.

This mission of "executive assistant in charge of race relations" is of particular significance, for one of the greatest changes in race relations in the United States since 1960 has been the development of a network of professionals in the federal government with a vision of eliminating racial discrimination and producing equality of both opportunity and results. They have power to move this vision toward fulfillment by bringing "pattern or practice suits" or by suspending payments of federal funds. Although subject to some influence from the White House and Congress, the persistence of the "race relations industry" in promoting affirmative action in education and employment even in the face of presidential reluctance during the Nixon and Ford administrations shows that it has indeed become part of the permanent government. As an example of this bureaucratic independence, Daniel P. Moynihan reports that

> ... even as President Nixon was assuring the AJC (American Jewish Committee) of his abhorrence of quotas, his Office of Civil Rights at HEW was preparing "guidelines" for Affirmative Action programs for colleges and universities which by most earlier understanding imposed quotas (Moynihan, 1973, p. 208).

These public servants find their projects subject to review by federal judges, they must operate within the boundaries laid down by Congress, and they find themselves in constant tension with Congress. Nevertheless they are engaged in one of the most extensive programs of social engineering in the nation's history. They are professionals, and they are acting as Everett Hughes predicted professionals will when he wrote in 1963, "Every profession considers itself the proper body to set the terms in which some aspect of society, life or nature is to be thought of, and to define the general lines, or even the details, of public policy concerning it" (Hughes, 1963a, p. 636). But these professionals not only have a vision, they also have power. The capability which an agency such as the HEW office of Civil Rights has of referring cases to the Attorney General for suit to bring about compliance with the Civil Rights Law is moderately more efficient than the procedure by which the British Race Relations Commission seeks injunctions in county courts after conciliation fails, but the power to terminate federal funds is far more awesome than any power the British race relations industry possesses. Largely through their dedication to promoting their long-range plan for racial assimilation, members of the American "race relations industry" have kept the subject of affirmative action, broadly conceived, in the forefront of political controversy—with busing, quotas, and timetables as specific issues. They have been influential in causing many universities to increase minority proportions in admissions of students and hiring of faculties; they have played a large part in the amazing dismantling of the dual school system in the South; and, along with the federal courts, they have sent thousands of school children on school bus rides across northern cities. Backed by the unwavering strategy of the NAACP and supported by the theories and research of the modern assimilationist school of social scientists, they have made advocacy of race-conscious affirmative action the touchstone of racial good will, despite the complexity of such issues as "reverse discrimination" and "benign racial classifications." The federal bureaucracy has taken up the torch which fell from the hand of the Civil Rights Movement. In 1965 Louis Lomax said cynically: "Let the Truth be told; Lyndon Baines Johnson is now the number one 'Negro' Leader!" (Lomax, 1965, p. 62). In 1977 it might be said, "The Civil Rights bureaucracy is the number one black organization!"

Certainly the mushrooming of government involvement in promoting racial equality may be taken as a sign of progress, although that progress is difficult to measure. But the nature of its ultimate goal may be debated, as is suggested by a statement made by Moynihan early in the development of the affirmative action strategy. He said:

> ... I am worried that having so far been unable to assemble the political majority that would enable the nation to provide a free and equal place for the Negro in the larger society by what are essentially market strategies (full employment, income supplementation, housing construction and such-like), we will be driven to institutional strategies involving government-dictated outcomes directed against those institutions most vulnerable to government pressure (Moynihan, 1973, p. 204).

Thus the promotion of seemingly drastic reforms does not necessarily signify that the U.S. "race relations industry" is, unlike the British, a revolutionary force inside the government. "Preferential treatment" and "affirmative action quotas'' of 10 or 15 percent do not constitute the kind of massive reparations to the black community demanded in the ''Black Manifesto'' adopted by the National Black Economic Development Conference in 1969. Nor is affirmative action an anti-establishment program in the sense of presenting a radical challenge to the existing system of monopoly capitalism which has made black unemployment a continuing crisis since 1957. Jack Rothman sums up what may be called the ''radical view'' of affirmative action as a liberal placebo in these words:

> It is also suggested that preferential treatment as an approach involves minor tinkering with the economic inequities of the system. Minorities at the bottom of the economic structure (blacks, Chicanos, Puerto Ricans) vie for a position with other minorities (Jews, Irish, Italians) who have only recently struggled up into the middle class. Meanwhile, comprehensive redistribution of wealth is sidetracked, and economic elites escape responsibility for helping to correct racial injustice, of which they are the major beneficiaries (Rothman, 1977, p. 42).

In an important sense, the rise of the race relations industry is a continuation of the Civil Rights, integrationist phase of the ''Black Revolution''—but not of the nationalist and separatist theme of black power. Thomas Blair, a black British sociologist, observes that many of the actors are the same:

> Many of the men and women who were involved in the boycotts, sit-ins, and freedom marches are now in well-paid executive, professional teaching and political positions. Government-financed anti-poverty programs, race-research centers, and urban-aid task forces, begun as the result of agitation in the ghettos, placed a generation of talented blacks in the managerial, technical, and paraprofessional posts that hitherto were the province only of whites (Blair, 1977, p. 187).

The very same liabilities that Asian and West Indian militants see in the British ''race relations industry'' may inhere in the United States civil rights establishment. First, there is a commitment to a thoroughgoing assimilationist philosophy which, a few years ago, would probably have evoked vigorous denunciations by such black nationalist heroes as Malcolm X and Stokeley Carmichael. The intellectual ferment which generated for blacks—and Chicanos and Puerto Ricans and Indians—a variety of goals and strategies has subsided with the decline of Black Power. The concept of community control of schools that remain black seems to have been abandoned; the implication that black children cannot learn in an all-black setting seems to be accepted both by members of the ''race relations industry'' and by the leaders of the NAACP. Black colleges, particularly private ones, must fight for their continued existence. What help they may expect from the federal government is designed to insure that they become less black and, desirably, less than half-black. Of assistance for private colleges Daniel C. Thompson writes:

> The federal government, too (like the foundations) has blatantly discriinated against Black colleges. According to all available pertinent information the financial support government

agencies have provided Black colleges is a relative pittance compared with what has been extended to white colleges. The federal government tends to deemphasize the role of Black colleges in its concern to promote the general welfare of this nation (Thompson, 1973, p. 247).

A second important point about the race relations industry is that it is not controlled by blacks, even though it is filled with people overflowing with good will toward the victims of discrimination. The Secretary of Health, Education and Welfare who created a storm by advocating minority quotas is not black but an Italian-American. How representative of blacks Patricia Harris, the black Secretary of Housing and Urban Development is, was questioned by the black psychiatrist, Alvin Poussaint, when he wrote of her exchange with Senator William Proxmire:

Ms. Harris' response, "Senator, I am one of them . . . I am a black woman, the daughter of a dining-car worker," may have reassured the Senate Banking, House and Urban Affairs Committee, but I doubt that it quieted the suspicions of the underprivileged. Many blacks can recall that black dining-car workers were well-paid and middle class compared to other blacks . . . (Poussaint, 1977, p. 56).

Poussaint goes on to argue:

Poor blacks have benefited from the urban riots of the 1960's and the civil rights movement. They are aware, however, that their sacrifices often opened the door to status jobs for middle-class blacks who gave little to the struggle (Poussaint, 1977, p. 56).

Poussaint's remarks suggest that the benefits of black protest have been spread differentially amongst blacks. For some, race relations has become a "growth industry" in the United States. In 1972 a group of sociologists studying black leadership in Providence, R.I., found evidence of this on the local level (Pfautz, Huguley and McLain, 1975, p. 460). Between 1962 and 1972 one of the most pronounced changes in the nature of black leadership was the increase in the proportion of leaders involved in occupations directly related to race relations or, in the authors' words, "in the race relations business." But another observation suggests a danger of the involvement of blacks in this growth industry:

Again, although training for leadership is inherent in their administrative roles, the new, younger, and often more militant leadership groups are exposed to co-option, for the funds as well as the decision-making in many of the agencies involved are typically more white than black (Pfautz et al., 1975, p. 465).

Here described, then, are the same dangers that black militants in Britain see in the race relations industry—co-option and control. But we must turn to black voices from the past, from the decade of the 1960s, to find warnings against these dangers in the United States. Robert S. Browne, one of the most ardent and articulate spokesmen for black separatism was one of many voices warning against the dangers of the assimilationist philosophy which now reigns supreme in the "race relations industry:"

> Understandably, it is the black masses who have most vociferously articulated these dangers of assimilation, for they have watched with alarm as the more fortunate among their ranks have gradually risen to the top only to be promptly "integrated" off into the white community—absorbed into another culture, often with undisguised contempt for all that had previously constituted their racial and cultural heritage. Also, it was the black masses who first perceived that integration actually increases the white community's control over the black one by destroying black institutions, and by absorbing black leadership and coinciding its interest with those of the white community (Browne, 1977, p. 25).

The prophets of black power, Stokeley Carmichael and Charles V. Hamilton, saw the same dangers in assimilation as did Browne. They went on, however, to a concern even more directly related to the burgeoning federal "race relations industry"—"the overall role played by federal funds in relation to the black liberation struggle." They wrote, in *Black Power*:

> In any case, the fact is that any federal program conceived with black people in mind is doomed if blacks do not control it. The fact is that the government will never "give" blacks everything they need economically unless they have the power to threaten enough in order to get enough (Carmichael and Hamilton, 1967, p. 183).

WHO HAS THE BLACK REVOLUTION?

These are strange, anachronistic sentiments from a revolutionary era that is recent but nonetheless past and almost forgotten. It was an era during which the loudest black voices were those demanding that the black revolution be wrested from the hands of white liberals. It was a time when not one but several varieties of black pluralism, nationalism or separatism competed with each other and with assimilationism for the allegiance of blacks. It was a time when a black leader could advocate black schools controlled by blacks without being branded an "Uncle Tom." White influence in black affairs was suspect, and federal power was particularly distrusted.

Rarely is such a spirit manifest today. The black revolution is dormant if not dead. Yet there has been no restoration of pre-1954-style white supremacy any more than there has been the realization of Black Power. The form of race relations, in terms of segregation in public places, has certainly changed drastically. How real and how secure has been progress in such areas as education, income, employment and housing remains a topic for endless debate. One thing seems to have been a definite outcome of the Civil Rights "Revolution"—the creation of a substantial race relations "industry" or "establishment" with its major segment in the federal government. By 1978 this "industry" had spawned 40 separate equal employment laws and regulations administered by 18 different agencies; yet one agency alone, the Equal Employment Opportunity Commission, had a backlog of 130,000 unresolved discrimination cases (*New York Times,* February 3, 1978, p. A 22). There are questions that still loom large for those minority leaders who still believe that basic changes are needed in American society, not just the opening of doors to let more "qualified" minority members in. One question is, "Has the race relations industry which has flowered in the United States fulfilled the black revolution or has it captured it?" Will the, "executive assistant in charge of race relations" be able to complete the job that the heroes of the sixties, from Martin Luther King, Jr., to Malcolm X, began?

It is doubtful that a race relations "industry" will be able to bring about such revolutionary changes on either side of the Atlantic. In Britain, the power to shape the law affecting race relations still lies in a House of Commons that contains no black members and a Home Office responsive to a party with no blacks high in its ranks. Whatever its good works in attacking individual instances of discrimination, combating racialist propaganda, and promoting harmonious community relations, the "race relations industry" is not a significant political force. It is not in a position to affect the distribution of political and economic power. Only a strong minority social movement, not in evidence in Britain at the present, would have a chance of wresting significant political and economic concessions from a government that is committed more deeply to harmony in race relations than to change.

In the meantime, the "race relations industry" creates an illusion of power where power may not exist. The image of a burgeoning force of meddling experts fostered by Peter Simple suggests that the Commission on Racial Equality has far greater police power than it actually has. An even older image of the "industry" held by some black militants portrays it as a "buffer institution" which has de-politicized race and permitted the Government to avoid dealing directly with Third World minorities (Katznelson, 1973). The central theme is that of co-optation. While at the time the Community Relations Commission was created and the Community Relations Councils (or Voluntary Liaison Committees) brought under its wing this image was probably very accurate, it may constitute an exaggeration ten years later. Far more than the government's support of the "race relations industry" is required to explain the failure of a militant Third World movement to develop in Britain since the brief flurry of Black Power activity in the late sixties.

In the United States, the public image of the "race-relations industry" is most likely to be that of a federal bureaucracy embroiled in controversies with school boards, contractors, employers and city governments over school busing plans, hiring quotas, aptitude tests, and other aspects of affirmative action. Frustration with the bureaucratic style of the "race relations industry" was expressed by a university chancellor, himself black, defending his administration against charges of not complying with federal guidelines. He said, "First, affirmative action policy is the right thing to do. Second, we have to satisfy the federal guidelines but HEW is out to satisfy a process and not a concept" (Bromery, 1978, p. 2). Nathan Glazer, one of the foremost critics of affirmative action, sees the "civil rights bureaucracy" as having adopted "statistical parity" as its goal (Glazer, 1975, pp. 33f). Glazer feels that this goal, embodying the concept of "equality of results," is not necessary because vigorously enforced antidiscrimination measures guaranteeing equality of opportunity would produce racial justice. A different query about the activities of various civil rights–equal opportunity agencies is whether they are not designed to produce changes that will be of primary benefit to upper and middle-class "qualified" blacks rather than to the black masses for whom massive unemployment and poverty are the basic problems. An economically radical movement which demanded to know why the United States economy has ceased to generate more jobs and higher *real* income for all its members might be more relevant to the plight of blacks than a campaign which stops with trying to obtain for them a bigger slice of a pie that is not getting larger.

The latter, however, seems to be the strategy to which the American "race relations industry" is committed. While the British phrase has not been adopted in the United States, there is already a widespread perception that there is yet another bureaucracy in Washington—the civil rights bureaucracy. Many people who sympathize with the goals and procedures of this bureaucracy applaud it. Many other people, however, will heap on it and its members all the opprobrium Americans have traditionally directed at "meddling bureaucrats." The *New York Times* refers to the "jobs rights thicket" (*New York Times,* February 3, 1978, p. A22). And Nathan Glazer, perhaps the foremost critic of the bureaucratically administered affirmative action programs, has predicted that this bureaucracy will follow the course of others when he says:

> We can be sure that when the last discriminatory act is performed in this country the antidiscrimination agencies will have reached a size that is far greater than it is today and that there will be no observable tendency for these agencies to propose reduction in their staffs and budgets as discrimination declines (Glazer, 1975, p. 214).

The concept of the "race relations industry" suggests, therefore, that to understand what is going on in race relations it is necessary to consider not only theory in race relations but also organizational theory and the history of bureaucracy. Crusaders for better race relations, like all crusaders, often fancy themselves as pure in heart and noble in purpose. Yet contemplation of the possibility that race relations may become an "industry" sensitizes us to the fact that individual motives may be quite mixed and that the organizational structures within which even "good works" are done may be constraining.

REFERENCES

Banton, Michael (1972), *Racial Minorities*. London: Collins.

Bennett, LeRone Jr. (1964), *The Negro Mood*. New York: Ballantine.

Blair, Thomas L. (1977), *Retreat to the Ghetto*. New York: Hill and Wang.

Blumer, Herbert (1969), *Symbolic Interactionism: Perspective and Method*. Englewood Cliffs, N.J.: Prentice-Hall.

Bromery, Randolph W. (1978), "Bromery Says HEW Didn't Notify UMass," quoted in Massachusetts Daily *Collegian,* Amherst, Mass. (February 16).

Browne, Robert S. (1977), "A Case for Separatism," in Raymond L. Hall, ed., *Black Separatism and Social Reality: Rhetoric and Reason*. Elmsford, N.Y.: Pergamon Press, 1977. (Article first published 1960.)

Carmichael, Stokeley, and Charles V. Hamilton (1967), *Black Power*. New York: Vintage Books.

Cox, Oliver C. (1949), *Caste, Class and Race*. New York: Monthly Review Press.

Dunbaugh, Frank (1975), "The Justice Department and Northern Integration," *Integrated Education* 13, No. 3 (May–June):11–13.

Embree, Edwin R., and Julie Waxman (1949), *Investment in People*. New York: Harper and Brothers.

Glazer, Nathan (1975), *Affirmative Discrimination*. New York: Basic Books.

Heineman, Benjamin W. Jr. (1972), *The Politics of the Powerless*. London: Oxford University Press.

Hughes, Everett C. (1963), "Race Relations and the Sociological Imagination," *American Sociological Review* 28, No. 6 (December):879–890.

———— (1963a), "Professions," *Daedalus* 92, No. 4 (Fall).

Jordan, Vernon E. Jr. (1976), "Blacks and American Foundations: Attitude and Outlook," in Mabel H. Smyth, ed., *The Black American Reference Book*. Englewood Cliffs, N.J.: Prentice-Hall.

Katznelson, Ira (1973), *Black Men, White Cities*. New York: Oxford University Press.

Lester, Anthony, and Geoffrey Bindman (1972), *Race and Law*. Harmondsworth, England: Penguin Books.

Lomax, Louis (1965), "The White Liberal," *Ebony* (August).

London Daily Telegraph, November 19, 1975, and January 23, 1976.

Moore, Robert (1975), *Racism and Black Resistance in England*. London: Pluto Press.

Morrison, Lionel (1976), *As They See It*. London: Community Relations Commission.

Moynihan, Daniel P. (1973), "The New Racialism," in *Coping: Essays on the Practice of Government*. New York: Random House.

Mrydal, Gunnar (1944), *An American Dilemma*. New York: Harper and Brothers.

New York Times (Feb. 3, 1978), "Clearing the Job Rights Thicket," p. A22.

Nichols, Lee (1954), *Breakthrough on the Color Front*. New York: Random House, pp. 65–72, 107–133.

Pfautz, Harold, W.; Harry C. Huguley; and John W. McClain (1975), "Charges in Reputed Black Community Leadership, 1962–72: A Case Study," *Social Forces* 53 (March):460–467.

Poussaint, Alvin F. (1977), "To Get and to Get Not," *New York Times* (March 13), p. 56.

Punch (1975) "Is There Black Room at the Top?" (December 10): 1085.

Rainwater, Lee, and William Yancey (1967), *The Moynihan Report and the Politics of Controversy*. Cambridge, Mass.: MIT Press, 1967.

Rees, Tom (1974), *Equal Employment Opportunity in the USA—Recent Developments*. London: The Runnymede Trust (August).

Rothman, Jack (1977), *Issues in Race and Ethnic Relations*. Itasca, Ill.: F. E. Peacock.

Schlesinger, Arthur, Jr. (1965), *One Thousand Days*. Boston: Houghton Mifflin.

Simple, Peter (1975), *A Choice of Peter Simple, 1973–75*. London: *The Daily Telegraph* (December).

Sivanandan, A. (1974), *Race and Resistance: The IRR Story*. London: Race Today Publications.

Stephen, David (1975), *Minority Rights and Minority Morale in the USA—How Relevant to Britain is U.S. Experience?* London: The Runnymede Trust (May).

Stouffer, Samuel et al. (1949), *The American Soldier: Adjustment During Army Life,* Vol. 1. Princeton, N.J.: Princeton University Press, pp. 586–599.

Thompson, Daniel C. (1973), *Private Black Colleges at the Crossroads.* Westport, Conn.: Greenwood Press.

Wax, Murray L. (1971), *Indian Americans: Unity and Diversity.* Englewood Cliffs, N.J.: Prentice-Hall.

AFFLUENCE, CONTENTMENT AND RESISTANCE TO FEMINISM:
THE CASE OF THE CORPORATE GYPSIES*

Margaret L. Andersen, UNIVERSITY OF DELAWARE

Great expectations for social change have often foundered on shoals of resistance located in the most unexpected places. This appears to be particularly true of neo-feminist expectations for change in contemporary American society, where the ratification of the Equal Rights Amendment appears to be in serious trouble because, in considerable measure, resistance to its intentions has emerged among those it would presumably benefit most—women themselves. In her very cogent analysis which follows, Margaret Andersen explores the sources of seemingly inexplicable antifeminism among American women. In doing so she draws our attention to the fact that when proponents of a policy initiative mistake their own visions of the good society for those of the people they are trying to help, their initiative can easily fall victim to needs and motives which they are unaware of.

THE QUIET OPPOSITION

Since the reappearance of feminism in the last decade, large numbers of women have become critical of their position in society. Moreover, programs of equal

Research in Social Problems and Public Policy—Vol. 1, 1979, pages 139–160
Copyright © 1979 by JAI Press, Inc.
All rights of reproduction in any form reserved.
ISBN 0-89232-068-0

opportunity and affirmative action and the increased availability of birth control and abortion have freed women from some of the restraints in their lives. But it is also true that resistance to feminism has placed many barriers in the way of policies intended to rectify sexual inequality. As recent events have shown us, many of those among the resistance have been women themselves.

For example, in June of 1975, the United Nations convened an International Women's Year meeting in Mexico City. One result of this meeting was the establishment of a national commission, later mandated by President Ford, to organize state meetings and a national women's conference. The state meetings were to adopt resolutions and elect state representatives to come before the national convention. In the summer of 1977, state meetings were held throughout the country. But, much to the chagrin of feminist supporters, several of these meetings were also attended by women who were opposed to feminist proposals. Since resolutions were adopted by democratic majorities and since, in some states, the conservative women outnumbered the feminist women, several states adopted resolutions which opposed ratification of the Equal Rights Amendment and denied women's rights to abortions.

When the national conference was held in November 1977, a coalition of women's groups opposed to feminism organized a second conference in Houston. Women protesting the feminist convention appeared at this meeting. In addition, some of the delegates attending the feminist conference represented antifeminist interests and campaigned there against feminist proposals. According to media accounts, antifeminists complained that feminist leaders had railroaded their own programs through the sessions and had dominated the meetings through parliamentary tactics. Media accounts of the conference made it appear that the meetings were marked by dissent and opposition; accounts by feminists at the meetings stressed the unity and cohesion of the proceedings. While we cannot yet evaluate the significance of resistance to feminism in this context, it is clear that women's resistance to feminism is a topic which needs further investigation.

Events at the Women's Year meeting, the current jeopardy of the Equal Rights Amendment, and the struggle to maintain the availability of abortion have all dramatized the existence of women's resistance to feminism. As of this writing, the ERA still needs ratification in three states by March 1979 if it is to become the law of the land. Likewise, the hard-fought battle for abortion rights is now threatened by the withdrawal of federal funds and the possibility of a national amendment to curtail all abortion rights. In both of these areas, many of the activists have been women. Their activities have resulted in a sobering perspective on the early faith of feminists that women's false consciousness would soon be overcome.

Women in these antifeminist lobbies are usually led by conservative opinion leaders and are heavily supported by the funds of existing political, religious, and commercial organizations. For example, much of the ERA resistance can be traced to Phyllis Schafly—long-time conservative opinion leader with the support of the John Birch Society. During the International Women's Year meetings, rumors also abounded that antifeminists had been supported and encouraged by the funding and organizational tactics of the Ku Klux Klan.

One could also interpret Anita Bryant's fight against homosexual rights as antifeminist activity since feminists have supported the rights of both women and men to free sexual association. In Bryant's case, the success of her antihomosexual campaign in Florida can be partly attributed to her conservative and religious charisma, as well as the public eye provided her by the Florida Citrus Commission.[1] Likewise, in the anti-abortion movement, political effectiveness is aided by the strong organization and extensive financing made available by the Catholic Church.[2] In each of these areas, it is clear that individual convictions have been backed by the well-organized and well-financed activities of political support groups.

Even in the less overtly political "Total Woman" movement, support for the movement has been generated by the vast organization of Marabel Morgan's publishing empire and celebrity appearances. Spurred by the publication of her book, *The Total Woman,* Morgan has encouraged women to rejuvenate their marriages "by catering to their man's special quirks—in salads, sex, or sports" (Morgan, 1973, p. 60). Although even some feminists would support these women's rights to better sexual experiences, there is no question that the movement is in specific opposition to the core of feminist thought. As one reviewer has described it, the central theme of Morgan's book is that "the way for a woman to be fulfilled as a human being is to subject herself to her husband" (Casler, 1976).

These political and social movements pose definable threats to the accomplishments of the women's liberation movement. They are well-organized, politically effective, and publically visible. But it is misleading to think of resistance to feminism only in these terms and as associated with right-wing politics. This image has been partly generated in the media where only the most zealous and outspoken have been portrayed. In fact, many women are much less certain of their reaction to feminism and they greet women's liberation more with ambivalence and limited support than with outright disagreement. These are women who are untouched by specific antifeminist organizations and philosophies. Although they are less publicly visible than are the organized resisters, they are found in every community and they embrace every political persuasion.

This paper is a discussion of one such group of women and their reactions to the women's liberation movement. It specifically focuses on a group of women who are well educated, affluent, and who think of themselves as liberal. Their attitude toward women's liberation is one of minimal support and they are opposed to changes in traditional sex role relations. They are women who live in traditional marriages in which their husbands provide their material security. Moreover, they are proud of their status and would not consider living in any other way. We know very little about women like this, other than that they constitute some vaguely defined "mainstream." Yet, most of us have met them and perhaps been perplexed by their reactions to women's liberation. These are women who, at cocktail parties and bridge clubs, might be quick to say, "Oh, I'm all for equal pay for equal work, but—I'm not one of those libbers!"

The particular women discussed in this paper were interviewed in their homes during January 1977. Only one of them worked full time and, based on their husbands' income, they are among the top 15 percent of the income classes in their city.[3] The women's husbands were corporate businessmen whose upwardly mobile careers had moved their families geographically on an average of once every three years. As a result, it was not unusual for the women to say: "If my husband's not promoted in three years, he moves to another company. . . . I don't really plan anything. I just live for today." And, "I've given up saying 'I will do such and such' because there were a couple of times when I thought our move was permanent and it was not. So now I just pretend it's permanent."

The husbands' frequent moves have created uncertain environments for the women. But, like many corporate wives, they have become "ambitious for their husbands, rather than for themselves" (Moss-Kanter, 1977, p. 106). As a result, the women's own educations, careers, and friendships were frequently interrupted or terminated as they followed their husband's successes.

These women are all relatively young; almost all are between their early thirties and their mid-forties. They are better educated than most American women, since most of them hold college degrees or have some college experience.[4] With the exception of two who had never worked and three who had held clerical jobs, all had held professionally skilled jobs and considered themselves highly capable and ambitious.[5] In addition, they consider themselves to be liberal on social issues and were proud to think of themselves as a group responsible for introducing progressive and innovative change to the traditional and class-conscious town in which they lived.[6]

Research has shown that women who support feminism tend to be well educated, young (under forty-five) and politically liberal. Sociologists have also claimed that women's participation in the labor force tends to enhance feminist awareness. Similarly, the women's liberation movement has been criticized as appealing primarily to upper-middle-class women. So, in a sense, women like these might be expected to support the women's liberation movement.

But, when asked about women's liberation, they make it clear that, although they think women's liberation may be good for some women, it is not important to them. They give their limited support to issues of equal employment opportunity for women, but since they are not working themselves, their interest is abstract and distant. In other areas, such as the dissolution of traditional sex roles, they are appalled by feminism and are quick to deny its relevance to their own lives. Their rejection of the more far-reaching criticisms which feminism has raised shows how feminism appears to women who had committed themselves to paths of financial dependence, marital commitment, and class attachment prior to the evolution of the women's liberation movement in the 1960s. Unlike those who overtly resist the feminist movement, women like these simply see no relevance of feminist issues to their own lives. Their opposition is an unspoken one which does not emerge from the organized activity of political groups, the support of church organizations, nor the mass-marketed media. Women like these are not politically organized, nor have they ever marched in opposition to feminism. Most would not even publicly campaign for their beliefs, even though, in personal conversation, their ideas are clearly and frequently expressed. They have escaped the attention of the press, as well as academic research, primarily because their opposition to feminism is so silent.

In spite of their omission from the media and from research, they are a significant group in considering feminist policies. To begin with, their traditional influence as wives and mothers contributes greatly to the formation of sex-role consciousness. But, in addition to their influence as mothers, their traditional roles put them in other positions of influence. With leisure time on their hands, many traditionally oriented women have sought involvement in community volunteer groups.

The particular women commented upon in this paper were all members of a local newcomers' group which some of them had organized. The club's purpose was to introduce incoming women to each other and to involve them in civic volunteer activities. Some of the women sit on boards of directors for local social service organizations and all of them have regular contact with social service clients (through their work in nursing homes, hospitals, and similar organizations.) Thus, although the women are traditionally engaged as housewives, they are not staying at home alone, uninvolved in commuity life, as many stereotypes would suggest. Many of them have contact with city officials, philanthropists, and community leaders—perhaps even more than do their husbands whose time is spent with business associates. As a result, their influence and potential input to social policy formation extends beyond the private realm of their families into local community life.

REACTIONS TO THE WOMEN'S LIBERATION MOVEMENT

The limitations which these women place on their acceptance of feminist philosophies is a correction to the impressions produced by opinion pollsters and the national press. Poll data has informed us that, since the 1960s, more persons (men and women alike) support women's right to equal employment, their right to choose abortions, and their rights to combine career and marriages (Roper, The Virginia Slims American Women's Opinion Poll, 1974; Harris Survey,

Spring 1976; Gallup Poll, March 1976). At first glance, their reports are encouraging for they indicate significant changes in national opinion over the last fifteen years.

But, as sociologists have pointed out, the polls only measure what people say they will do, not what they actually will do (Deutscher, 1973) and they treat individual opinions as if they existed apart from social alignments (Blumer, 1969). Also, even though the polls may accurately reflect public opinion, there is no reason to believe that majority opinions will emerge victorious in real political contests. Not to assume otherwise is to ignore the process of interest group formation, party politics, and the unequal distribution of power. In spite of our democratic ideology, the American political process does not always follow the will of the majority. Feminist journalists sardonically recognized this in a recent wishful headline: "If Polls Could Vote!" (*Ms.*, July 1977).

Considering these criticisms, some conclusions drawn from the polls can be deceptive. For instance, in the fall of 1976, *The Washington Post* ran a feature article carrying the headline, "Feminist Movement Goals Have Wide and Growing Support" (September 28, 1976). At first glance, one might assume that feminism has become a majority opinion. Reading further, one learns that Harvard political scientists Verba and Orren have found that support for women's issues is generally higher among men than among women. Furthermore, their conclusion that feminism is "widespread" comes primarily from asking "whether women are better off having careers and jobs, just as men do, or if they are better off raising families." Their findings are that, among young people (under forty-five years of age), 63 percent of the men and 57 percent of the women favored careers and jobs for women. For those over forty-five, only 39 percent of the men and 25 percent of the women favored careers versus families. Without the age breakdown their findings show that 41 percent of all American women believe that women were better off in careers. Their conclusions that feminism has "widespread support" seem hardly warranted by the results of this particular item.

Their conclusions are even more questionable when one reviews their other findings. For instance, they find that half of all women agree that "if a company has to lay off part of its labor force, the first workers to go should be women whose husbands have jobs." Also, they find that more than half of their sample of women agreed that "the majority of American women do not agree with the leaders of the feminist movement." It would seem these women are probably correct since Verba and Orren's own research lends itself to the conclusion—equally plausible to that of *The Washington Post*—that more than half of all American women still do not support even the more moderate feminist goals!

The important point that this and other polls have overlooked is that the endorsement of equal employment rights for women is not equivalent to support for feminism on the whole. Feminists themselves have argued that sex inequality runs deeper than job discrimination and their philosophies are critical of all realms of traditional male-female relations. Although the removal of formal barriers of discrimination is an important feminist goal, it is by no means the singular theme of women's liberation. Opinion polls which use such restricted data to claim widespread support for feminism are both faulty and misleading.

Sociological research confirms this point. Investigators have found that a majority of women do support egalitarian rights in the labor market, but that most women also continue to support the traditional sex divisions of labor (Mason and Bumpass, 1975). Research has also shown that support for feminism is not a unilateral commitment and that the various issues of the women's liberation movement tend to be clustered around separable themes (Welch, 1975). Since each cluster of issues gains support from sociologically distinct groups, it is feasible to find groups who would support issues of equal employment without endorsing other issues of women's liberation. This same research has also found that women's support for specific feminist proposals is greater than their support for the general idea of women's liberation (Welch, 1975).

The women who were interviewed for this paper have a similar response to women's liberation. They are not completely opposed to women's liberation, but they are largely uninterested. Some do not detail specific objections, but claim that feminism just does not concern them:

> I haven't given it much though. I'm a homebody.

or,

> I'm not interested at all in women's liberation. I don't believe in it. I mean, what's the big deal?

Most believe that women's liberation is of benefit to women who work, but that they, as housewives, don't experience any disadvantages. As they said,

> I can't say as I've ever been at a disadvantage as a woman. I can't say as I've felt that way really. Maybe if I were out working, I'd have more opinions on that.

and,

> Not being a career person, I don't feel any disadvantages.

In their responses, the women express support for equal employment opportunities for women, but they don't see this issue as affecting their lives. As the polls would predict, these women will support the idea of equal pay for equal work.[7] But, even with her qualified support, each denies that she is a "women's libber" and some go so far as to restrict equality only to certain jobs. Their words make it obvious that, even with their moderate support for equal opportunity, many women think of feminists as an alien group with whom they do not identify. Indicative of this reaction are the disclaimers about feminists which many attach to their support:

> I do go along with a lot of their thoughts—for instance, equal pay for equal work. I think some of the rules and regulations of industries and different companies, as far as women are concerned, are ridiculous. Some of the regulations in my own profession [nursing] are ridiculous. But I don't consider myself a woman's libber.

After using the same disclaimer, another related her doubts about women's ability to perform traditionally male jobs:

> I'm not a libber and I never would be a libber because I think they carried it too far. If a woman can do a job, fine. I think she should be entitled to apply for that job on the same basis as any other human. I think she should be accepted for her qualifications—not for her sex. I think she should be paid the going rate. She shouldn't be paid higher or lower. She should be accepted for her qualification alone. That part I'm for—equal rights.

She continues,

> But, I would not feel secure if a woman were patrolling my block as a policewoman. I would feel less secure if my house was on fire and a woman fireman came up the ladder to carry me down. I think there are some jobs that a woman can do. I think there are some jobs definitely that a woman shouldn't do. I do not support the ERA because it sets quotas and you might have to hire someone that you didn't like.

Their objections to "libber types" demonstrate that feminists have offended their traditional concepts of womanhood and femininity. For women who maintain traditional concepts of sex role identity, feminist criticism is likely to appear as an affront to self. The same traditions of sex role behavior which feminists have criticized are those which these women define as the special privileges of being a woman. Their reservations about women's liberation come in part from their recognition that feminism asks them to redefine these traditional identities. Consequently, most of their first objections to feminism focus on the issues of chivalry and femininity. Characteristic of their disgruntled response are comments like the following:

> I go along with a lot of their ideas, like equal pay for equal work. But I don't think I'd want to stop having all the niceties that a gentleman does for a lady—like opening doors and taking them out to dinner.

and,

> I think it takes away from a woman's femininity when she's too aggressive.

They realize that feminism challenges traditionally assumed differences between men and women. Their concern with the symbolic issues of dress, manners, and style indicates that they understand the link between these differences and differences in economic and social power. One woman explicitly links her fears that the abolition of chivalry and femininity will mean women will have to be just as powerful and self-sufficient as men:

> I support women's liberation to a certain extent. I think it's doing better than in the beginning. At least, it seems to be defined better. I thought in the beginning it was kind of crackpot. And like the other day, I saw some lady on television and I wanted to say, "Oh, why are you dressing like a man?" She just looked so ridiculous. I feel like women should get the pay, but I don't want women to run the world. I still want somebody to open the doors—pay the bills.

Feminists argue that chivalrous codes are the symbolic means by which men keep women in their place. Interpreted in this light, the etiquette of sex roles is the charade in which the dependent status of women is acted out. But the same behaviors which feminists find so objectionable are the ones which these women see as advantages. When asked to describe any advantages and disadvantages they have had as women, they only relate the advantages. Their descriptions portray the preferred status they believe they have:

> Being a woman does have its advantages. I don't think a man would talk to a woman the way he would a man. He'd respect her more. He might think she's crazy with something she'd say. But he'd not come out and tell her. A man would tell a man if he really disapproved of what he said.

and,

> I suppose every woman has felt like she's had an advantage—like when they drive into a service station and really need something done. You talk real sweet to the guy and they take you first. The only disadvantage is in wages.

These women appear to be valuing foolishness, cunning, and manipulation. But, within a traditional orientation toward sex roles, they transform these characteristics into respectable attributes of personal identity.

In a similar vein, some women express fears that the downfall of femininity will also bring about the disappearance of romantic love. That men and women should share responsibilities and opportunities implies to them a cold and unemotional state of affairs:

> I would like to remain as a female and be treated as a female. I want doors opened for me and be treated as a woman. I think the women's movement is taking a little of this away. It's making the man feel the woman is his equal and that is going to the extreme.

She went on to say,

> I wonder what it will be like ten years from now? How will a man feel about a woman? Will he feel about her as someone to be protected and very feminine or will he think of her as an equal—just someone to live with and share expenses with?

By couching their objections to women's liberation in terms of threats to love and chivalry, the women implicitly acknowledge the challenge which feminism poses to the underlying structure of male/female relations. Feminism undermines what they think of as love, proper manners, and social respectability. It is no wonder then that the most common qualifier to their support for women's liberation is their annoyance with what they perceive as militance and extremism. In every interview, the women quickly volunteered their disdain for feminists' style:

> I feel sympathetic to the goals. But I don't feel sympathetic to the shouters.

and,

> I can't go along with the very radical. They're leaning a bit to far.

Considering the range of feminist styles, it might be assumed that their disapproval is in reference to the most radical of feminist activists. But, in fact, their image of an extremist is one which most feminists would see as moderate:

> I'm sympathetic with the women's movement, but not with the extremes. But, then, I tell my husband, if we didn't have the extremes, we couldn't get to the middle. Some of the very far-out women—Gloria Steinem and some of those—are a little too outspoken. Not too liberated, but outspoken.

The portrayal of Steinem as a "typical extremist" reflects the narrow limits of these women's support for women's liberation. But, more than that, her selection also indicates the foreign quality of the feminist movement in the experiences of these women. Because of her national visibility, Steinem is the most available name for them to choose. Using her as the representation of a "typical radical" likely reflects the women's lack of familiarity with feminist leaders and ideas more than it reflects a specific objection to Steinem's particular philosophy and style. Were the women more accepting of the relevance of feminism to their lives, they would recognize a host of other names from which a spectrum of radicalism to moderation could be established. Their perceptions of militance are an indication of the lack of pertinence they think women's liberation has to their lives.

It is significant that the feminist activities which they most object to are also those which would most alter their own situations. Since they have no interest in working, the job reforms they support create little impact on their lives. They are undisturbed by their reliance on their husband's economic support and believe that their position is preferable to having their own careers:

> My husband's always been the one who took care of me and always opened and shut the doors. I like this sort of thing. I love to be taken care of. I have nothing against someone who

doesn't want it that way. I feel that, if women are capable, they should be paid the same as a man—if they have the training. But when these extremists go the other way—no way! They have such a downgrading look on a man. Like I say, I've always been taken care of and they seem to want no part of it.

Another said,

I'm very content the way I am. If I had to go to work I would. But I'm in a position where I don't have to.

One woman even said she thought women's lives were preferable to those of men. As she said,

Men have it much harder. They have to go out in the world and work every day.

As long as their support for feminism is restricted to the workplace, then they can define it as a movement which has no significance to them. The limited degree to which they support feminism is only hypothetical because it creates no change in their own status as women. Even in the face of financial difficulties, most would not want to work if they could avoid it:

I'm more or less satisfied. I'm not that happy with this house. . . . I suppose I should get a job. Things are tight financially and they will be for another year. . . . So except for being a financial bind, there wouldn't be anything else that I'm dissatisfied with. I'd like to get the house fixed up. I think we'd be a lot happier because we left a brand new ranch home and had to buy this one in a hurry. I just figure if I can get out of the house a couple of times a week, I can forget it.

Unlike the depression-wrought middle-class housewives that Friedan described in *The Feminine Mystique,* these women are exuberant about their lives. They express no dissatisfaction in their roles as housewives and they are glad to have the economic support of their husbands:

I really have enjoyed the fact that I have been in a household of boys. And I have enjoyed the fact that I have a husband who certainly has been able to provide the things that we enjoy.

They do not consider themselves dependent on their husbands—certainly not in a debilitating way. In fact, most emphasize their individuality and personal freedom, even though, in doing so, they rely on their husband's name to identify themselves:

I'm not a great women's libber. I love being Mrs. [husband's name] and have loved every minute of it. What I fight for, in essence, is "know me for me."

They believe they are personally content and they claim to live exceptionally good lives. They believe they are fortunate as women and are unlike those who are discontent with their roles. Each believes she has been especially lucky because she has found "the right man":

> Every person has to be fulfilled, but I think the feminists put women in a position they don't want to be in. Most of my friends don't work and they are happy. I am satisfied and always have been. I think a lot depends on your husband, too.

and,

> If I do have a feeling of inferiority, my husband is the one who has been a booster.

In sum, these women think of women's liberation as a movement of misfits. Although they think that other women might need more satisfaction, they do not include themselves among them. Their disinterest in feminism is perhaps best represented in the words of a woman who said: "I'm not one of those people who feels non-liberated."

CLASS, CONTENTMENT, AND FEMINISM

The contentment expressed by these women provides a context in which resistance to feminism can be understood. Their reports of contentedness stand in direct contrast to the wealth of emerging information on the distress of middle-class housewives. This information, in both the academic and the public arena, chronicles the latent despair which many women experience as part of their roles as wives and mothers.

Specifically, contemporary social research is now exposing the widespread occurrence of alcoholism and drug abuse among middle-class married women (Chambers, 1971; Gunther, 1975). Other studies document the mid-life depression which career housewives experience when their roles are dissipated by the absence of grown children (Bart, 1970). Also, in the particular case of corporate wives, social scientists find that they experience high rates of depression as a response to their frequent relocation and feelings of displacement (Seidenberg, 1973; Weissman and Paykel, 1972).

Even without going to the academic literature, the public has been informed of the various "identity crises" experienced by adult women. For instance, Sheehy's best seller, *Passages,* told wide audiences that mid-life crises (for both women and men) are not only common but predictable. Others have discredited the myth of magnificent motherhood (Lazarre, 1976; Rich, 1976) and challenged the credibility of the "happy housewife" mystique (Lopata, 1971; Oakley, 1974a and 1974b; Glazer-Malbin, 1976). And, most people have heard the rhetoric of feminists which claims that no man is so exceptional that he justifies a sacrificed career, unending housework, and a total absorption in the lives of others.

In the face of this research and testimony, women's accounts of the perfection and satisfaction of their lives seems artificial. We have to wonder how likely it is that corporate wives who move so frequently, terminate their careers, and lose their friends will feel undisturbed by these events. Most do report the loneliness and isolation they feel in the initial stages of a move:

> My life is perfect. I reached a period when I like myself. I liked what I did. There was a time when I felt—well, where I couldn't do things. But a lot of women feel like that with small children. I think age has a lot to do with it. . . .

> But I'm passed that point. To come past that point and to like yourself is the most wonderful thing in the world. It was myself—nobody else—who moved myself to that. I think it's just periods of events that happen in your life and then it finally comes to you and you realize that you like yourself. . . .

> Not that I always thought that I didn't like myself. But there were periods of time when I wanted to be important. That meant most everything—to be recognized—and now that's not important to me. . . .

> I've never had any big things happen to me in my life. I'm just a regular person who is happy. I've got a marvelous, most beautiful husband and two great children. Everything just could not be any better.

In a sense, these are women without a sociological imagination—women who, in the words of C. Wright Mills, would interpret their difficulties as personal troubles, not public issues (Mills, 1959). They are privately oriented women whose satisfaction stems from the families and possessions they are oriented to. Their belief that satisfaction is derived only within the personal realm prevents them from seeking alterations in the external world (Turkel, 1977). With this orientation, they are unlikely candidates for a social movement which has always emphasized that "the personal is political" (Hanisch, 1970).

Women who do become feminists usually do so out of the content of their immediate experience. Events like unwanted pregnancies, dissolving marriages and dead-end careers often act as precipitating situations to a woman's interest in and initiation to feminist activity. In the case of corporate wives, we have a group of women constrained by the class and status orientations affiliated with their role. Among women, they are some of the closest benefactors of an economic system which many feminists argue is the core of sex inequality (Mitchell, 1971; Zaretsky, 1976). These women have major commitments to the existing class structure. Their homes, their clothing and their leisure time to participate in volunteer work are all products of the surplus time and money their economic standing brings. It is from this background that they develop their contentment and "personal growth." In this context, it is interesting that their only criticism of this system is that more women should be admitted to it. But to ask them to change more than the entrance requirements so as to redistribute economic and power resources is asking them to challenge the fundamental basis of their current experience. Without a precipitant crisis in their personal lives, which their class position tends to protect them from, it is unlikely that they would support a movement which forces them to consider these issues.

In accordance with the literature on housewife despair, there is the possibility that their accounts of contentment are unauthentic and that, behind the veneer of their satisfaction, lies genuine discontent and unhappiness. Since social actors come to "believe in the parts they play" (Goffman, 1959), it is difficult to establish the actual sincerity with which their accounts are produced. But, even if the women's contentment is false, we can understand their continued resistance to feminism.

Existing literature on community power and corporate influence argues that the civic participation of corporate employees is "motivated by a desire to present the corporation to the citizenry in as favorable a light as possible" (Pelligrin and Coates, 1956: 414; also, Mott, 1970). The sexist bias of this literature is evident in its omission of the role of wives because wives' participation in charitable activities, volunteer work, and hostess networks also enhances her husband's status and that of his company.

It is unlikely that their volunteer work is consciously motivated by a desire to enhance the status of the corporation. In the women's own eyes, volunteering brings them a chance to meet other women, at the same time that they satisfy their learned roles of compassion and nurturance (Gold, 1971). As one woman said,

> I have always been involved in hospital volunteer work and there is service to the community. But I have, very frankly, just enjoyed working with the people and that is my selfish motivation.

We can only conclude that the status benefits the women accrue from their civic work are the unintended consequences of their search for friendship and affiliation. Nevertheless, the women come to believe they have community reputations to protect. Some explicitly acknowledge their reluctance to act in ways that would mar their or their husband's reputation. For instance, one woman who quit her job rather than challenge what she saw as the sexist attitude of her boss commented:

> Why hurt your husband in the process? I have to live in this city. Maybe someone else would whose husband was not in the position mine is. But I can't. No matter what I do or say, I still must watch what I say. He is in a company which is owned here and he's on the Board of Directors at the country club.

It is feasible to speculate that the women's sense of community prominence and their commitment to civic duty also pervades their presentation of self in a research encounter. If so, their accounts of contentment have been biased by their sense of community standing. Without knowing the truth of their claims, we must take their accounts at face value. But we also know that they describe feminism as "crackpot" and extremist. Additionally, their support for feminism is extended only to the most "respectable" goals of the movement. If their desire to appear publicly respectable does permeate their accounts of contentment, then we should know that they would not affiliate with a social movement which associates them with an "unrespectable, lunatic fringe" (Turner and Killian, 1972).

The constraints on their roles as corporate wives places the analysis of resistance to feminism in a context different from that argued by feminists and by those who think of feminist resistance as always tied to right-wing politics. In the latter case, we have already seen the differences in the quiet disinterest of the corporate gypsies, compared to the ardent, antifeminist troops. But, in feminist analysis, the theme has predominated that women's resistance to feminism is a question of misguided socialization and "false consciousness." Borrowing their rhetoric from Stokeley Carmichael and the Black Power movement, they have charged that "the enemy has outposts in your head" (Kempton, 1970). Their analysis makes the claim that with the proper resocialization, women will redefine their status relative to men and will, therefore, seek transformations in the status quo.

This perspective was central to the "consciousness-raising" techniques developed by the women's movement in the late 1960s. As the women's movement developed, feminists knew that many women would resist their analysis. They described examples of women's resistance to feminism as believing that "our man is the exception and that we, therefore, are the exception among women" and that "individual solutions are possible" (Peslikis, 1970). But they believed that continued consciousness-raising would bring women to see themselves in political terms. As one early advocate of consciousness-raising wrote, ". . . consciousness-raising is a program planned on the assumption that a mass liberation movement will develop as more and more women begin to perceive their situation correctly" (Sarachild, 1972).

This perspective was also consistent with dominant themes in the academic literature which emphasized the idea that sexism is a learned pattern of beliefs originating in the socialization process. Since social scientists had for years developed the idea that the socialization process was central to the building of social selves, it was perhaps inevitable that this perspective would become a major theme in the growing fields of the psychology and sociology of sex roles. This perspective has generated volumes of research on socialization practices, male/female stereotyping, and sex role identity.[9] But it is also true that, as a theory, socialization has produced an equal number of facile and highly limited explanations of sex role phenomena. At the same time, in the women's movement, "consciousness-raising" has become a shared vocabulary for describing the process by which women alter their definitions of themselves and their situations.

There are several problems associated with the socialization theme. First, it has a tendency to place the conditions of women's beliefs in the past, rather than within the immediate experience of the person. Second, it assumes an image of human beings as passive recipients of a culture which is externally imposed on them. Finally, it tends to put the responsibility for continuing sexism on abstract processes and, as such, absolves real human actors from responsibility for their behavior.

One feminist critic recently opened discussion of these ideas. She writes:

> This seemingly enlightened analysis is a fraud. Its vague, passive jargon pins the reponsibility for bad treatment of women on amorphous "roles" and "forces," which, unlike human beings, are not accountable to anybody. . . . Its fraudulence is not just a matter of trivial and linguistic muddle that smart people will penetrate. It tells two big lies, which appear to be almost universally believed. First, it says that the problem is so awesomely complex and due to such obscure "forces" that even with the best will in the world we won't be able to understand it, let alone solve it, for goodness knows how long. This certainly takes the heat off daddies and male teachers (Geng, 1976: 50).

An alternative point of view is one which emphasizes the particular and ongoing conditions of women's lives in which their beliefs are generated. Also, women should be seen as active creators of the meaning of their lives, not mere receptacles for the culture's traditions. This perspective sees human actors as making their choices within the context of the material resources available to them. In the case of resistance to feminism, this explains that the class interests of certain groups of women place limitations on their willingness to support feminist ideas. The tendency in feminist circles to make heroines of all women obscures this point. Corporate wives stand closer to the high end of the distribution of material resources than all but the wealthiest of American women. Of course, since they are financially dependent on their husbands, they are not the immediate beneficiaries of economic privilege. Moreover, their future security depends on the continuing prosperity and economic support of their husbands. But, as long as that support is maintained, the privileges of marriage allow them the economic and social resources that other women would like to capture.

With the appearance of feminist protest, these women are faced with a dilemma. As feminists might like them to do, they are not likely to change their situation and forego the resources they now have. Consequently, they can either give their support to feminist ideas but maintain an inconsistency between their beliefs and behavior or they can adapt their beliefs about feminism to the behavior systems in which they live. In fact, the latter is what they do and it explains why they can call themselves liberal, support the limited goals of reform in the workplace, yet not alter in the least their traditional concepts of the roles of women and men. Seen in this way, their quiet resistance to feminism is not the result of their past socialization, but is a cognitive solution to the constraints they experience in their roles as affluent wives.

CONCLUSION

The resistance to feminism described by the women in this paper is not unique to corporate wives. Disclaimers to support for feminism can be heard from many who are unwilling to risk their status by demanding a more equitable system for everyone else. In the nineteenth century, Harriet Taylor Mill portrayed resistance to feminism as integrally connected to the power and material resources available to women. She wrote,

> Women, it is said, do not desire—do not seek, what is called their emancipation. On the contrary, they generally disown such claims when made in their behalf, and fall with acharne-ment [sic] upon any one of themselves who identifies herself with their common cause.
>
> . . . Their position is like that of the tenants or labourers who vote against their own political interests to please their landlords or employers; with the unique addition that submission is inculcated on them from childhood, as the peculiar attraction and grace of their character (Mill, ''Enfranchisement of Women,'' in Rossi, 1970a, pp. 117–118).

If we take Mill's ideas seriously and if we listen to the themes of resistance expressed by the corporate gypsies, then we must recognize the centrality of women's class interests to the character of their orientation toward the women's movement. Consistent with Mill's view is the recognition that women now benefiting from the status quo are unlikely to support radical social change. Their desires for public respectability, as well as the affluence they derive from their husbands, prevent them from associating with a movement they define as an extremist movement and one which is unlikely to succeed. Especially consider-ing the documentation of wage discrimination by sex, it is unlikely that these women would earn comparable incomes if they did declare financial indepen-dence. Until there is the real prospect of creating a society structured upon feminist ideals, asking them to accept the responsibility for their own support is like asking someone to take a reduction in their wages so that everyone else will be better off.

This paper emphasizes that resistance to feminism is not restricted to women of right-wing politics, nor is it found exclusively among less-educated women. Such stereotypes of feminist backlash assume that equality between the sexes could be accomplished if only we could re-educate women and persuade them to adopt liberal politics. By shifting the concern with resistance to feminism to include the better-educated and more affluent, we also shift the responsibility for obstructing social change to those with the greatest access to social, economic, and political resources.

Unfortunately, this thesis raises some disturbing issues for those interested in establishing a world based on equal rights for both sexes. Although they have not developed a wholly negative response to feminism, these corporate wives have clearly expressed the limitations of their support. Moreover, by virtue of their community activities, they are women who can potentially influence the future direction of social policy. Through their volunteer work, they act to implement policy in social service organizations. Their contact with social service clients puts them in the distinct position of bridging the distance between social classes. Were they to use this experience to realize radical support for these clients, they could be an effective voice in bringing new considerations to the business and governmental leaders with whom they maintain personal associations. But, in these interviews, the women make it clear that their class and respectability are at stake and are to be protected. Even though volunteering is personally important to them, they are not likely to relinquish the class and status rewards which they currently receive. Most persons are unwilling to support changes which would reduce their own material benefits, even if for the good of some abstract whole. The corporate gypsies are no exception and, as a result, they approach their association with the community poor primarily for the personal satisfaction it gives them—not for the social change they can generate.

Additionally, their influence indicates that it may become increasingly difficult in the future to translate feminist goals into actual social policies. The rhetoric of the women's liberation movement leads us to believe that feminism speaks to all women—regardless of differences in class, race, education, and politics. But these women who might be expected to be among those reasonably receptive to the feminist message do not think feminism represents them and they are unwilling to lend their support to most of the movement's goals. Under some circumstances, they might support limited programs of wages for volunteer labor, the re-entry of older women to job and educational systems, and, perhaps, enhancements in the status of household labor. But changes in the sexual division of labor or in social definitions of femininity challenge the very basis of their current complacence. Consequently, they are most likely to campaign for programs which would confirm their traditional attachments to affluent men. Callous thinkers might hope that their personal contentment and material affluence would be interrupted by disruptions in their personal lives and material security. But, as long as their support is maintained by a system resting upon sex role inequities, we will not be able to depend on them as agents of social change. As much as feminists would like to enlist their support, it is improbable that this will occur. Past optimism among feminists that these women are on their side has blurred the distinction between those changes feminists would like to see and those they are likely to see. Future activities should more carefully recognize the characteristics of assumed constituencies before counting on their support.

We have already begun to feel the backlash against feminism generated by conservative advocates of women's place. We have probably yet to feel the impact of the more silent opposition. Their moderate support for reform policies might bring encouragement to some. But their objections to the broader concept of equality between the sexes make it clear that what Rossi once called an "immodest proposal" (1964) is a more radical vision of social change than those of the affluent classes are willing to support.

FOOTNOTES

*The author thanks Sally Bould, William Chambliss, Jan DeAmicis, Sandra Harding, Randall Stokes, and Gerald Turkel for their helpful comments on an earlier draft of this article.

1. Source: *New York Times,* March 3, 1977, p. 27.

2. The National Abortion Rights Action League has distributed information documenting the support of the Catholic Church for the Right-to-Life Movement. According to their reports, every local diocese has been asked to establish a right-to-life committee. Between January 1976 and March 1977, these dioceses donated over $900,000 to the National Committee for a Human Life Amendment. (*Source:* Gelb and Palley, 1977; National Abortion Rights Action League, Information Sheet, mimeo.)

3. Twenty women were interviewed. The one woman who worked full time held a secretarial job to supplement their family income. Three others worked part-time and none of the women, whether working or not, expressed any desire to hold a full-time job in the future. More than half of them earned over $25,000 per year. Of the twenty interviews, nine fell in the $15,000-$25,000 bracket; eight, $25,000-$50,000; two, $50,000-$100,000; one did not respond on income.

4. One-third of the group held college degrees, one of these also had her M.A. Most of the others had some college experience, ranging from one year to near completion. But, for them, college had ended when they married or had children. Two had recently returned to finish degrees, although one of them dropped out "when she got too many complaints from her husband" that she was giving too much time to her studies.

5. Among them was a former college instructor, an artist, a craftswoman, several teachers, skilled technicians, nurses, a merchandize buyer, and a business entrepreneur.

6. The women lived in a mid-size (population 70,000) southern city which is part of the recent expansion of the "sunbelt." This town like others in the sunbelt, has experienced rapid industrial growth in the last twenty years. Consequently, much of the new money in this town comes from outsiders like these women. They self-consciously think of themselves as changing old southern traditions and bringing new life to an elitist town.

7. The women were split on the issue of the Equal Rights Amendment. A few thought it would obliterate all distinctions between the sexes. Others thought it would create quota systems which they objected to. This is consistent with data from the polls which show that support for the concept of equal opportunity declines when real behavioral alternatives are suggested (Verba and Orren Poll, *The Washington Post,* September 9, 1976).

8. Unlike regular careers, volunteer work also allows them freedom of entry to and withdrawal from a "job market" without detrimental effects on their career progression.

9. For an excellent review of these studies see Weitzman (1975).

REFERENCES

Adams, Margaret (1971), "The Compassion Trap," in Vivian Gornick and Barbara Moran, eds., *Women in Sexist Society*. New York: Basic Books, pp. 555–575.

Bardwick, Judith, and Elizabeth Douvan (1971), "Ambivalence: the Socialization of Women," in Vivian Gornick and Barbara Moran, eds., *Woman in Sexist Society*. New York: Basic Books, pp. 225–241.

Bart, Pauline (1970), "Mother Portnoy's Complaint," *Transaction/Society* 8(November–December):69–74.

Blumer, Herbert (1969), *Symbolic Interactionism*. Englewood Cliffs, N.J.: Prentice-Hall.

Casler, Lawrence (1976), "Review Essay: The Total Woman; the Joy of Being a Woman," *Journal of Marriage and the Family* (November):789–792.

Chambers, Carl (1971), *Differential Drug Use Within the New York State Labor Force*. New York: New York State Narcotic Addiction Control Commission.

Deutscher, Irwin (1973), *What We Say, What We Do*. Glenview, Ill.: Scott, Foresman.

Dixon, Marlene (1969), "The Rise of Women's Liberation," Betty Roszak and Theodore Rosak, eds., *Masculine/Feminine*. New York: Harper & Row.

Freeman, Jo (1970), "The Building of the Gilded Cage, in Jerome Skolnick and Elliot Currie, eds., *Crisis in American Institutions*. Boston: Little, Brown.

Friedan, Betty (1963), *The Feminine Mystique*. New York: Norton.

Gallup Poll (1976), Field Enterprises, Inc.

Gelb, Joyce, and Marian L. Palley (1977), "The Interest Group System and the Politics of Moderation," unpublished manuscript, presented at the meeting of the Northeast Political Science Association (November).

Geng, Veronica (1976), "Requiem for the Women's Movement," *Harper's* 253(November):49–68.

Glazer-Malbin, Nona (1976), "Housework," *Signs* 1(Summer):905–923.

Goffman, Erving (1959), *The Presentation of Self in Everyday Life*. Garden City, N.Y.: Doubleday-Anchor.

Gold, Doris B. (1971), "Women and Voluntarism," in Vivian Gornick and Barbara Moran, eds., *Woman in Sexist Society*. New York: Basic Books, pp. 533–554.

Gunther, Max (1975), "Female Alcoholism: the Drinker in the Party," *Today's Health* (June).

Hanisch, Carol (1970), "The Personal Is Political," *Notes from the Second Year: Women's Liberation—Major Writings of the Radical Feminists*. New York: Radical Feminism.

Harding, Sandra (n.d.), "Is the Equality of Opportunity Principle Democratic?", unpublished manuscript, University of Delaware (Newark).

Harris Survey (1976), Louis Harris and Associates (Spring).

Hole, Judith, and Ellen Levine (1971), *Rebirth of Feminism*. New York: Quadrangle.

Kempton, Sally (1970), "Cutting Loose," *Esquire* (July):53–57.

Lazarre, Jane (1976), *The Mother Knot*. New York: Dell.

Loeser, Herta (1974), *Women, Work and Volunteering*. Boston: Beacon Press.

Lopata, Helena (1971), *Occupation: Housewife*. New York: Oxford University Press.

Mason, Karen Oppenheim, and Larry L. Bumpass (1975), "U.S. Women's Sex Role Ideology, 1970," *American Journal of Sociology* 80(March):1212–1219.

Miller, Jean Baker (1976a), *Toward a New Psychology of Women*. Boston: Beacon.

———— (1976b), "Psychoanalysis, Patriarchy and Power: One Viewpoint on Women's Goals and Needs," *Chrysalis* 2, Los Angeles, Calif.

Millett, Kate (1970), *Sexual Politics*. Garden City, N.Y.: Doubleday.

Mitchell, Juliet (1971), *Woman's Estate*. New York: Pantheon.

Morgan, Marabel (1973), *The Total Woman*. Old Tappan, N.J.: Fleming H. Revell Co.

Moss-Kanter, Rosabeth (1977), *Men and Women of the Corporation*. New York: Basic Books.

Mott, Paul E. (1970), "The Role of the Absentee-Owned Corporation in the Changing Community," in Michael Aiken and Paul Mott, eds., *The Structure of Community Power*. New York: Random House, pp. 170–179.

Ms. (1977), "If Polls Could Vote" (July):90.

National Abortion Rights Action League (1973), "Public Opinion Polls Since the Supreme Court Decisions of 1973," Washington, D.C.: *Fact Sheet*.

National Commission on the Observance of International Women's Years (1976), *To Form a More Perfect Union: Justice for American Women*. Washington, D.C.: Government Printing Office.

NOW (National Organization for Women) (1971), Resolution on Volunteerism. Presented at the 5th National Conference. Los Angeles (September).

—— (1973a), "Volunteer—Why Not? Analyses and Answers," Chicago Task Force on Women and Volunteerism.

—— (1973b), "Volunteerism—What It's All About," Berkeley Women and Volunteerism Task Force.

Oakley, Ann (1974a), *The Sociology of Housework*. New York: Pantheon.

—— (1974b), *Woman's Work: A History of the Housewife*. New York: Pantheon.

Oppenheimer, Valerie Kincade (1977), "The Sociology of Women's Economic Role in the Family," *American Sociological Review* 42(June):387–406.

Pelligrin, Roland, and Charles H. Coates (1956), "Absentee-Owned Corporations and Community Power Structure," *American Journal of Sociology* 61(March):413–419.

Peslikis, Irene (1970), "Resistance to Consciousness," *Notes from the Second Year: Women's Liberation—Major Writings of the Radical Feminists*. New York: Radical Feminism.

Platt, Anthony (1972), "The Triumph of Benevolence: the Origins of the Juvenile Justice System in the U.S.," in Abraham Blumberg ed., *Introduction Criminology*. New York: Random House.

Rich, Adrienne (1976), *Of Woman Born: Motherhood as Experience and Institution*. New York: Norton.

The Roper Organization, Inc. (1974), The Virginia Slims American Women's Opinion Poll, Vol. III.

Rossi, Alice (1964), "Equality Between the Sexes: An Immodest Proposal," *Daedulus* 93:607–52.

—— (1970a), *Essays on Sex Equality: John Stuart Mill and Harriet Taylor Mill*. Chicago: University of Chicago Press.

—— (1970b), "Women—Terms of Liberation," *Dissent* 17 (November).

—— (1972), "The Roots of Ambivalence in American Women," in Judith Bardwick, ed., *Readings on the Psychology of Women*. New York: Harper & Row, pp. 125–127.

Salzman-Webb, Marilyn (1970), "Media strategy," *Women: A Journal of Liberation* (Summer).

Sarachild, Kathie (1970), "A Program for Feminist 'Consciousness-Raising,'" *Notes from the Second Year: Women's Liberation—Major Writings of the Radical Feminists*. New York: Radical Feminism.

Scott, Marvin, and Stanford M. Lyman (1970), "Accounts," in Gregory P. Stone and Harvey A. Farberman, eds., *Social Psychology Through Symbolic Interaction*. Waltham, Mass.: Ginn-Blaisdell, pp. 489–509.

Seidenberg, Robert (1973), *Corporate Wives—Corporate Casualties?* New York: American Management Assoc.

Sheehy, Gail (1974), *Passages*. New York: Dutton.

Tavris, Carol (1973), "Who Likes Women's Liberation and Why: The Case of the Unliberated Liberals," *Journal of Social Issues* 29:175–198.

Turkel, Gerald (1977), "Privatism and Orientation Toward Political Action," unpublished manuscript, University of Delaware (Newark).

Turner, Ralph, and Lewis M. Killian (1972), *Collective Behavior*. Englewood Cliffs, N.J.: Prentice-Hall.

The Washington Post (1976), "Feminist Movement Goals Have Wide and Growing Support," (September 28).

Weissman, Myrna M., and Eugene S. Paykel (1972), "Moving and Depression in Women," *Transaction/Society* 9(July–August):24–28.

Weitzman, Lenore (1975), "Sex-Role Socialization," in Jo Freeman ed., *Women: A Feminist Perspective*. Palo Alto, Calif.: Mayfield Publishing Co.

Welch, Susan (1975), "Support Among Women for the Issues of the Women's Movement," *Sociological Quarterly* 16(Spring):216–227.

Zaretsky, Eli (1976), *Capitalism, the Family and Personal Life*. New York: Harper & Row.

DRIFT AND DEFINITIONAL EXPANSION: TOWARD THE HYPOTHESIS OF RACE-SPECIFIC ETIOLOGIES IN THE THEORY OF CRIMINAL DEVIANCE

Michael Lewis, UNIVERSITY OF MASSACHUSETTS

Anthony Harris, UNIVERSITY OF MASSACHUSETTS

The persistence of a major crime problem in American society is as perplexing as it is confounding. Some experts have recently taken the position that social scientists, with their interest in causality, really have little to offer policy-makers as they strive to reduce criminal incidence. They aregue that causal attribution is really irrelevant to policy and that, on the contrary, policy efforts should focus on control and deterrence mechanisms. Michael Lewis and Anthony Harris argue an opposite position in the following paper. In their view it is not an emphasis upon causality which is the problem but an *unrefined* emphasis upon causality which leads to unproductive attempts to reduce crime. By positing race-specific etiologies of criminal deviance they draw our attention to important policy implications which they believe can be ignored only at considerable risk to our anticrime efforts.

Research in Social Problems and Public Policy—Vol. 1, 1979, pages 161–177
Copyright © 1979 by JAI Press, Inc.
All rights of reproduction in any form reserved.
ISBN 0-89232-068-0

INTRODUCTION: THE "TWO WORLDS OF RACE" AND CRIMINAL DEVIANCE

In this paper an attempt will be made to explore the impact of racial difference on the etiology of criminal deviance. The starting point of our exploration rests on the question: Do criminally deviant youths constitute a homogeneous group with respect to their self-definitions and perceptions of opportunity irrespective of their racial backgrounds, or do they constitute racially separate deviant sub-groups? It shall be argued that if black and white youthful offenders are basically indistinguishable in terms of identity characteristics and perceived opportunity, we would be led to conclude that within this society's youthful population, offenders and potential offenders are likely to violate the law for essentially the same reasons, regardless of racial background. If, alternatively, black and white offenders differ from one another in these terms, there would be an important empirical basis from which to argue that the etiology of criminal behavior (and youthful criminal behavior in particular) varies according to differences in experience inherent in the castelike separation of the "two worlds of race."

An argument of this latter type would necessarily suggest that existing "color blind" theories of deviance and its genesis should be reformulated along racially specific lines. To the extent, moreover, that such theories presently inform prevention and rehabilitation programs, the implication would be that such programs should be modified in a manner consonant with the reformulation and validation of these theories. While we do not suggest that a definitive conclusion can as yet be reached with regard to these alternative positions, we believe that there is enough available evidence to suggest that white and black offenders differ in important ways from one another and that no single "color blind" etiological formulation can account for the genesis of their criminally deviant behaviors.

The starting point of the analysis is a study of remanded black and white youthful offenders. Based on a sample of 234 inmates in 1971, Harris (1976) found a number of suggestive racial differences. While some of these differences were relatively strong, and some relatively weak, a pattern emerged from the data which appeared to justify a substantive, castelike interpretation: that, in short, the subjective effects of criminal identity ought to vary by race, with whites experiencing a greater sense of stigma than blacks for given levels of criminal self-identity. Given little in the way of other, potentially confounding background differences between the blacks and whites sampled, including age (the mean for both races at about 22 years), education (the mean for both groups at about 10 years), and family origin socioeconomic status (both groups coming from predominantly lower-SES origins),[1] the findings in the Harris study seemed all the more suggestive in terms of the past and future role of "caste" in deviance theorizing.

More specifically, in this study, the following differences were observed:

whites who, by virtue of their imprisonment, had been officially labeled as "criminal," scored significantly lower on a measure of "straight" identity than did blacks so labeled ($\dot{X}$ = 14.32 versus 15.32, "t" = 1.82), and marginally higher on a measure of criminal identity ($\dot{X}$ = 15.82 for whites and 15.40 for blacks, "t" = 0.76). In substantively related terms, for whites the correlation between degree of criminal identity and a measure of the stability of self-imagery exceeded that for blacks (r = − .25 versus −.07, "z" = 1.41), as did the correlation between criminal identity and self-esteem (r = −.36 for whites and −.09 for blacks, "z" = 2.07). A measure of the relative rationality or expected value of criminal to "straight" choice stood at .351 for whites and .434 for blacks ("t" = 5.24). Finally, this measure, and a measure of past criminal income, were found to be negatively correlated with self-esteem for whites (r = −.15 and −.28, respectively), but positively correlated with self-esteem for blacks (r = .15 and .18, respectively). For given levels of deviant self-definition and commitment to deviant choice, then, the whites in the Harris sample appeared to have more difficulty than the blacks in maintaining their sense of self-worth and personal stability. To a significantly greater extent than was the case for the blacks, the whites in the Harris study also perceived it to be more rational to remain "straight" than to take up a criminal career.

In reflecting on the pattern of these findings, we concluded that it was reasonable to draw two major implications. First, for the whites, getting caught for the choice of criminal behavior appeared to remove them to a greater degree from a moral and behavioral universe which they continued to regard as legitimate than getting caught so removed the blacks. And second, in consequence of this, deviant identification and commitment generally seemed to exact a more significant price in the psychological well-being of the white group as compared to the black group. These implications, in turn, suggested to us the potential utility of race specific hypotheses concerning the etiology of criminal deviance. We believe these hypotheses, though by no means unequivocally evidenced in available data, bear serious consideration in future theory and research. In the following we shall 1) develop these etiological implications as fully as possible, 2) present additional empirical evidence supportive of the potential worth of these hypotheses, 3) address the issue of future work in the area once race is brought back into the analysis, and 4) address possible policy implications of our hypotheses.

ETIOLOGICAL IMPLICATIONS: THE HYPOTHESES OF DRIFT AND DEFINITIONAL EXPANSION

If, as the Harris findings suggest, whites have considerable difficulty in justifying their criminally deviant behaviors and identities—i.e., they feel removed from the straight moral universe and they are apparently troubled by this circumstance—neither affinity for or commitment to deviant values as posited by

Miller (1958), nor the disavowal of mainstream straight values as posited by Cohen (1955), would appear to be powerful explanations of the genesis of white criminal deviance. Both the Miller and Cohen arguments imply an element of moral justification which, if present among the whites, would seem to have rendered them less troubled about their moral isolation than they appear to have been. It also appears that for the whites, the suggestion that a sense of blocked legitimate opportunity will lead to criminal deviance as an innovative route to conventional success (Merton, 1957; Cloward and Ohlin, 1960) has minimal salience. If the ''structured strain''/differential opportunity formulations were operative, it would appear that whites would not, as they *did*, have found it clearly less rational to opt for criminal deviance than to remain straight.

Rather, the whites' sense of moral and psychological isolation, as well as their sense of the nonrational character of the choices they have made suggests that David Matza's *drift* formulation (Matza, 1964) may be the most powerful etiological characterization of their journey into criminal deviance. It is important to realize that drift implies a situation wherein the choice of rule-breaking behavior does not in itself imply commitment to a moral schema exogenous to conventional expectations, nor does it imply rational calculation of instrumental gain as the motivational source for such a choice. In light of the Harris findings on white offenders consider the goodness of fit of the following drift scenario.

A white youth is most likely to begin his criminally deviant career in a manner perhaps best described as mindless. He finds himself in a situation where the prohibitions against doing wrong are *neutralized*. Among his peers he is challenged to act. While in the abstract he may understand the criminal ''wrongness'' of the proposed act, in the immediate context he comes to believe—usually with the encouragement and reinforcement of his peers—that the abstract definition is inapplicable and that, consequently, any implication of moral violation is inappropriate. In effect, he traverses a great moral distance without confronting the realization that he has done so. Stealing a car is wrong, but he's not stealing a car, he's just going to have some fun and take a vehicle for a ride! If, however, he is apprehended and thereby forced to confront his behavior as a violation, as a case of prohibited wrongdoing, he will find it difficult to maintain this neutralization and avoid consciousness of wrongdoing. If he is apprehended (and it must be remembered that all those in the Harris study had been apprehended) he is forced to confront the disjunction between his behavior and his standards. People in authority force such a confrontation upon him; he faces a consortium of powerful adults. The police, a judge, a probation officer, the prison psychologists, his parents, all strive to impress him with the fact that he has violated not merely their morality but his *own* as well. He becomes progressively disenchanted. In retrospect the process of neutralization seems never to have occurred. What was adventure, an expression of his masculinity or just having a good time, he now recognizes as a crime. Our prototypical white—never having rejected conventional moral expectations, having instead neutralized them in specific situations—now judges himself to have violated these expectations. He suffers the collectively imposed stigma of deviance, and to a certain extent, at least, he acquiesces in its imposition. He is morally and psychologically isolated. In short, having "messed up" behaviorally he is now "messed up" cognitively, emotionally, and morally.

If Matza's drift formulation is consonant with the Harris findings on white offenders it would appear to be markedly less so with regard to the findings on their black counterparts. For the black offenders, criminal identity and involvement did not imply a strong sense of moral and psychological isolation from nondeviant blacks and the everyday character of the black experience. Relative to the whites, being identified as a criminal was of little or no moral and psychological consequence for the blacks. As such, we see it as reasonable to entertain the hypothesis that for them criminal choice—or the genesis of criminal deviance—was *not* a function of the suspension or neutralization of conventional morality, that is, of drift. Drift rests on the assumption of commitment to a morality which cannot justify the behaviors engaged in; in these terms the conscious juxtaposition of criminal behavior against the putative stigma of arrest and incarceration should result in a strong and self-deprecatory consciousness of deviant identity. This seems to be the way the whites interpreted the meaning of their experience, but not the blacks. The latter did see themselves as deviant but somewhat less so than did the whites see themselves; and whatever blacks' sense of deviance it did not appear to lead them into extensive self-deprecation.

If the drift scenario does not appear to account for the etiology of criminal deviance among the black offenders, neither do the normative or contra-cultural formulations of Miller and Cohen. While in the Harris study it is true that the blacks perceived going or being "straight" as less rational than did the whites, it is nevertheless also true that in the absolute the blacks perceived straight options to be more rational than "crooked" or deviant options. It is therefore difficult to assume that their criminally deviant behavior is the result of a normative commitment which, in its anticonventional emphasis, leads them into conflict with the law. Put simply, the choice of criminal options among the black offenders did not appear governed by commitment to criminogenic norms. The blacks found it more attractive to "go straight" than to "go crooked" (albeit to a lesser extent than the whites); but having gone crooked and having been apprehended appeared to be of little personal consequence to them. In light of this characterization the following etiological scenario of black criminal deviance seems to offer the best fit.

The fact that black ghettos are characteristically located in the heart of major metropolitan areas, together with the fact that white-dominated mass media are everywhere to be experienced, virtually assures the incursion of mainstream influences into these communities. Blacks are at once attracted to mainstream expectations such as self-mastery, autonomy, and personal success, and are (because they are black) excluded from the possibility of realizing these expectations in the precincts from which they emanate—an excruciating dilemma! In such a circumstance mainstream expectations could be disavowed (Merton, 1957; Cohen, 1955), but for most, the attraction of these expectations proves much too powerful for such a rejection. These expectations are, after all, the tenets by which whites seem to live and whites, as every black can testify, have had pretty much their own way in American society.

If mainstream expectations cannot be disavowed, the choice for blacks is one between sustained frustration and, we hypothesize, a *definitional transformation* of the conventional opportunity structure into one in which some semblance of these expectations can be realized. Given the joint conditions of subjectively maintained conventional success norms and (objectively) very limited access to the realization of these norms, one major alternative to felt frustration involves an expanded definition of morally legitimate—if sometimes illegal—activities. In these terms, differential access to the conventionally defined array of acceptable activities may well lead to a unique if not radical redefinition of what concrete activities fall within this array. Such redefinition is likely to involve a functional increase in the cognitive band width of the category of noncensurable (sometimes illegal) activities. This cognitive transformation, in turn, may well lead to behavioral commitments which, by conventional standards, stand outside the narrower category band width. Where such *"innovative conformity,"* from the mainstream perspective, might be seen as beyond the categorical bounds of what is legitimate, moral, and legal, from the subjective point of view it is within the bounds of conventional legitimate and moral activity—even though known to be illegal. While some may see in this assertion considerable similarity to the "strain"/opportunity theory conception of "innovative" deviance, the similarity between the two is, however, only minimal. In the "definitional expansion" formulation, from *the point of view of the actor,* both ends and means do *not* differ in kind from those characteristic of the American mainstream, whereas "innovative" deviance implies similar ends but intrinsically (objectively and subjectively speaking) dissimilar (deviant) means for their achievement.

Given scarce resources and severely limited access to conventionally acceptable activities (both in terms of means and ends), then, the structure of behavioral options in the black ghetto is just as likely as not (or perhaps even more likely) to include as approved options those which violate the law. To the degree that this is so, violating the law from the perspective of the ghetto resident has little self-definitional meaning; it may not even mean that the violator—both in his own terms and in those of the people with whom he regularly interacts—has ceased to "go straight." If *neutralization* is likely to be the initiating factor in the genesis of white criminal deviance, then we suggest that *definitional expansion* is likely to be the initiating factor in the genesis of black criminal deviance.

While some behavioral options in the ghetto happen to violate the law of the larger civil community, they paradoxically afford opportunities—from the ghetto resident's point of view—for increasing the possibility of realizing mainstream expectations. The numbers runner can be straight (honest) and usually is, even as he breaks the law. The street hustler asks and gets fair exchange for a "hot" color-television set. The war ministers of two fighting gangs try to reduce conflict and succeed in ironing out truces complete with codicils on territorial sovereignty (Lewis, 1970). Through the process of *definitional expansion* illegality subjectively loses its deviant character. Black offenders in the Harris study appeared to be bothered little if at all by apprehension and awareness of their "official" criminal identity, even while they endorsed straight vs. criminal options. In the context of definitional expansion one can be straight even while civil authority says one is criminal.

We suggest, then, that most whites, even poor ones, live and act in the mainstream and when they are apprehended they are more likely than blacks to experience moral trauma in recognition of their criminality. We suggest that most blacks, on the other hand, live and act in a world where behavioral (means-ends) norms are the same in kind as those existing in the mainstream, but where the options for their realization are in mainstream terms more frequently illegitimate, immoral, and illegal. In the ghetto, apprehension means that one has been in violation of a law—but probably not of a morality.

Based on what we believe to be the substantive implications of the Harris findings, what has been proposed thus far may be summarized as follows:

1) Consonant with the well-documented implications of the American racial dichotomy, *the etiology of criminal deviance is likely to be different for whites and blacks.*
2) The *normative affinity formulation* (Miller, 1958) probably does *not* account for much of the criminal deviance found among whites or blacks.
3) The *contra-cultural formulation* (Cohen, 1955) probably does *not* account for much of the criminal deviance found among whites or blacks.
4) The *drift formulation* (Matza, 1964) probably offers the best etiological account of criminal deviance among whites but is probably less powerful when applied to blacks.
5) An extension of the *"structured strain"/differential opportunity argument* (Merton, 1957; Cloward and Ohlin, 1960)—*the definitional expansion formulation*—probably offers the best etiological account of criminal deviance among blacks but is probably less powerful when applied to whites.

In short, we suggest that the "color blind" approach to the etiology of criminal deviance is probably in error; that some of the standard etiological formulations (standard even though they have never been subjected to rigorous empirical assessment) are likely to be of little use in understanding the genesis of criminal deviance—whether among blacks or whites; and that those formulations which render powerful accounts of such deviance are likely to do so in a manner which must be described as racially specific. Our argument thus far does not lead us to suggest that these etiologies represent racially *exclusive* processes, but rather, that there is reason to hypothesize that the processes in question are distributed differentially enough by race to warrant their characterization as race-specific.

ADDITIONAL EVIDENCE FOR THE HYPOTHESIS OF RACE-SPECIFIC ETIOLOGIES[2]

Our claim has not been that the hypothesis of race-specific etiologies in criminal deviance has been tested and supported. In the previous section the Harris (1976) study simply served as a major empirical stimulus to the *induction* of this hypothesis. Substantive support, *not* for the validity of the etiological scenarios we have proposed, but rather, for the *empirical appropriateness* of their induction, may be found in several studies of black and white youths.[3] In this sense, the findings to be cited do not test our hypothesis. Rather, they lend credibility to the worth of testing it in future research.

Differential Moral Polarization

As was found for the Harris offenders, Short and Strodtbeck (1965) found differences between black and white gang boys suggesting that whites perceived a greater distance between nondeviant and deviant moral dimensions than did blacks. The subjects in this study were asked to characterize their membership cliques in terms of a series of pared adjectival opposites (e.g., good–bad; kind–mean; helpful–troublesome; etc.). In eight of nine comparisons on those pairs which are relevant, the whites' self-descriptions suggested a markedly greater separation of nondeviant and deviant moral dimensions.[4]

In the same study gang boys were asked to indicate the amount of time they spent doing domestic chores as well as the extent of their delinquent involvement. On the assumption that domestic activities and delinquent activities represent two potentially separate and distinct moral realms, and that, on this basis, commitment to one realm precludes commitment to the other, we should expect to find negative correlations between degree of commitment to one realm and degree of commitment to the other. For each of four types of gangs Short and Strodtbeck identified, the correlation for whites was indeed negative, but for blacks was *positive*. Cross-race differences in these correlations for each of the four gang types were significant.[5] These findings clearly lend substantive support to our observation that in describing themselves, whites generally perceive greater polarization between deviant and nondeviant moral dimensions than blacks generally do.

In related terms, Schwartz and Stryker (1970) found that white and black school boys (aged 12–15) identified by school personnel as "bad" (i.e., seen by teachers and principals as likely to come into contact with the criminal justice system) offered very different perceptions of the extent to which they were viewed by significant others in a consistent manner. Through the well-validated use of semantic differential techniques, these boys were asked to rate themselves according to the way they believed they were perceived by teachers, mother, father, best friend, boys in general and girls in general. The data indicate that the whites perceived much less consistency in the way they were evaluated by significant others than did the blacks. This finding would seem to be quite suggestive: if the reported perceptions of the white and black ''bad'' boys do in fact accurately depict the way they are evaluated by significant others, then it would appear reasonable to conclude that, relative to the blacks, the whites were experiencing a greater breakup of their reference group as they gravitated toward deviant identities. It would seem that white ''bad'' boys (boys deemed likely to become labeled as criminally deviant by the criminal justice system) were, by virtue of a bifurcation of their reference group, getting a message that is substantively consistent with both the Harris and the Short and Strodtbeck findings. As the whites moved toward deviant identities, perceived reference group evaluations of them were polarizing to a greater degree than the correspondingly perceived evaluations of the blacks. As they gravitated toward deviance, that is, whites were seemingly aware of a greater separation between deviant and nondeviant moral spheres than were blacks in precisely the same situation.[6]

Sense of Self-Worth

Earlier in this paper we suggested, on the basis of the Harris findings on self-esteem, that deviant identification exacted a more significant price in the psychological well-being of incarcerated whites as compared to incarcerated blacks. Consistent with this suggestion we would expect that racially differentiated samples of nonincarcerated but *officially identified* gang delinquents should reveal higher black than white self-esteem. Short and Strodtbeck found this to be true of the black and white gang boys they studied (1965). Schwartz and Stryker (1970) found the same thing to be true of a racially differentiated sample of ''bad'' boys. In what may be an ancillary but nevertheless intriguing finding, Short and Strodtbeck also pointed out that the black gang boys perceived themselves as smarter than did the white gang boys.[7] These two findings together with the Harris findings strongly suggest that, on the whole, deviant identification is more psychologically detrimental to whites than to blacks.

Rationality of Criminal Choice

In his study, Harris found that white offenders believed it to be considerably less rational than did blacks to take up criminal careers. Although both whites and blacks perceived greater rationality in going straight as opposed to going crooked, the whites did so to a significantly greater extent. One indicator of the perceived rationality of going straight is the extent to which the straight opportunity structure is understood as being responsive to efforts in pursuit of vocational success. It is reasonable to argue that to the extent that the legitimate opportunity structure appears responsive to such efforts, it will also appear to be more rational to go straight than to go crooked. Since there are fewer risks in pursuing legitimate opportunity as opposed to deviant opportunity, one would assume that the greater the perception of legitimate responsiveness the greater the probability of choosing the straight option. To the extent that this is so, and in light of the Harris finding to the effect that whites perceived greater rationality in going straight than did blacks, we should expect that similar samples of white and black criminal deviants would perceive the responsiveness of the legitimate opportunity structure differentially—that whites would perceive that structure as more responsive than would blacks. Short et al., in a study of gang boys (1965), found that whites perceived the legitimate structure of occupational opportunity to be somewhat more open than a structure of illegitimate vocational opportunities. Blacks, on the other hand, were found to perceive greater illegitimate as opposed to legitimate opportunity. Although not quite as marked, Schwartz and Stryker's (1970) findings are exactly parallel to these for their sample of "bad" boys (black and white).[8] These findings would appear to be consonant with Harris's; and taken together, all three findings suggest that delinquent whites more than delinquent blacks are likely to view their criminally deviant acts as alienating. In this instance they are more likely to see their deviance as a violation of rationality—as unreasonable. We argue, therefore, that whites are more likely to view their behavior as censurable.

EXTENSIONS AND CONCLUSIONS

There would appear to be ample substantive consistency between the Harris findings and those just cited to suggest that the etiological implications we have drawn from the Harris study are not sample-specific and that they warrant empirical test in future research. White and black youthful offenders and potential offenders do seem to differ at the aggregated level in terms of central tendency. Though there is undoubtedly overlap between the groups, it would appear theoretically justifiable to treat blacks and whites as separate groups of actors who, when they enter into deviance, may well do so on essentially different bases. The findings we have looked at all suggest that, in terms of its *subjective meaning,* conventionally defined deviance is in fact *deviant* in the eyes of most white youths and that, as a consequence of this, the drift-neutralization scenario is likely to provide the most powerful etiological account of their deviant acts. On the other hand, the findings suggest that, *again in terms of its subjective meaning,* conventionally defined deviance is not nearly as deviant in the eyes of comparable black youths; that given the limits upon legitimate opportunity which blacks most often confront, realization of mainstream expectations for exemplary and "successful" behavior will as likely as not depend upon the exercise of options which civil authority defines as illegal and that, consequently, the definitional expansion arguement may well provide the most powerful etiological account of black criminal deviance.

From the point of view of whites, criminal deviance appears to be aberrant behavior, behavior they characteristically engage in only when they are able to neutralize prohibitions which they themselves endorse—behavior which, when they recognize its deviant quality, becomes a source of guilt and personal mortification. From the point of view of blacks, criminal deviance appears to be a label that civil authority, *white-dominated* civil authority, imposes upon certain of *their* behaviors—behaviors that do not in their view differ in substance from other behaviors which such authority regards as legitimate or nondeviant. For blacks it appears to be a matter of charter. Honesty, initiative, creativity, salesmanship, and the exercise of autonomy are all allowed and even encouraged by civil authority in some precincts but prohibited by that authority in others. The social location of blacks is such that more frequently than not, opportunities for the expression of these highly valued qualities fall outside the range of acceptability and legitimacy as this range is conventionally determined. As such, blacks frequently do not have a charter to do what, in their view, is no different from what it is that others are often encouraged to do. Thus while civil authority may regard these behaviors as criminally deviant, blacks may well see no reason to do so. Under this condition, to be labeled as criminally deviant is therefore of no consequence to the way one sees oneself. When, in this position, the label costs one's freedom, guilt is not experienced—one is not mortified by the realization that one has done something "wrong." On the contrary, when in these terms "criminal deviance" costs blacks their freedom, they are more than likely to see it as but one more injustice visited upon them because of their racial identity. From their point of view, they are not deviant even if they act outside the law, so long as the forms their behaviors take do not violate mainstream normative expectations. Structured exclusion from the precincts of legitimate activity renders the strictures placed upon black's behavior by civil authority illegitimate in their eyes; consequently, we argue, blacks feel justified in violating these strictures more easily than whites—if not also with a far stronger sense of impunity.

There is no question that the argument we have presented in this paper remains implicational, speculative, and in need of direct empirical evaluation. We have simply scratched the surface of an important but curiously neglected issue. In these terms it would seem considerably useful to conduct further research on the specific issue of caste-related aspects of deviance in general and criminal deviance in particular. Concretely, we would suggest that in conducting such research more attention be paid to both the trait and construct validation of measures *across* racial groups in pre-testing. All too frequently this is not done, the result either being the potentially misleading conclusion that race variance is an artifact of class variance or, perhaps worse, that one of the groups ought to be dropped from the analysis (usually blacks).

In suggesting that what many regard as general theories of deviance may not be general at all, we are, necessarily, suggesting that measurement ought to be sensitive to this possibility as well. In this sense, the trait validation of measures, accomplished separately for each racial group [as in Rosenberg and Simmons' (1971) work on self-esteem], is a necessary prerequisite for cross-racial analysis. By no means, on the other hand, should construct validation be necessarily sought for each group with the same criterion variable as the reference point. Insofar as a particular theoretical expectation guiding a concrete effort at construct validation is unspecified with respect to race, we should expect the criterion variable, say a measure of self-esteem, to be related to the variable being validated, say a measure of criminal identity, in the same fashion for both blacks and whites. As we have precisely argued, however, we might well want to specify such a theoretical expectation by race. Given this, it should be anticipated that construct validation of such a measure will vary by race. If this is not perceived in advance, the observation of certain data patterns (i.e., weak, in opposite directions by race, etc.) may well lead to the unwarranted assumption that the measure is invalid (i.e., not "meaningful") for one racial group (usually blacks), when in fact it is perfectly valid in terms of trait validity and under a race-specified, construct validity expectation.

If further research should support our contention that etiologies of adolescent criminal deviance are likely to vary according to the social location of those who come to be regarded as deviant, then it would not be in error to suggest that deviance theorists develop, to a greater extent than they have, approaches which are more sensitive to *situated* causation. It is clear that if further inquiry should bear out our hypothesis that black and white adolescents violate the law (when they do) for essentially different reasons, then our present conceptions of why it is that criminal deviance occurs will have to be modified to allow for greater awareness of the differing phenomenologies of such deviance. If our argument in this paper is correct, then it must be understood that some of what we regard as the overgeneralized character of extant etiological formulations is a function of the fact that their proponents have not attended to the situated subjective meanings given to objectively deviant behaviors by those who engage in them. Since situations vary for included as opposed to excluded groups, it is not unreasonable to propose that the subjective readings members of these groups have of these behaviors—behaviors held by sociological observers to have the same meaning for members of both groups—will in fact vary substantially; and, as a consequence of this, that the reasons for initiating such behaviors are likely to differ for each group even though sociologists have argued otherwise.

Although our etiological interpretations of different patterns of self-perceptions among black and white youthful offenders are *ex post facto,* were they to be validated by direct test, then it might pay students of deviance as well as those interested in the prevention of crime to explore their policy implications. When dealing with drift, the key to prevention and rehabilitation is likely to be found in the extent to which the neutralization process can be controlled among potential and experienced offenders—if indeed it can be. When criminal deviance is a function of definitional expansion and if, as a result of this, apprehension and recognition of one's criminality is of little personal consequence (apprehension and incarceration being an acceptable price to pay for seizing the opportunity to be someone and do something), then intervention by street workers, psychologists, psychiatrists, social workers, and parole officers is likely to have little or no impact. Definitional expansion, it should be realized, is a strategic response to structural blockage—a situation not predisposing to personal reformation. From this perspective even minimal social-structural awareness of the offender's part suggests to him nothing to be ashamed of and, therefore, no reason to change.[9]

When and if groups like blacks are no longer structurally excluded we might expect a change in the etiology of their criminal deviance in the direction of the drift scenario. At this point, race would no longer be etiologically significant. While historical and age-graded events such as unemployment and adolescent frustration play a role in facilitating neutralization at various points in individual life-cycles, through the use of professional and paraprofessional therapists our society is prepared at least in principle to deal with such difficult periods in individual lives. By no means, however, are we now prepared in principle or practice to deal effectively with difficult lives created by large-scale structural exclusion.

Assuming the validity of our argument, the existence of race-specific etiologies would of course imply the necessity of race-specific policies for the reduction, if not the prevention, of criminal deviance among the target population of potential youthful offenders. Campaigns to increase the provision of youth services—the availability of guidance personnel and general opportunities for the wholesome expression of youthful exuberance—under this assumption, make sense only when whites are the objects of such initiatives. The provision of extensive youth services may very well maximize the extent to which the neutralization process among white youths can be controlled. But for black youths any increased provision of such services is likely to be irrelevant to the etiology of their deviant behaviors and consequently ineffective as a strategy for the reduction of criminal offense. If, as we argue, neutralization is not etiologically significant for blacks, then it will do very little good to attempt to control it through intensive guidance and the redirection of youthful energies. And if we persist with the youth services strategy where blacks are concerned, in spite of the likelihood that it will fail, we run the risk of exacerbating the criminogenic social circumstances in which so many black youths find themselves. In this light consider the following hypothetical scenario.

Faced with the unsettling problem of increasing criminal incidence among young people, campaigns for the *provision* of more extensive youth services prove successful. Because such services address the etiological crux of criminal deviance among white youths there is a measurable reduction in their observed criminal offenses. Because, alternatively, such services are irrelevant to the etiology of criminal deviance among black youths no concomitant reduction in their rate of criminal offense is recorded. For a period of time criminal justice policy-makers respond to this lack of measurable positive effect by redoubling their youth service efforts. Convinced by their apparent success with white youths that they are on the right track, they reason that the lack of success among black youths is merely a function of the fact that their generally disadvantaged position in American society necessitates more extensive services relative to those provided for whites. Services are thus extended in the ghettos, with little positive impact. The criminal justice policy-makers, noting their continuing lack of success with the blacks, despair of the prevention, service-oriented strategy and opt instead for the maximization of a policing strategy. Provision of youth services in ghetto areas is reduced while monies for intensified law enforcement become available. The ghettos come more and more to resemble containment areas under the control of enlarged police contingents empowered to enforce the law with aggressive determination. Where black youths are concerned "stop and frisk" and intense surveillance become the order of the day. From the perspective of those who are the recipients of such attention mainstream society represented by the "man" appears increasingly repressive and inhospitable. As such, whatever motivation they possess for trying to "make it" in that society is diminished, while their propensity for realizing mainstream values in activities which, from the point of view of those in the mainstream, are deviant—their propensity for *definitional expansion*—is intensified. The outcome of all this, contrary to the ostensible intentions of the criminal justice policy-makers, is an increase in the incidence of youthful offenses among blacks.

Whether or not this scenario will unfold in the predicted manner is of course open to question. But if we are correct about the existence of race-specific etiologies, and if these racially specific etiologies are as we have characterized them, failure on the part of policy-makers to take etiological differences into account can only render the reduction of criminal deviance more problematic than it even now appears to be. If we are correct about the etiological centrality of *definitional expansion* for black youths, then any policy discourse which neglects structural reallocation of mainstream opportunities as largely unimportant or unrealistic in the planning of anticrime strategies to be used with black youths—is likely to generate an approach which, we feel, can hardly be anything other than counterproductive.

Anti-crime policy that ignores this issue is, we believe, policy likely to be doomed to failure. As noted above, when and if blacks are no longer structurally excluded from mainstream opportunities, the etiology of their criminal deviance may be expected to shift from definitional expansion to drift and neutralization. At that point, the provision of services strategy might very well be employed to positive effect. Until then, however, color-blind anticrime policies, such as the universal application of the youth services strategy, are likely to be ineffective where black youths are concerned precisely because they are etiologically irrelevant.

FOOTNOTES

1. In addition, the Harris sample shows a higher rate of disrupted family of origin status than do comparable youths in the general U.S. population (U.S. Bureau of the Census, 1968:22), and it shows this disruption at a higher rate for blacks than whites (Harris, 1973). Apart from this, however, and as noted in the text, comparisons between the two racial groups reveal little in the way of background differences. Comparisons on this score include: "seriousness" of criminal histories, age at first arrest (the mean for both races at about fifteen years), the number of times and total time imprisoned previously (the mean for both races at about 1.7 times and two years, respectively), and months since last prior imprisonment [the mean for both groups at about twelve months (Harris, 1973)]. Such similarities might well be expected of samples drawn from a correctional setting and, by reducing the possibility of confounding factors, make the job of more interesting racial comparisons easier.

2. Though to some extent the findings to be cited are based on similar theoretical frameworks and consequently similar measurement techniques, because of their remaining disparity and difference of detail, and given the present purpose of this paper—to suggest race-specific, hypothetical scenarios for criminal deviance—we shall attempt to minimize the presentation of data in the analysis and, instead, focus on the substantive meaning of such findings. When necessary, particularly salient data will be reported in following footnotes.

3. These represent the small set of scholarly attempts to assess differences between black and white youths in their perception of legitimate and illegitimate opportunities.

4. The full set of polar adjective pairs we have identified also includes friendly-unfriendly; clean-dirty; polite-rude; studious-lazy; obedient-disobedient, and cool-square. Scoring was accomplished by first noting the difference between mean-scores for each of the two paired adjectives according to race. This difference was taken to measure the degree of moral separation between deviant and nondeviant attributes of membership cliques; the greater the difference scores the greater the perceived separation. These difference scores were then compared across race. In eight of nine such comparisons difference scores were higher for whites than they were for blacks. [See p. 149 in Short and Strodtbeck (1965).]

5. As indicated in Table 5.3 (p. 105) in Short and Strodtbeck, significant white-black differences are found in the correlation between delinquent involvement and performing domestic chores for each of the four types of delinquent gangs identified. Thus, for "conflict" gang boys, the r stands at −.14 for whites and .42 for blacks; for gangs marked by sexual activity, the same r is −.21 for whites and .38 for blacks, for "retreatist" gang boys, the r is −.18 for whites and .04 for blacks; and for "protest" gang boys, r is −.07 for whites and .19 for blacks.

6. The relevant correlations are as follows [p. 83 in Schwartz and Stryker (1970)]: on the evaluation dimension, r = .43 for blacks versus .30 for whites; on the activity dimension, r = .49 for blacks versus .32 for whites; on the potency dimension, r = .39 for blacks and .37 for whites; and on an "interpersonal quality" dimension, r = .54 for blacks and .40 for whites. In all cases the r's indicate greater consistency for the significant others of the blacks.

7. On a measure of self-evaluation [p. 60 in Short and Strodtbeck (1965)], white gang boys

showed a mean of 4.88, while black gang boys showed a mean of 5.26. Similarly, on a measure of "smartness," $\bar{X}$ for whites was 5.14, but for blacks was 5.79 (p. 63). On a measure of self-evaluation [p. 76, Schwartz and Stryker (1970)] white "bad" boys showed a mean of 18.68 while black "bad" boys showed a mean of 17.86 (the higher the score the lower the self-evaluation).

8. There is, in this regard, a striking parallel between the Harris data and the Short et al. data (1965). The blacks in Harris's study showed a mean of .434 and the whites a mean of .351 on a measure of the relative perceived rationality or expected value of criminal to "straight" career choices (the measure, REV_c). For this variable, then, the black mean (.434) stands in a ratio of 1.24 to the white mean (.351). Taking Short et al.'s questions indexing the perception of illegitimate opportunity (Q 14–20) and those indexing the perception of legitimate opportunity (Q 7–11 and 23), and (a) reverse scoring those items which deny opportunity (items 7, 9, 10 and 20) and then (b), generating two means within each race which reflect "degree of agreement" that illegitimate/ legitimate opportunity is available for self, we find the following. For blacks, the perception of legitimate opportunity stands at .487 and that of illegitimate opportunity at .641. To yield the analogy to the Harris measure of REV_c, we then take the ratio .641/(.641 + .487) [see Harris (1975)], to yield a relative rationality of criminal choice score of .568 for blacks. Since for whites the perception of legitimate opportunity stands at .589 and that of illegitimate opportunity at .524, the same process yields a surrogate measure of "REV_c" of .470 for Short et al.'s whites. The ratio of these two "REV_c" scores (.568 for blacks and .470 for whites) yields a black/white differential of 1.21— strikingly close to the analogous Harris differential of 1.24. (It may be noted in addition that if the same procedure is used on the Short et al. items appearing in Schwartz and Stryker, for the latter, the analogous "REV_c" score is .509 for blacks and .497 for whites. The differential for Schwartz and Stryker's sample, then, understandably lower than in Harris and Short et al. because of the middle-class basis of Schwartz and Stryker's sample, is nonetheless in the same direction, standing at 1.02.)

9. Indeed, intervention efforts may seem increasingly unwarranted and, as a consequence, incarceration increasingly inequitable. In this light it is interesting to note the role of black inmates in the politicization of the prison experience. It is the black inmate to a much greater extent than the white inmate who has come to articulate imprisonment in political terms. He is in jail not for offending a moral code but because he has offended a law which in its political inspiration has victimized him.

REFERENCES

Cloward, Richard, and Lloyd Ohlin (1960), *Delinquency and Opportunity*. New York: Free Press.

Cohen, Albert V. (1955), *Delinquent Boys*. Glencoe, Ill.: Free Press.

Harris, Anthony (1973), "Deviant Identity, Rational Choice, and Cognitive Simplification," unpublished Ph.D. dissertation, Princeton University.

———— (1976), "Race, Commitment to Deviance, and Spoiled Identity," *American Sociological Review* (June).

Lewis, Michael (1970), "Structural Deviance and Normative Conformity," in Daniel Glaser, ed., *Crime in the City*. New York: Harper & Row, pp. 176–199.

Matza, David (1964), *Delinquency and Drift*. New York: Wiley.

Merton, Robert K. (1957), "Social Structure and Anomie," in R. K. Merton, *Social Theory and Social Structure*. Glencoe, Ill.: Free Press.

Miller, Walter (1958), "Lower-Class Culture as a Generating Milieu of Gang Delinquency," *Journal of Social Issues* 14(3):5–19.

Rosenberg, Morris, and Roberta Simmons (1971), *Black and White Self-Esteem: The Urban School Child*. Monograph. Washington, D.C.: American Sociological Association.

Schwartz, Michael, and S. Stryker (1970), *Deviance, Selves and Others*. Rose Monograph ASA.

Short, James; R. Rivera; and R. A. Tennyson (1965), "Perceived Opportunities, Gang Membership, and Delinquency," in *American Sociological Review* 30(February):56–67.

Short, James Jr., and F. Strodtbeck (1965), *Group Process and Gang Delinquency*. Chicago: University of Chicago Press.

U.S. Bureau of the Census (1968), "Marital Status and Family Status: March, 1968," Current Population Reports Series P-20, No. 187, Washington, D.C.

CROWDING AND SLUMS:
A STATISTICAL EXPLORATION*

Harvey M. Choldin, UNIVERSITY OF ILLINOIS

There is an ongoing debate among urbanists over the causal factors responsible for rates of social pathology in urban communities. Some argue that demographic and ecological characteristics such as high density and overcrowding are primarily responsible for high rates of pathology. Others point to social structure as the primary source of pathology. A definitive determination regarding the locus of causation would of course have significant implications for the development of policy intended to reduce the presence and impact of social pathology in urban communities. Such a determination would indicate what factors and conditions are most in need of remedial intervention if the incidence of pathology is to be significantly reduced. While a definitive finding on cause yet eludes us, Harvey Choldin has undertaken an analysis which begins to shed light on the relative causal potency of demographic-ecological as opposed to social structural variables with regard to the incidence of social pathology. In the following paper Choldin reports a number of findings which must be taken seriously if we are truly interested in maximizing the human serviceability of the urban environment.

The research literature on urban population density and social pathologies contains several unresolved issues. This literature centers about the "density-

Research in Social Problems and Public Policy—Vol. 1, 1979, pages 179–194
Copyright © 1979 by JAI Press, Inc.

pathology hypothesis" that high density produces pathologies such as aggression, stress, poor health, social breakdown, etc. [The hypothesis and literature are reviewed in Choldin (1978).] Sociological research on this hypothesis proliferated following the publication of ethological work by Calhoun (1962, 1965) and other biologists and psychologists who demonstrated that abnormally high densities had harmful effects upon various animals, including rodents, cats and deer. Sociologists and psychologists then attempted to discover this effect among humans. Their studies were designed at varying scales, from the small group to the nation-state, and it is the community and neighborhood scale which will be considered in this paper. Sociologists brought social structure to the forefront of the debate, asking whether social structure was more important than density in generating pathologies. Two unresolved issues are whether density makes a difference once social structure is taken into account and whether poverty is more important than race and ethnicity as structural variables. Another issue pertains to the dimensions of density, especially household crowding: what does the statistical relationship between household crowding and pathology at the neighborhood level mean?

Given the fact that social structure is related to subcommunity pathologies, which structural variable, if any, is crucial? The broad issue regarding social structure is that most of the variance in pathology rates is accounted for by social structural variables; density adds but little explained variance. Galle, Gove and McPherson (1972) showed the importance of structural variables, but used an index which combined race, nationality and socioeconomic status of census tracts in Chicago. Choldin and Roncek (1976) showed that race was a more predictive variable than income in a relatively small city.

In the recent series of density-pathology reports (Galle, et al., 1972; Freedman, 1975; Gillis, 1974), density has frequently been an insignificant variable, but household crowding has often had a substantial relationship to pathology rates. Crowding may be a component of density, but may also be independent of it (Webb, 1975). Roncek (1975) in a review of thirteen urban ecological studies reported that they consistently found levels of crowding to be directly related to crime or delinquency rates. In most of the studies this was an incidental finding and it was not treated theoretically.

Whether population density or household crowding is the central variable in the density-pathology hypothesis has become a persistent issue in this literature. "Density" is a shorthand expression for the gross population density of an area, representing the census population divided by the amount of area. In the United States, it is conventionally expressed as persons per acre or square mile. Crowding is the extent to which the residents of a given set of dwellings occupy them beyond some level of occupancy, the level representing an agreed-upon housing standard. The U.S. standard is one person per room (American Public Health Association, 1950, 1969), which is extraordinarily high by world standards. The extent of crowding in a given residential area is expressed as the percentage of the population living in dwellings occupied at more than one person per room. It is possible to have very dense residential areas with no crowding. The persistent controversy has been over the effects of density as opposed to crowding (Schmitt, 1966; Jacobs, 1961; Freedman, 1975; Booth, 1976; Galle and Gove, 1975; Michelson, 1970). One group has contended that high density is harmful while crowding is tolerable, whereas others have argued the opposite, and some have used the concepts more or less interchangeably.

A discussion of the relationship between crowding and pathology at the neighborhood level is likely to draw one into the ecological fallacy (Robinson, 1951). Crime rates, for example, may be social facts, pertaining to the subcommunity. The proportion of crowded households may also be treated at this level. But, given subcommunity statistics, to say as some investigators have, that the people in crowded households are subject to "interpersonal press" which leads them toward criminal acts is to commit the fallacy. It is still necessary to explore the meaning of crowding levels, at the subcommunity level.

One measurement problem in the density-pathology literature which is treated in this paper is that of disparate indicators of pathology which may have different relationships to density and social structure. In the urban ecological studies there have been several pathologies studied—from tract-level rates of incarceration to rates of tuberculosis (Schmitt, 1966). Typically, studies have looked at two or more of them in relation to density/crowding and social structure. In some cases, some of them have been related to the independent variables in one way, while others (such as suicide and mental illness) have not. In this study we have devised a composite neighborhood pathology index, which is of interest even apart from the density issues.

What is the nature of the modern urban slum is the question behind the more specific research issues. Is it to be defined environmentally, in terms of degraded conditions, or socially and behaviorally, in terms of social position and particular events, or by some combination of environmental and social terms? One serviceable definition of the slum is proposed by Clinard (1966), who states that such an area is characterized by a complex of environmental conditions, such as dilapidated housing, and social characteristics, such as higher-than-average rates of crime, delinquency and vice. Two other positions to be considered in this paper are those of Jacobs (1961) and Newman (1972), both architectural specialists who emphasize environmental variables, and Shaw and McKay (1942). These sociologists advanced a neighborhood theory which states that social structural integrity and a pervasive value system, linking family, church, school, etc., generate informal local social control which prevents crime and delinquency.

In sum, this report explores the density-social structure-pathology issues at the intraurban level. Within the cluster of social structural variables, the effects of poverty and race-ethnicity are separated. Within the spatial variables, the effects of density and crowding are separated and crowding is considered as a subcommunity variable.

METHOD

This report is based upon analysis of 1970 census tracts of the city of Los Angeles, which is an excellent case for a study of density/crowding, SES/ethnicity, and pathology. Although it is often cited as a prototypical spread city, Los Angeles actually has a great range of densities. This city also has a wide range of socioeconomic levels, including a large middle and upper-middle class, unlike some other large cities which have lost these segments of the population. Los Angeles has two large minority groups, Mexican Americans and blacks, most of whom live in segregated sections of the city. The city is very large, with a 1970 population of 2.8 million.

The housing and density pattern in Los Angeles is certainly sufficiently urban to make it a suitable case for a study of variation within a single community.[1] The 48 densest tracts in the city exceeded 23,000 residents per square mile, which is quite high, even by U.S. big city standards. Chicago's citywide average in the same year was about 16,000 (Los Angeles' citywide average was 6,000). In Los Angeles there were approximately 150 tracts denser than one standard deviation above the mean of all tracts. The city also had a greater proportion of housing in multi-unit structures than most cities. In the typical U.S. city, about one-third of the units are in multi-unit structures, the more common type of dwelling being the single-family detached house. In Los Angeles, more than 40 percent of the housing was in multi-unit structures.

The data originate in the census, in records of public agencies, and in geographical measurements. The census provided age, family and household, occupation, education, ethnicity and race and housing. Agency reports generate the pathology rates, including crimes, fires, suicides, etc.[2] Geographical measurements yield distance from city center and population density. The statistics all refer to census tracts—there were 725 in 1970—which are used as surrogates for neighborhoods.

The attempt to produce a pathology indicator required the combination of several measures of negatively valued phenomena occurring in neighborhoods. The phenomena represent numerous and various undesirable incidents, such as violent crimes and fires. The statistical task was to find several which co-varied in their distribution across neighborhoods. We obtained data on nine negatively valued phenomena and calculated tract-level rates. They were: deaths (which yielded a Crude Death Rate); assaults, robberies, homicides, attempted suicides, two types of fires, juvenile delinquency arrests, and substandard scores on 6th grade reading tests. These were subjected to a factor analysis and seven proved to be highly intercorrelated. The two which did not correlate as highly were Crude Death Rate and attempted suicides. The rest were combined into a neighborhood pathology index[3] which became the principal dependent variable for much of the analysis. The burden of the analysis was to account for the distribution of pathology rates across the areas of the city.

The principal statistical tools employed are correlation and multiple regression. The objective in the use of regression is to extricate the effects of the various causal variables. The first attempt is to compare the effects of density and crowding versus the social structural variables. The second effort is to examine the separate effects of ethnicity and race versus poverty in relation to the pathology levels. The proportion of young males residing in the tracts is also considered in the analysis, since this has been shown to be related to certain crime rates in other studies.

While statistical relationships will be generated at the aggregate level, the analysis will not fall into the statistical fallacy. The fallacy occurs when individual-level explanations are superimposed upon aggregate-level statistical relationships. In this case, the statistics and the interpretation will remain at the aggregate—neighborhood—level.

FINDINGS

The intercorrelations among independent variables are at the center of this entire problem. In most cities there is a coincidence, over space, among income, ethnicity/race, and environmental conditions. The problem in the series of intraurban density-pathology studies has been to separate the effects of these causal variables.

The zero-order correlation matrix (Table 1) indicates the extent of interrelationship among the main predictor variables. The matrix shows that the variables are not unrelated to each other, but the greatest r = .69. None of the correlations approach unity and we consider the correlations to be sufficiently low to permit multiple regression without multicollinearity.

The regression analysis shows that density is not related to pathology, although crowding is. Density has a zero-order correlation of .35 with pathology, but partial correlation and regression analysis reveal that this is spurious. A partial correlation shows that controlling for SES vitiates the apparent relationship between density and pathology. (The partials are not reported here in tabular form.) The standardized regression coefficient for density-pathology is trivial even though it is statistically significant. Density is judged to be unimportant and is dropped from the remainder of the analysis.

Crowding, on the other hand, is one of the best predictors of pathology. In the multiple regression it is the second-best predictor. Probing the crowding-pathology relationship with various controls shows that it is strong. In partial correlation analysis it survives controls for SES and ethnicity.

Social structure is also highly related to pathology rates, the most powerful predictors in this cluster being percent Black and SES. The results of the 14-variable multiple regression, shown in Table 2, are similar to those reported in Galle, et al. (1972). If these variables are the first entered into a regression equation and crowding follows, it adds very little explained variance.

Two additional variables which were theoretically interesting prove to be

Table 1. Zero-Order Correlations Among Selected Independent Variables, Los Angeles Census Tracts, 1970.

	SES	Density	Crowding	% Black	% Spanish	% Over 60	% Under 5	Males 15–19	Distance from CBD
SES	1.000	−.529	−.675	−.409	−.361	−.282	−.281	.139	.577
Density		1.000	.350	.293	.161	.266	.058	−.108	−.499
Crowding			1.000	.343	.695	−.110	.645	−.030	.448
% Black				1.000	−.216	−.104	.354	.019	−.340
% Spanish					1.000	−.068	.425	.019	−.303
% Over 60						1.000	−.547	−.479	−.463
% Under 5							1.000	.190	.032
Males 15–19								1.000	.303
Distance from CBD									1.000

Table 2.   Standardized Regression Coefficients
(Los Angeles Census Tracts, 1970).

Pathology Index with:	Beta =	r =
% Black	.481*	.686
Crowding	.430*	.652
Males 15–19	.228*	.138
SES	−.128*	−.620
Structure + 50	.125*	.026
% Over 60	.095*	−.052
% Under 5	.076*	.466
% Spanish	−.066*	.189
Stability	.061*	.152
Density	−.054*	.352
Parksite	.026	.029
% Husb-Wife fam	−.008	−.286
% Family Units	−.002	−.186
Distance from CBD	−.001	−.394
R^2 =	.736	
R =	.858	

*Significant at .05 level. Significance not indicated for r's.

related to the pathology rate: presence of large apartment structures and the presence of males aged 15–19. Some other variables hypothesized to be related to pathology were shown to be unrelated. They are: stability/transiency of the population, presence of intact-family households, distance from city center and the presence of children and older people. These are dropped from further analysis and an attempt is made to find an abbreviated set of predictor variables.

Regressions with several subsets of the original predictors revealed that five variables accounted for almost all the variance explained. They are: crowding, SES, percent black, number of teenaged males, and type of housing. This list is irreducible in that none of these, used as controls, eliminates the effects of another. We prepared regressions with these five variables plus percent Spanish for the city as a whole and within black and Chicano tracts.[4]

The city-wide regression indicates that the pathology index is highly related to crowding and the percent black in tracts (Table 3). Following these, pathology is related to the presence of teenaged males and it is inversely related to socioeconomic level. Finally, the housing type in a neighborhood seems to have a slight relationship to the dependent variable in that areas with higher proportions of single-family houses have somewhat lower pathology rates.

The rest of the analysis treats racial and ethnic differences. At the outset in the regression analysis, black and Chicano sections of the city appeared to be different. The proportion black of a tract was highly related to the pathology level, whereas the proportion Chicano had a weak negative relationship to pathology. Neither of these findings was an artifact of low-income levels, since SES did not

LIST OF VARIABLES

Demographic:

% UNDER 5	*Percent of population ages 0–4 (Source:* 1970 census)
% OVER 60	Percent of population ages 60+ *(Source:* 1970 census)
MALES 15–19	*Number of males ages 15–19 (Source:* 1970 census)
STABILITY	*An index composed of percent of pupils transferring out of schools* in the tract, 1971, *percent of pupils transferring into schools* in the tract, and *percent of population residing in same residence, 1965–1970 (Source:* L.A. Board of Education, via State of the City file and 1970 census)

$$STABILITY = .75566 \left[\frac{\text{transfer in} - 28.6427}{8.7858} \right]$$
$$+ .22907 \left[\frac{\text{transfer out} - 21.3387}{6.7697} \right]$$
$$- .02973 \left[\frac{1965\text{-}1970 \text{ nonmovers} - 44.5928}{12.6200} \right]$$

Social Structural:

SES	An index composed of *median family income, median years of schooling completed, % of adult males unemployed,* 1970 *(Source:* 1970 census)

$$SES = .12948 \left[\frac{\text{EDUCATION} - 12.0445}{1.5855} \right]$$
$$+ .81803 \left[\frac{\text{INCOME} - 8836.9570}{4561.1467} \right]$$
$$- .07598 \left[\frac{\text{UNEMPLOYMENT} - 7.2660}{3.9210} \right]$$

% BLACK	*Percent Negro (Source:* 1970 census)
% SPANISH	*Percent Spanish surname or Spanish language (Source:* 1970 census)
% HUSB-WIFE FAM	*Percent of household units composed of husband-wife families (Source:* 1970 census)

Environmental:

% FAMUNITS	*% of housing units comprised of single-family detached structures (Source:* 1970 census)
STRUCTURE 50	*Number of structures with 50 or more housing units (Source:* 1970 census)
DISTANCE FROM CBD	*Radial distance from City Hall* (calculated from digitized tract centroids supplied by ISSR, University of Southern California)
PARKSITE	*Number of parks within the tract (Source:* Los Angeles Parks Department, via CAB State of the City file)

obliterate the pronounced differences between the effects of the two ethnic/racial variables in the multiple regression. Socioeconomic levels in black and Chicano tracts are both low as is indicated in Table 4. The interplay among the predictor variables is different in black and Chicano tracts (Table 3).

The black tracts have the highest overall pathology level, and within these areas two variables are prominently related to pathology. The presence of males

Table 3. Standardized Regression Coefficients, Short Model

	All Tracts	Black Tracts	Chicano Tracts
Crowding	.453*	.266*	.089
% Black	.439*	—	.339*
Males 15–19	.189*	.640*	.712*
SES	−.161*	−.316*	.011
% Spanish	−.099*	−.080	—
% Family units	−.064*	−.169*	−.218*

*Significant at .05 level.

aged 15–19 is the most important predictor of pathology. Socioeconomic status is highly negatively related to the pathology index as it is elsewhere.

In the Chicano section, the presence of males aged 15–19 is also extremely highly related to the pathology index. Neither crowding nor SES is related to the dependent variable. Areas with higher proportions of single-family housing units are likely to have lower pathology rates.

DISCUSSION[5]

It is clear that the simple density-pathology hypothesis may be rejected on the basis of the findings. The hypothesis stated that high pathology levels should be found where high density is found. Within the multivariate analysis, density had a small negative relationship to the pathology rate, not the positive relationship which had been hypothesized. The positive zero-order correlation initially suggests that there might be some relationship between density and pathology, but the further analysis shows that the other variables associated with density are the more important ones. [Indeed, the negative sign of the density term in the regression suggests that poor, sparsely settled districts might have more pathology than poor dense ones. Roncek and I have found this in more intensive analyses of two other cities (Roncek and Choldin, 1977).]

The difference between the correlation and regression coefficients means that density and pathology do co-vary across the areas of the city to some extent,

Table 4. Means and Standard Deviations of Selected Variables, City-Wide and by Race/Ethnicity (Los Angeles Tracts, 1970)

	Total City		Black Tracts		Chicano Tracts	
	$\bar{X}$	SD	$\bar{X}$	SD	$\bar{X}$	SD
Pathology	.004	.985	1.296	1.020	0.429	0.625
SES	.006	.942	−0.704	.428	−0.742	0.390
Stability	.002	.971	8.177	.711	−0.403	0.618
Density	16.016	9.983	30.269	7.715	19.886	9.762
Crowding	3.229	2.488	4.741	1.712	7.654	1.803

although this correlation is not nearly as high as between pathology and some other variables. But, the regressions show that this is a spurious relationship. The more important relationships are between pathology and other variables. This finding is consistent with those in a series of other intraurban studies which also found that density variation within the city is not related to pathology rates, once social structural variables are taken into account (Choldin, 1978).

The finding that density does not have a positive association with crime tends to support Jacobs's (1961) argument regarding density and neighborhood life. Jacobs asserts that high density is a positive attribute of urban neighborhoods. She says that high density and street life suppress crime. If there is high density, plus shops along streets, there will be shopkeepers, shoppers, and passers-by and the street area will be constantly under informal surveillance. Thus street crime will be suppressed because the would-be attacker cannot act without witnesses. The simple availability of relatively large numbers of people means that the place is never abandoned and unprotected against criminals. Our finding that density does not correlate with pathology is consistent with Jacobs's argument, especially insofar as we found a negative relationship between density and pathology in the regression analysis. The findings regarding crowding were quite unlike those for density, however.

Crowding was closely and consistently related to the pathology rate, a finding which corresponds to those of similar intraurban studies (Roncek, 1975; Galle et al., 1972; Gillis, 1974). Several density-pathology studies have switched from population density to household crowding as an independent variable. For example, after decomposing the components of density, Galle et al. found that the density element most closely related to pathology was persons per room.

This shift to the use of crowding as a substitute for density is methodologically questionable. The justification for the switch has been that crowding is a component of density (Winsborough, 1961), that density is a function of crowding. However, crowding and density may vary independently. A city may have dense areas without crowding, as in prosperous areas in Manhattan, or it may have low-density areas with crowding, as in Watts. Among the Los Angeles census tracts, the correlation between density and crowding is only .35.

The shift to the use of crowding within a test of the density-pathology hypothesis is also theoretically questionable. To assert that high density causes pathology is to say that there is something about the community or neighborhood which is harmful. To assert that crowding causes pathology is to say that there is something in the household which is harmful. This latter statement should then be tested with household data.

There are plausible arguments suggesting that crowded housing should be pathogenic and equally plausible ones saying it should not. Mitchell (1971) found that crowded housing in Hong Kong led to the children's leaving the apartment and being out of the scrutiny of parents for much of the day. Choldin et al. (1975) found that within graduate student families in the United States, crowded housing led to the fathers' spending much time outside the household and, hence, out of touch with children. Plant (1930) stated that crowding exposed children to too much adult backstage activity and thus prevented moral development by depriving the child of any adult role models. Alternatively, Michelson (1970) suggests that tight quarters should foster consideration and cooperation within the family. There are innumerable stories of cooperative behavior among highly crowded urban immigrant families in U.S. history.

Despite this theoretical background, we contend that the ecological urban studies, including this one, do not indicate that crowding causes community pathologies. It is simply not possible to test the current theories with ecological data. There is no way to know, for example, that the residents of the crowded households within the tracts with high crowding levels are the persons who commit the assaults and other acts which contribute to high pathology rates.

Crowding should be viewed as an effect rather than a cause. It seems to be a function of some of the same forces which generate the elements of the pathology index, particularly poverty and minority status. The data show that crowding has a strong negative relationship to SES and it is higher in minority areas. It occurs more toward the city center than away from it. In particular, crowding is highest in poor minority areas where there are many small children. Crowding is evidently a good indicator of housing deficiency. It is an effect of poverty and fertility and is more like an urban pathology itself than a cause of other pathologies.

Some of the control variables, which were hypothesized to be related to neighborhood pathology proved to be unrelated. Transiency presumably showed that the residents of an area were coming and going and were thus unable to forge a stable social order. This proved not to be the case. The presence of family units with husband, wife and children present was hypothesized to be negatively related to pathology rates. Other studies have shown that familistic neighborhoods tend not to have high pathology rates (Choldin and Roncek, 1976; Roncek and Choldin, 1977). Other studies have shown that female-headed households are likely to be subject to various kinds of problems. This Los Angeles study does not confirm the familism hypothesis.

The neighborhood theory of Shaw and McKay (1942) also pertains to these observations about familism and age composition. It states that stability and familism support an integrated pervasive value system and a local social system which has effective informal controls over deviant behavior, and, hence, tends to suppress crime and delinquency. In this analysis, transiency and familism prove to be unimportant, while the presence of teen-aged males, race, and poverty are major variables. We must conclude that the general hypothesis is not useful in this case, since the other three variables are so powerful.

A second general hypothesis suggests that it is the population at risk of victimization in a neighborhood which determines the crime rate there (Boggs, 1965; Choldin and Roncek, 1976). Thus, a neighborhood with numerous elderly persons, who might be defenseless victims, would be expected to have a high crime rate. This proved not to be the case in the present analysis. Evidently, the presence of potential perpetrators of crimes, young males, is more predictive of the rates of events than is the presence of potential victims.

The finding that tracts with multi-family housing were more likely to have higher pathology rates is consistent with Newman's argument about urban environments. Newman (1972) argues that certain types of urban environments are *defensible spaces*. Such areas must be peopled and must be physically arranged in such a way that their occupants can distinguish between locals and strangers and may see and stop disruptive behaviors. He found that particular types of apartment buildings and projects were unlikely to have defensible space.

The density-social structure model does not seem useful in understanding the distribution of pathology in the city. Social structure is related to pathology, but so are the presence of teen-aged males and the type of housing in the neighborhood. In particular, the highest pathology rates are found in areas which are black and poor, and which have teen-aged males and multi-family housing. In more general terms, it is elements of social structure, age composition and environment which make a difference.

It is also clear that social structure is not an undifferentiated factor influencing the distribution of pathology. It is not correct to say that pathology rates are a simple function of minority status and poverty. Blacks and Chicanos represent large, poor minorities which have been discriminated against in the city. Each occupies a large area of old housing. Within each of these minority areas the pathology pattern is different.

The black areas have much higher pathology rates than the Chicano. Both minority areas are poor and have more crowded housing than the city average. In both, the most powerful predictor of pathology, by far, is the presence of teen-aged males.

The difference between the black and Chicano areas is that the former have considerably higher pathology rates. Within the Black areas, SES is a powerful variable, poorer areas having more pathology. But in the Chicano areas, SES makes no difference. The density-social structure-pathology model makes no provision for such complexities, treating minority status and poverty in an undifferentiated manner. Another interpretation is suggested to interpret these differences.

Perhaps the length of time in the city explains the difference between these two minority groups. The Chicano population has been in Los Angeles from the beginning of the city and has grown with the community. Much of the black population arrived recently in the great migration from the rural South after World War II. The Chicanos have developed more of a socially integrated community with linkages between family, church, voluntary associations and the like. The blacks, at an equivalent level of poverty, are a newcomer population to a considerable degree, with a much higher level of transiency than the Chicanos.

Thus, among the Mexican Americans, poverty does not make a difference. What differentiates areas is the presence of teen-aged males who are potential gang members, and the presence of multi-family housing, some of which consists of public housing projects. Shaw and McKay's (1942) more general theory thus helps to interpret the difference between these two minority areas. It suggests that the long-resident Chicano population, even though it is poor, developed a pervasive neighborhood social organization, which maintained social control, while the more transient newcomer population of blacks did not, and hence, it experiences a higher level of the pathologies.

The construction of a neighborhood pathology index is a reminder that many of the negative phenomena of the city are concentrated in particular sub-areas. The factor analysis which produced the index showed that when a variety of eleven pathology indicators were examined, nine were highly intercorrelated, even though they seemed, substantively, to be quite disparate. Three types of crimes, two types of fires and delinquency arrests were associated and they were all correlated with low performance on school tests. The only two which were not related with the others, were the Crude Death Rate, which is presumably a function of the age structure, and attempted suicide, which is not as severely class-biased as the other phenomena. In a sense, the composite pathology index represents an ecological behavioral operational definition of a slum.

This index also opens a direction for social area analysis and factorial ecology to expand in the study of the social geography of the metropolis. These methods use census data to discover types of neighborhoods and their distribution over space (Rees, 1970). The methods regularly generate three social dimensions: socioeconomic status, familism, and race/ethnicity. The addition of this other type of data from municipal agencies adds another dimension to this portrayal of the neighborhoods. It is demonstrated that census tracts vary along this pathology dimension in addition to their SES, familism and race/ethnicity. Furthermore, interrelationships between pathology and the three conventional dimensions are shown in this analysis.

Definitions of the slum usually contain a physical and a behavioral dimension. One leading definition (Clinard, 1966) says that a slum is an urban sub-area with degraded environment including deteriorated housing and it also contains high rates of crime and delinquency. The crowding-pathology data further indicate the connection between these two dimensions. The pathology index shows that slum areas have high rates of fires as well as of crimes and that in these areas the school performance of the children is measurably lower than in the rest of the city. The crowding level shows that in addition to having high pathology rates, they also have inferior housing.

In terms of public policy, the argument reminds us of one obvious point: improving housing and reducing crowding cannot eliminate poverty and discrimination.[6] It continues to be true, however, that many of the urban poor occupy the lowest-quality housing in the community and much of it is substandard. This study, like others, suggests that large apartment projects are not good environments for the urban poor. But, even more strongly, it shows that more basic social facts, social structure and age composition of the population, underlie the distribution of urban pathology.

SUMMARY

The initial problem addressed was the density-pathology hypothesis, which states that the parts of the city with the highest levels of population density will have the highest levels of various pathologies. A related problem was whether household crowding, which has been studied in other inquiries, is a reasonable substitute for density. The density-pathology hypothesis has become embedded in a model which states that both social structure and density contribute to pathology. Multivariate analysis of 1970 data on Los Angeles census tracts showed that population density has only a spurious relationship to pathology. For this reason the hypothesis was rejected. The analysis showed that social structural and demographic variables were highly related to pathology levels, as was household crowding. However, it cannot be logically demonstrated in an ecological study that crowding causes neighborhood pathology. Crowding cannot cause poverty and minority status but poverty and minority status can and probably do cause crowding. Thus, the crowding-pathology hypothesis at the community level should be rejected as illogical. Crowding itself should be seen as an indicator of slum conditions, generated by a complex of social structural and demographic phenomena.

FOOTNOTES

*The author is grateful to the Rockefeller Foundation and the Center for Population Research of the National Institute for Child Health and Human Development (grant no. RO 1 HD08031), for support of this research. Los Angeles non-census data were generously provided by D. Craig Avery of the Community Analysis Bureau, City of Los Angeles, and Census data were provided by Leo Schuermann and Linda Fullmer of the Institute for Social Science Research, University of Southern California. An earlier version of this paper was presented at the 1976 meeting of the American Sociological Association in New York City.

1. This analysis shows that Los Angeles does have a discernible density gradient. Previous investigators, including Guest (1973) and Edmonston (1975) stated that the density gradient in Los Angeles and similar spread cities is almost flat. Duncan et al. (1962) indicated that the growth and aging of residential areas in that city does not move toward a peaking of occupancy. The 1970 tract data indicate that there is a gradient, although it is not steep. The correlation between distance from CBD and density is − .50. Although much of the city is settled at moderately low densities, there are many high density tracts, or "peaks" in the surface of the distribution.

2. The State of the City file (City of Los Angeles, 1973, 1974) contains tract-level data from many local agencies. This includes information from the school board, police department, parks department, etc. See notes to Table 3 for specific items.

3. In this study we were able to obtain data on the most extensive list of pathologies since Schmitt's study of 1950 data for Honolulu. Our 1970 data for Los Angeles census tracts include the following pathologies: deaths (yielding Crude Death Rate), assaults, robberies, homicides, attempted suicides, fires (structural), fires (nonstructural), juvenile delinquent arrests, average 6th grade reading scores. Seven of these nine indicators were highly intercorrelated (mean correlation = 0.52). The two which did not correlate as highly were Crude Death Rate and number of attempted suicides. This left three types of serious crimes, juvenile delinquent arrests, two types of fires and the rate at which children perform on reading tests. Presumably, some other pathology indicators such as morbidity would have cohered with these, but they were not available for study.

A factor analysis yielded the following formula for a pathology index:

$$\text{PATHOLOGY} = 0.00886 \left[\frac{\text{MURDER} - 0.4932}{1.1628} \right] + .72692 \left[\frac{\text{ASSAULT} - 32.5745}{33.7028} \right]$$

$$- .05832 \left[\frac{\text{ROBBERY} - 17.2561}{23.8147} \right] - .00854 \left[\frac{\text{JUV ARREST} - 34.2629}{35.0704} \right]$$

$$+ .08128 \left[\frac{\text{TYPE 1 FIRE} - 48.4471}{36.666} \right] + .14325 \left[\frac{\text{TYPE 2 FIRE} - 24.7184}{18.4249} \right]$$

$$- 0.21786 \left[\frac{\text{READING} - 41.9241}{19.0670} \right]$$

4. A tract was labeled black if more than 50 percent of its population was Negro, by census designation. Of the 136 tracts so labeled, over 100 were more than 75 percent Negro. This, of course reflects the scarcity of integrated neighborhoods. A tract was labeled Chicano if more than 50 percent of its population was designated "Spanish heritage," persons of Spanish language or surname. There were 68 such tracts. About half of these were more than 75 percent Spanish, which indicates that this group is somewhat less segregated than the blacks.

5. In the discussion, the pathology index is discussed as though it were a crime rate, or at least these results are compared with those of urban crime studies. The pathology index is used in this way because the heaviest loading within its formula is for the number of assaults occurring in the census tract in the year.

6. At an earlier time in the history of urban reform some thought that poor environment caused poverty and it was argued that removing slums would cure poverty. This sort of environmental determinism has long since been rejected in the social sciences.

REFERENCES

American Public Health Association (1950), *Planning the Home for Occupancy*. Chicago: American Public Health Association.

———— (1969), *APHA-PHS Recommended Housing Maintenance and Occupancy Ordinance*. Washington: U.S. Department of Health, Education, and Welfare, Public Health Service, Consumer Protection and Environmental Health Service, Environmental Control Administration, Bureau of Community Environmental Management.

Boggs, Sarah L. (1965), "Urban Crime Patterns," *American Sociological Review* 30(December):899–901.

Booth, A. (1976), *Urban Crowding and Its Consequences*. New York: Praeger.

Calhoun, J. B. (1962a), "A Behavioral Sink," in *Roots of Behavior*, E. L. Bliss, ed., New York: Harper, pp. 295–315.

———— (1962b), "Population Density and Social Pathology," *Scientific American* 206:139–48.

Choldin, Harvey M. (1978), "Urban Density and Pathology," *Annual Review of Sociology* 4:91–113.

Choldin, Harvey M.; Ellen Jacobsen; and Gayle Yahnke (1975), "Effects of Crowded Dwellings on Family Life," *Sociological Symposium* 14(Fall):69–76.

_____, and Dennis Roncek (1976), "Density, Population Potential and Pathology: A Block-Level Analysis," *Review of Public Data Use* 4:19–30.

City of Los Angeles (1973), *State of the City Data Base*. Los Angeles: Community Analysis Bureau.

_____ (1974), *The State of the City: A Cluster Analysis of Los Angeles*. Los Angeles: Community Analysis Bureau.

Clinard, M. B. (1966), *Slums and Community Development: Experiments in Self-Help*. New York: Free Press.

Duncan, Beverly; George Sabagh; and Maurice Van Arsdol, Jr. (1962), "Patterns of City Growth," *American Journal of Sociology* 67: 418–29.

Edmonston, Barry (1975), *Population Distribution in American Cities*. Lexington, Mass.: Lexington Books.

Freedman, J. L. (1975), *Crowding and Behavior*. San Francisco: W. H. Freeman.

Galle, O. R., and W. R. Gove (1975). *Crowding and Behavior in Chicago, 1940–1970*. Madison, Wis.: Center for Demographic Ecology, University of Wisconsin.

Galle, Omer; Walter R. Gove; and J. Miller McPherson (1972), "Population Density and Pathology: What Are the Relations for Man?" *Science* 176(April 7):23–30.

Gillis, A. R. (1974), "Population Density and Social Pathology: The Case of Building Type, Social Allowance and Juvenile Delinquency." *Social Forces* 53(December):306–315.

Guest, Avery M. (1973), "Urban Growth and Population Densities." *Demography* 10(February):53–69.

Jacobs, J. (1961), *The Death and Life of Great American Cities*. New York: Random House.

Mitchell, R. E. (1971), "Some Social Implications of High Density Living," *American Sociological Review* 36:18–29.

Michelson, William H. (1970), *Man and His Urban Environment*. Reading, Mass.: Addison-Wesley.

Newman, O. (1972), *Defensible Space*. New York: Macmillan.

Plant, James S. (1930), "Some Psychiatric Aspects of Crowded Living Conditions," *American Journal of Psychiatry* 9:849–60.

Rees, Philip H. (1970), "The Factorial Ecology of Chicago." in *Geographic Perspectives on Urban Systems*, Brian J. L. Berry and Frank E. Horton, eds., Englewood Cliffs, N.J.: Prentice-Hall, pp. 276–290, 306–397.

Robinson, W. S. (1950), "Ecological Correlations and the Behavior of Individuals," *American Sociological Review* 15(June):351–357.

Roncek, Dennis W. (1975), "Density and Crime: A Methodological Critique," *American Behavioral Scientist* 18(July–August):843–860.

_____, and H. M. Choldin (1977), "Urban Crime Rates: Effects of Social and Spatial Variables at the City Block Level." Chicago: Department of Sociology, University of Illinois. (mimeographed)

Schmitt, Robert C. (1966), "Density, Health and Social Disorganization," *Journal of the American Institute of Planners* 32(1):38–40.

Shaw, Clifford R., and Henry D. McKay (1942), *Juvenile Delinquency and Urban Areas*. Chicago: University of Chicago Press.

Webb, S. D. (1975), "The Meaning, Measurement and Interchangeability of Density and Crowding Indices," *Australian and New Zealand Journal of Sociology* 11:60–62.

Winsborough, H. H. (1961), "A Comparative Study of Urban Population Densities," Ph.D. thesis. Chicago: University of Chicago.

ISSUES IN COMBINING SOCIAL ACTION WITH PLANNING: THE CASE OF ADVOCACY PLANNING

Rosalie G. Genovese, BROCKPORT-CORNELL

MANAGEMENT STUDIES PROGRAM AND

ST. JOHN FISHER COLLEGE, ROCHESTER

In the final paper of this volume we return to the issue of professionalized social reform and possible alternatives to it. Recently some urban planners, dissatisfied with the ''establishment'' orientation which dominates their efforts, have attempted to become advocates for the less-powerful in planning controversies. In her paper Rosalie Genovese explores the possibilities and limitations of such an approach. Her detailed analysis of three attempts at advocacy planning is particularly useful in highlighting the organizational and political obstacles which constrain professionals when they attempt to ally themselves with the underdog in policy disputes.

During the 1960s, practitioners in various professions, their clients, and sociologists re-examined the role of professionals in society and challenged

Research in Social Problems and Public Policy—Vol. 1, 1979, pages 195–224
Copyright © 1979 by JAI Press, Inc.
All rights of reproduction in any form reserved.
ISBN 0-89232-068-0

traditional definitions of professionalism. Their focus was on the special status of professionals in society and on two core characteristics, expertise based on an abstract body of knowledge and service to others, which are considered essential to achieving that desired status.[1] Practitioners in various occupations and professions who were critical of elitism and the special status of professionals sought ways to introduce (or reintroduce) activism and social change concerns into their work.[2] They especially wanted to develop roles for themselves in social change efforts.

At the same time, what has been termed the "revolt of the client" occurred as clients challenged professional autonomy on various grounds: inadequate professional expertise, unfounded claims of altruism, and delivery systems which either did not work or were too efficient, going beyond the limits of their power (Haug and Sussman, 1969:156). In effect, laymen were objecting to the control over their lives exercised by professionals. In the field of urban planning, for example, residents opposed many government decisions on the grounds that they were better able than the experts to understand community needs and a plan's impact on their neighborhoods. Therefore, community residents demanded a voice in decisions on whether to build a highway that would destroy a community or housing that would require demolition of existing housing and relocation of many families.

Advocacy planning, proposed as a new form of practice in urban planning, reflected some planners' dissatisfaction with their occupation's dominant physical planning orientation and the adverse impact that past planning decisions, especially in the area of urban renewal, had on some people's lives. They also believed that planning decisions had too often reflected middle-class and business interests and they sought to redress past inequities by giving the poor and underrepresented access to technical knowledge and skills. In this way, they hoped to give the disadvantaged greater influence in the planning process.

Therefore, a study of advocacy planning as a new orientation within urban planning contributes to our knowledge of how social and political activism may become institutionalized within occupations and professions. Moreover, we can learn more about the obstacles to achieving this objective and the conditions which seemed associated with success. For example, when advocacy planning was put into practice, it became apparent that it could develop in different directions, leading to different fates. It could become an accepted career alternative within urban planning or a social experiment which flourishes briefly and then dies out, much like a social movement which fails. In the latter instance, it would represent an attempt at reform or radical change which frequently arises during a period of ferment or upheaval in society and leaves its imprint on an occupation or profession, but falls short of major change. City planning itself began during one such period in American history and traces its roots partly to the reform movement which developed before the turn of the century (Scott, 1969:40).

A case study of three advocacy planning groups in a large metropolitan area explored these questions and issues.[3] For the purposes of the study, advocate planning groups were defined as groups of planners and architects (a) who offered technical assistance to community groups, (b) whose members were guided by their personal, social and political values, and (c) who encouraged client groups to participate in the planning process and gave them a determining voice in decision making.

The research consisted primarily of unstructured interviews and an analysis of published and unpublished documents. In addition to members of the three advocate planning groups, planners who worked in universities, government, and community agencies were also interviewed. Several well-known advocate planners in another city were interviewed for comparative purposes. The metropolitan area chosen was particularly good for this study because it is the location of several planning and architecture schools whose faculty and students were interested in working with communities and receptive to innovation and experimentation.

These three groups represent two of the most frequent organizational arrangements for advocacy planning, namely, governmental and university auspices. The group which is being called "Ideological Advocates" (IA) is one of the oldest and best-known advocate planning groups and has received federal funding since 1969. It was formally established in 1966, although several of its founders had already been working informally on community projects for several years. The other two university-affiliated groups were begun with seed money from foundations. They both had only one or two paid staff members and depended primarily on student volunteers. "Community Services" (CS) began as a graduate course in the planning department of a large university in the spring of 1968. Its first director, who had also helped found IA, developed a program for students who wanted their training to include community work. When its original grant money ran out, the university provided more limited financial support for the group. Student enrollments in the program ranged from about 20 to 60. "Technical Assistance to Communities" (TAC), the third group, began in the school of architecture and planning of another university in 1968. About 15 or 20 students enrolled each term, most of them in architecture with a few in planning.

One way for advocacy planning to become a major force within urban planning was by gaining recognition as a new segment. Bucher defines segments as "groupings of professionals who share both an organized identity and a common professional fate" (Bucher, 1962:51). As they develop within the parent occupation, nascent segments resemble social movements. While some segments "make it" and become established career choices, others die out or remain relatively small and marginal to the mainstream of the occupation. However, a nascent segment may continue, owing to the persistence of a small, committed group, and become recognized at a later time under more favorable conditions. Bucher's analysis of clinical pathology as a successful segment indicates that a new segment goes through the following steps in becoming established: (1) it develops a claim to an area of work, (2) it proclaims its mission, (3) it defines work roles and relationships, and (4) it creates associations to promote its interests (ibid.:51).

The questions which this research sought to answer were (1) why did advocacy planning seem unlikely to succeed as a new segment, (2) why did it develop in several directions with different implications for urban planning's future, and (3) what does this experience tell us about social action in occupations and professions in general? Two readily apparent differences between advocacy planning and clinical pathology may provide clues to their fates. Advocacy planning did not arise in response to new knowledge or technological discoveries, but got its impetus from the interests and values of practitioners. Its social action character might provide a less solid basis than new knowledge or skills for establishing the segment's legitimacy. Its success rested largely on external conditions outside practitioners' control and its fate was linked to events in the larger society. A second difference stems from the fact that city planning, the parent occupation, was not a full profession like medicine, but a semi-profession struggling to attain this higher status.

Advocacy planning's emergence in urban planning was part of the larger movement to change inequalities in American society which arose during the 1960s. In urban planning itself, its way had been paved by the critical look some practitioners were taking at the occupation's ideology and influence and the resulting emphasis on social planning to compensate for the narrowness of physical planning.[4] At an American Institute of Planners' Conference in 1964, Paul Davidoff criticized the values which frequently underlie planning decisions, especially the support of the status quo and middle-class interests (Davidoff, 1964: 125–131). Instead, he proposed that planners consciously adopt as their mission assisting the disadvantaged. However, Davidoff's proposal did not require planners to depart radically from traditional practice. Their basic functions would still be technical, but they might also help clients to strengthen their organizations and improve their effectiveness.

> The planner acting as advocate brings to his client social knowledge about urban planning and the rules governing the development and implementation of plans. He helps them by performing services they may not be prepared to carry out. For example, the techniques of non-violent protest have become familiar and successful. But protesting is not planning. Solutions to current problems are required.... Moreover, the advocate planner has the responsibility of protecting his clients from undue procedure and from plans that are not well supported in reason or fact (Davidoff, 1964:129).

The advocate planner would seek clients among groups without access to planning assistance, providing them with needed technical knowledge and skills. Planners would gain from this assistance since they could work with groups whose values were compatible with their own. In contrast, traditional planners in governmental agencies usually had little or no communication with the people affected by their plans, and planning consultants' "clients" were often the builders and developers of facilities, rather than the eventual users.

According to Davidoff, the mission of advocate planners was to work vigorously for equal opportunity so that all could participate fully in their society. The implication is that proposals which lead to a more equal sharing of resources were to be supported and those which would benefit the affluent at the expense of the impoverished were to be strongly opposed.

In a second article, Davidoff expanded on his concept of advocacy planning (Davidoff, 1965:331–337). He proposed that planners become advocates for what they deemed proper, offering their expertise to groups with little or no say in the planning process. By representing the interests of the underrepresented, planners could help change existing inequalities. Thus, Davidoff urged planners to drop professional claims of value-neutrality which were often untrue in practice. His position was that planners have a responsibility to make their values known and reflected in their work.

How planners should go about creating this form of practice was not spelled out in great detail, although Davidoff suggested several possible institutional arrangements. In what has been called the "pure" form of advocacy planning, a planner would be hired by, and responsible to, a community group. However, since most groups have limited resources, planners might also consider working under the auspices of independent organizations, i.e., those which represent neither government nor communities. The following special interest groups were named: "Chambers of commerce, real estate boards, labor organizations, pro- and anti-civil rights groups, and anti-poverty councils" (Davidoff, 1965:334). Ad hoc groups formed to oppose a specific policy and political parties were other possible employers. Such suggestions reflected Davidoff's belief in pluralism. He thought that any of these groups might engage in the planning process by preparing plans to counter those of government agencies.

Soon after Davidoff's proposal appeared, the planning journals began to carry reactions, critiques, and counterproposals.[5] Some writers emphasized the need to politicize planners and planning. As advocacy planning was put into practice, planners soon came face to face with the issue of acquiring power for themselves and their clients, recognizing that "planning decisions are decisions about who gets what in the city. . . . Planning decisions, in other words, are political decisions" (Piven, 1970:34).

A basic difficulty underlying Davidoff's proposal helps explain the different conceptions of advocacy planning which developed. Davidoff makes the assumption that technical expertise can help disadvantaged groups influence planning decisions in their favor. But if planning is political, then community groups need more than expertise, they need political power if they are to affect planning. Otherwise, alternative plans are likely to have little or no effect on decision making: "A plan, of itself, is not a force; it is not capable of releasing the necessary federal subsidies or of overcoming the inertia of the city agencies'' (Piven, 1970:35).

Moreover, a debate arose about the political ideology underlying Davidoff's proposal. Planners' attitudes toward the extent of change needed in this country and their general political world views led them to define advocacy planning's mission and functions in different ways. Some planners rejected the reform liberal ideology on which advocacy planning rested, especially the assumption that "the system" was basically sound but malfunctioning.[6] As regards the proposal's stress on planning, responsiveness to people, and changing the unequal distribution of political power; Kravitz complained that advocate planners erred in their willingness to accept regular, politically defined mechanisms and processes (Kravitz, 1970:263). Also, Rein has pointed out that incremental politics give the poor only short-term gains, rather than the power and influence that permit them to bargain and significantly affect decisions (Rein, 1971:306). Therefore, planners who were committed to more radical change did not see advocacy planning as the answer.

Critics also charged that advocacy planning efforts could be counterproductive if their consequence was to reduce pressure for more basic change (Kravitz, 1968:38–46). In a similar vein, Funnyé charged that planners might help to "defang" the poor. He saw government programs as "inherently diversionary" because they sought to substitute make-work projects for more meaningful forms of confrontation (Funnyé, 1970:35). Thus, a major criticism of advocacy planning was that it might prolong the present system by neutralizing dissent and protest.

Davidoff's use of the adversary system, borrowed from law, as a model was another target of criticism. Its assumption is that "each side has an advocate, each advocate is competent and fully devoted to the interests of his client, and from this structure justice will emerge" (Wexler, 1970:1059). But many would argue that the adversary system, which is at the heart of common law, has not worked adequately for the poor. Additional difficulties arise when the concept is transferred to planning. First, planning traditionally has placed high value on consensus and the reconciliation of divergent interests, but advocate planners do not necessarily agree that there is one best plan to which all parties will eventually agree. Second, planning possesses no established mechanism for resolving conflicts, like the judge or jury in law. Who makes decisions on competing plans? The answer is usually the government agency, one of the parties in the contest. Moreover, the two sides in a planning contest are not always clearly defined. If community residents oppose a proposed urban renewal plan, who are their adversaries—the developers of the project, the local government which approves it, or the federal government which established the program in the first place? Therefore, the adversary system as a model could pose considerable difficulties for advocacy planning in practice.

Although critics of the Davidoff proposal were explicit about its weaknesses and limitations, they did not seem to have a viable alternative to substitute. They tended to see themselves as part of a larger movement for change and adopted New Left values of community, participation, and decentralization, as well as major concerns for equality and justice. However, they did not specify how planners could translate these values into their work.

ADVOCACY PLANNING'S FAILURE TO BECOME A RECOGNIZED SEGMENT WITH URBAN PLANNING

The three groups in this study all began with the objective of providing technical assistance to community groups. Before IA was established the planners and architects who had already begun to assist communities in their spare time thought of their work as counterplanning. When this group was able to have a full-time director, thanks to support from another organization, its activities in transportation, housing and urban renewal continued to be guided by the mission of providing technical assistance. However, IA's mission changed as it went through several stages in its history.

Community organizing soon replaced technical assistance as the group entered its second stage. There were numerous reasons for this shift. Communities which were not organized could not profit from technical assistance. During this period, IA's grant from a federal agency included the condition that it provide assistance to working-class white communities in the metropolitan area, as well as to black and Puerto Rican inner-city neighborhoods. These new client groups were less well organized than their inner-city counterparts and needed help in this area. Staff members had learned that communities had to display their political muscle if they were to have impact.

The politicization of the group continued and accelerated with the hiring of a new director who was not interested in planning. During this third phase, IA's mission was defined as political education and radical politics. Its goal was to help build a grass-roots movement for social change. Since staff members held a range of political philosophies and were trained in various disciplines, they had difficulty agreeing on how to translate these goals into action and how to define their work.

It was not clear what special competence the staff could offer communities in these new areas. Moreover, as IA members increasingly identified themselves as activists, their occupational identity weakened. Under the new director, having the "right" values became a more important criterion for hiring than having technical skills. Both the group's interest in providing technical assistance and its ability to do so diminished. IA began to resemble a social movement group rather than practitioners trying to develop and gain acceptance for a new form of practice.[7]

Ideological Advocates' board of directors, which included some of its founders, was disturbed by the organization's drift away from its original mission, but
seemed reluctant to force the staff to make the changes in work and goals which it
thought necessary. Several directors resigned and some staff members, unhappy
about the group's new directions, also left. Therefore, although advocacy planning as conceived by Davidoff did not signify a radical departure from traditional
planning practice, it was transformed into something quite different in IA's case.

The goals of the other two groups remained the same over time, partly because
university auspices limited the degree to which they could experiment. Since
their resources were limited, they did not develop into full-fledged organizations,
but remained in a fairly embryonic stage. Community Services and TAC had a
twofold mission: to provide technical assistance to communities and to socialize
students in urban planning and architecture to new activities, values and clients.
Some faculty members objected to the social and political change goals of advocate planners, fearing that such innovations were "unprofessional" and could
lead to the deprofessionalization of urban planning.[8] For example, by making
their values known and championing their clients' interests, advocate planners
went against the tradition in the professions of objectivity and value neutrality.
Urban planners, who has taken great pains to create their image as expert advis-
ers to officials and politicians, were now being asked to become partisans.
Furthermore, when advocate planners questioned the effectiveness of their occupation's knowledge and activities and criticized the Establishment positions and
alliances of traditional practitioners, they increased the segment's "radical"
image. Even the goal of more egalitarian relationships with clients was resisted
by other planners who thought this trend would work against their goal of full
professional status for urban planning. Since professionalization attempts usually
involve making an occupation's knowledge base more specific and technical and
thus farther removed from the lay person's understanding, there was a tension
between the mystification and demystification aims of these two groups of practitioners.[9]

The advocate planning groups also were unsuccessful in accomplishing two
other steps in establishing a new segment. They were not able unequivocally to
carve out a distinct area of work as their province or clearly establish their
legitimacy with clients, officials, and the public, although some members did
gain recognition *as individuals*. The two directions taken by advocate planners
meant that they were seeking jurisdiction over different areas of work which
called for different bases of legitimacy.[10] Planners who defined their mission and
work in terms of providing technical assistance sought legitimacy in this area and
measured their effectiveness in these terms. Although building a playground or
rehabilitating a building were modest accomplishments when measured against
more ambitious social change goals of other advocates, yet these concrete gains
provided them and their clients with a measure of satisfaction. On the other hand,

advocate planners who turned to organizing and radical politics were not always able to convince clients that they possessed special qualifications for this work or that their efforts would lead to change. Since building a grass-roots movement is a long-term project, activists and their clients found it difficult to measure their effectiveness or point to signs of progress.

The basis for claiming legitimacy was a special problem for advocate planners. It varied according to the group to be influenced and the planners' mission. Professionals depend heavily on their expertise to convince others to let them intervene. Since advocate planners rejected elitism in favor of egalitarianism, they were understandably reluctant to use this basis for legitimacy, especially with clients.

The approaches taken by IA members at different stages of the organization's evolution are interesting. Its founders said that they consciously emphasized their expertise at the beginning: "Much time, particularly at the beginning, was devoted to the process of legitimation, that is getting people used to us and convincing them that we were not a bunch of freaks, that we were responsible and so were our critiques." Although one prominent official referred to them as "tinker toy boys," their academic credentials and the quality of their work eventually convinced officials (and clients) that they were competent to criticize official proposals and prepare alternatives. As IA's mission was redefined, members spent less time on technical tasks and more on organizing, political strategy, and political education, areas in which planners had no claims to special competence. They had to vie with community organizers, political scientists, social workers and others for jurisdiction over this work.

University-affiliated groups used their free services as a basis for legitimacy with clients. They only entered a community at its invitation:

> We are here to do the community's bidding, to see that it gets what it wants. Since the communities that need advocates are usually those which the present system most neglects and since advocate planners tend to be concerned with social justice, a rough "fit" does prevail (Hartman, 1970:38).

In practice, university groups faced difficulties because clients were sometimes reluctant to give full responsibility to students. Clients also worried that course deadlines and exams would take priority over community needs. At issue, too, was the fact that students' commitment was short-lived, although some students continued their work long after their courses had ended.

An important problem for advocate planners was to work out their relationships with new client groups. Professional socialization often left planners ill-equipped to work with low-income clients. Their training was directed toward working with other professionals, government officials and businessmen who shared middle-class values and "spoke the same language." Since those who acted as experts with all the answers were quickly rejected as paternalistic by community groups, many planners emphasized working *with* clients. They tried to let clients make decisions and carry out their wishes.

In addition to a "servant" role, advocate planners could also adopt the role of teacher and try to transfer knowledge to clients. Sometimes they taught planning skills, at other times they wanted to educate clients politically. As IA changed, its members began to be like missionaries building a grass-roots movement for change. However, strains developed when IA members and clients held conflicting values or disagreed on issues. Client groups that wanted technical assistance free of ideological overtones looked elsewhere for help.

Faced with these differences in mission and work among advocate planners, some clients became confused about what assistance they would receive. Advocates who were not trained planners or architects tended to stress organizing and other activities rather than technical services. However, it is a sign of urban planning's semiprofessional status that those who lacked formal training could still offer planning assistance. One of IA's most successful advocates was not a planner and said that he obtained the technical information he needed from his co-workers. Furthermore, in the case of IA, clients were aware of its internal tensions as members directed much of their energy toward reaching a consensus on the organization's mission and functioning. Helping clients seemed a secondary concern. A community group representative commented that she didn't see how IA members could help them when "they couldn't even get their own heads together." Another referred to IA during that period as "an asylum for radicals."

Legitimacy was not easy to achieve with officials and agency planners either. Physical planners in governmental agencies often regarded advocate planners as traitors whose criticism of colleagues' work was unprofessional. They viewed advocate planners as adversaries and referred to them as "manipulators pulling strings." Attitudes of officials and administrators at various governmental levels ranged from opposition to acceptance, to willingness to give advocates a role in the planning process.[11] Much depended on the officials and planners in a given situation. In its later stages, IA's staff became ambivalent about whether it even wanted to establish good working relationships with agencies, fearing that they would be co-opted and have their principles compromised. Critics of the group suggested that this made it less effective since it lacked access to the information which sympathetic agency sources could provide.

Without successfully firmly establishing their legitimacy and laying claim to a specific work area, advocate planners' potential for institutionalizing the new segment was negligible. Practitioners were unable to establish advocacy planning on an independent basis, as required for "pure" advocacy. Although the university seemed to offer good possibilities, CS and TAC faced opposition to their programs within the planning and architecture departments where they were located. The positions of both groups were precarious in their respective universities and their survival was in doubt almost from the beginning. Community

Services' situation was somewhat special because its director was the center of controversy within the department and he was the object of personal animosity. He was especially criticized for siding with the community against the university on the issue of university expansion. Opposition to him personally and to the program was considerable, especially among older, tenured faculty members. When his contract was not renewed, student protests were followed by several years of investigation by various university and faculty committees.

Although TAC did not have this problem and existed in an environment which was more receptive to innovation, it too suffered a decline when its foundation funds were exhausted. Both universities withdrew their largely token support when budgets became tight and the militant campus atmosphere subsided. Without vocal student and faculty demands for socially oriented programs like advocacy planning, universities seem unlikely to support such nontraditional and often controversial activities. Therefore, the outlook for institutionalizing advocacy planning under university auspices does not seem favorable.

Ideological Advocates represented the other major hope for institutionalizing advocacy planning—under government auspices. Although such sponsorship admittedly might entail constraints, IA's staff did not find the work limited in this way, nor did they consider their primary loyalty to be to the funding agency. Moreover, support continued despite the organization's social movement characteristics and radical political objectives. (It is not clear how aware the funding agency was of the organizational changes that had occurred, since the group was not closely monitored after its first year of funding.) Nevertheless, most governmental programs directed toward solving social problems or accomplishing social change now have been either discontinued or greatly reduced, so advocacy planning's chances for support in the future are not good. Moreover, there are few other potential sources of support. While foundations in the 1960s funded many innovative programs, they did not provide long-term funding.

Not only does a nascent segment need to institutionalize its activities, but it must recruit new members to insure continuity. These recruitment efforts often resemble the proselytizing of a social movement. Newcomers' commitment is more likely to persist if they see the promise of lifelong careers in the new segment. Otherwise, the nascent segment might be forced to rely on a constant supply of recruits whose interest will be transitory.

Recruitment was no problem for advocate planning groups. In the 1960s many students chose careers in planning in the belief that they could work for change. They were also receptive to appeals from anti-establishment social movements. However, enrollment in a university program did not necessarily signify commitment to a career as an advocate planner. Students had diverse reasons for choosing CS or TAC: dissatisfaction with traditional courses, desire for "real life" experiences to counterbalance the "ivory tower" and "elitist" orientations of other courses, and a chance to test their skills. Sometimes the reasons were practical: the work was available, interesting, a way of earning money under work-study assignments. Of course, many enrollees were already committed to community work and advocacy when they joined the groups and they planned careers which would allow them to do "socially meaningful" work.

The work histories of IA members may provide more reliable indications of planners' commitment to advocacy planning careers. As one of the few advocate planning groups which offered paid enrollment, IA received many applications. However, while applicants in the early years were interested in advocacy planning, later applicants tended to be more committed to organizing and radical politics. Ideological Advocates' staff turnover suggests that advocacy planning may not be a long-term commitment. More than half of the twenty-two staff members in October of 1969 had left by the beginning of 1971. Furthermore, one-half of those employed at the beginning of 1971 had left by the end of the year. Six had been there since 1969. Among those who left by the beginning of 1971 were four planners and one architect. In addition, five board members who resigned during this period were architects or planners. Although this turnover is related to the turmoil within the organization, it also reflects members' differing attitudes toward their careers and skills.

An analysis of work experiences of advocate planners in the three groups reveals no one characteristic pattern. The later experience of IA board and staff members was varied. Careers of board members and others committed to using their occupational background and skills proceeded along traditional lines in education and government. Five former board members concentrated on their academic careers and published books and articles based on their advocacy planning experiences. A former board member who worked in several city government positions was later to be appointed to an important state government office, transforming him from a persistent critic of the state's policies and performance to its top policy maker in this area. Two staff members took positions with city agencies which they thought allowed them to advocate the interests of communities. One of them commented that his IA experience unexpectedly had convinced him to try this more structured work situation and to attempt to bring about change "within the system."

Only a few pursued careers which were close to advocacy planning. An architect and IA founder became the president of a real estate development firm that had built numerous low-income housing projects. He was also subsequently appointed to an important position on a state agency board. Another former board member, whose career as an advocate seemed established, headed a community-based architectural firm that had built several housing projects with community groups as developers.

Others followed different paths. A former director, whose work history included a significant career change before joining IA, increasingly considered himself an activist and had become more concerned with policy issues at the societal level than with strictly planning issues. When interviewed, he was with a nonprofit policy research group working on alternative social structures. His successor, an experienced organizer, had also left IA and was teaching at an experimental college. Several other former staff members were not pursuing careers or had "dropped out."

Community Services members tended either to continue with advocacy and community work or to go on for additional graduate training. Among those who went to work for IA were a former assistant director and an administrator. Several also were working for the community-based architectural firm headed by the former IA board member. It is not possible to predict whether these positions reflect relatively permanent career directions or short-term choices.

Technical Assistance to Communities (TAC) members seemed the most committed to technical work. Several got jobs with developers, both profit-making and nonprofit firms. Others who wanted eventually to work in the community development area saw the need for additional training and went on to get graduate degrees, often in business.

Advocacy planning may only be feasible as an individual activity, given its failure to become institutionalized. Yet even on an individual basis, advocacy planning is a difficult career to establish. In the metropolitan area studied, there was actually only a small number of planners and architects dedicated to advocacy planning. They had to explore all possibilities for financing their activities. They frequently found that the only way they could work with communities was under the auspices of established agencies, with the constraints which this arrangement entailed, or as volunteers in their free time.

Moreover, interviews with advocate planners revealed that it was extremely difficult to sustain the advocate role for long periods of time. The time and energy invested were great and the rewards or victories few. Informants reported that some of the area's most effective advocate planners turned to other work when they were "burned out" after several years of intense activity. Practitioners may consider advocacy planning a stage in their careers, perhaps during training or between graduation and the beginning of more permanent careers: "The professional wants a stable job with an agency. There's no alternative. This is a deterrent to doing something. The community can't pay, therefore they get lots of volunteer work. This can be good caliber because people are really interested, but there is no long-term commitment to the community."

Based on the study of these three groups, the conclusion reached was that advocacy planning would not succeed as a segment. No permanent setting for advocacy developed and it was clear by the end of the study that it was not growing in this metropolitan area. Advocate planners, both those associated with the three groups and others, evaluated its potential in the same way. They gave various reasons for its failure. A former CS director stated that the conditions which had given rise to advocacy in the first place no longer existed. Another former advocate with IA thought that communities needed other kinds of assistance as they moved into development. Interestingly, community groups which were named sponsors of housing projects often did not hire advocate planning groups but turned to established firms. It is not clear why. It might have been a matter of prestige or the security of their past work.

Another former IA member thought that the group was important not for its concrete accomplishments, but for its "sense of strategy." In *After the Planners,* Goodman, himself a disillusioned advocate planner, recounted the story of another who wanted to make a film of advocacy planning projects across the country, but was dismayed to find that there did not seem to be any (Goodman, 1972:63). For his part, Goodman concluded that advocacy planning lacked the ability to change the basic distribution of resources in our society.

Despite this pessimistic assessment of advocacy planning, it should be recognized that the groups studied had numerous successful projects, notably in transportation and housing. (Perhaps the film-maker did not wait long enough for some of the housing to be built.) They also helped communities oppose undesirable projects or obtain facilities or services. In addition, they helped somewhat to strengthen community groups and transfer knowledge to community leaders and residents. To some extent, advocate planners realized their often-stated goal of doing themselves out of a job as communities developed needed resources within their own boundaries. Some communities in the process became less receptive to outside assistance, a reaction not unique to the area studied. In one city, an advocate planning and architecture group relocated when a community publicly rejected them.

FUTURE DIRECTIONS FOR ADVOCACY PLANNING

Advocacy planning's failure to lead to major changes in urban planning is perhaps not surprising, since as Krause has noted most reformist groups end by preserving rather than changing the essential functional role of the occupations they wish to reform (Krause, 1971:216). Yet segments, like social movements, often continue in modified form, rather than dying out completely. Furthermore, experiments like advocacy planning may have considerable impact on an occupation or profession, even when they do not become major directions. As Gusfield noted, collective action often produces less change than intended, but it may still influence public opinion or lead to governmental reforms (Gusfield, 1970:500–01). Advocacy planning's emphasis on the political nature of planning, its concern about needed social change, and its client orientation have all influenced urban planning practice and the socialization of planning students. For example, because the adverse social consequences of governmental policies like urban renewal have been widely recognized, social factors in planning are not ignored today as they were in the 1950s and early 1960s.

Furthermore, it is likely that advocacy planning will continue in more modest forms and with more circumscribed objectives, just as social movements often settle for more limited goals as the price for survival. The experiences of the three advocate groups studied indicate how advocacy planning may continue. If we look at their experience and the literature on advocacy planning, there are two crucial dimensions to their work. First, advocate planning groups had to decide whether their major frame of reference was their occupation and use of its skills or political action. As we have seen, tensions arose for advocate planners when they tried to use their technical knowledge and skills to further their social action and social change goals.

The groups studied resolved the issue by placing primary emphasis either on technical assistance or on social and political action. In his survey of advocate planners, Ross came to a similar conclusion. He found that they could be dichotomized into two main polar types—professionals and radicals (Ross, 1976:477). This conclusion was based on their memberships in various types of organizations and their career interests and objectives.

A second major decision for advocate planners in setting organizational goals was whether to work for change primarily in the local area, either at the group or community level, or to concentrate on change at the institutional or national level. The choice of a target for change efforts reflected individual and group beliefs about where their work would be most effective. These two dimensions can be combined into a property space to provide four possible future directions for advocacy. More generally, they suggest alternative ways of integrating social and professional activism into professional work. For example, social workers who wanted to work for change had experiences similar to those of planners and they resolved their dilemma in similar ways, choosing to serve clients or to concentrate on social action and social change goals.[12]

University-affiliated advocacy planning and community-oriented groups belong in Cell 1. Although the two groups that were studied did not become institutionalized, a few groups had more success. The Pratt Institute Center for Community and Environmental Development, associated with the Pratt Institute

		Scope and Focus of Change	
		Short-Term Local Groups or Communities	Long-Term Societal Institutions
Major Frame of Reference and Definition of Work	Planning	Traditional　　　　　1 Advocacy Community-based Planning Community development corporations	Ideological　　　　2 Advocacy Social Policy Planning "Inside" Advocacy
	Political Action	Community　　　　　3 organization Community control	Social movement　4 Radical politics Policy analysis

in Brooklyn, has been in existence since 1963 (ASPO, 1977:20). However, like TAC and CS, this group also found that affiliation with a planning department created difficulties and for a time it functioned independently of the school. More recently it has operated on closer terms with it. Its director, Ron Shiffman, attributed the change to the fact that the interests of those now directing the department and those of the advocacy group are not so far apart.

The Pratt Center differs significantly from TAC or CS with regard to finances. With an annual budget of $250,000, it does not have the uncertain existence of the other two groups. It can afford a professional staff of fourteen architects and planners, as well as having the services of four volunteer architects and about twenty students. Shiffman is convinced that technical assistance is not effective when provided on a volunteer basis by those active for only short periods of time. He believes that a core staff is essential, supplemented by others with shorter-term commitments. Comments made by CS directors expressed similar concerns. They found community clients often ambivalent about having students work on a project for a term.

Technical assistance is the mission of the Pratt Center. It does not do community organizing, although its members often work with organizers. Another goal is to demystify the planning profession. Thus, members' professional identification is strong, although they also want to see changes in the occupation and in its relationships with government and clients. Some completed projects include: construction of 42 housing units for families displaced by factory expansion; a 12-block miniplan for a Puerto Rican group in the Bronx; and the establishment of the Pratt Architects Collaborative to provide varying types of technical assistance. Housing units for the elderly and the rehabilitation of several Manhattan buildings are additional planned projects. Although its work is technical, the Center's efforts to form a coalition group composed of 64 neighborhood groups to lobby on a citywide basis for action to benefit neighborhoods reveals its awareness of political realities (ASPO, 1977:20).

Planning and architectural firms whose work is primarily with community clients also belong here. Their work is similar to that of the traditional firm, but they have a strong orientation to community clients and participatory processes. Helping the disadvantaged and working for equality are important to these groups. Planners who work for community development corporations (CDCs) fit here too. If CDCs had the resources to hire planners, they could provide a congenial setting for advocate planners. Advocate planners would be responsible to the organization which hired them, an advantage not found in some other arrangements. Their work could be both technical and change-oriented, another positive factor. Furthermore, planners' personal goals and values could be compatible and even synonymous with those of the organization.

Groups that want to use their planning knowledge and skills to work for change at the institutional level fall into Cell 2. Such groups may define their mission as ideological advocacy. This term was coined to refer to planning groups which did not have a specific community group as a client, but were working to further the interests of certain population groups like the disadvantaged or low-income people. Suburban Action, headed by Paul Davidoff is a good example (Davidoff et al., 1970:12–16). It is using legal means to open up housing in the suburbs to low-income people. Also in this category are organizations engaged in social policy research and planning whose mission is to accomplish institutional change. Health-PAC, a New York City health advocacy group, performs such a function in the health-care field. Urban policy is an evident area of interest for planners, but they still must vie with other practitioners trying to establish a claim to this area.

Since social policy is such a growing field of interest, planners need to develop their own specialized knowledge and skills to convince the public and officials to grant them jurisdiction in this interdisciplinary field. In some planning schools, social policy already is a major area of specialization. As a nascent segment, social policy faces problems similar to those of advocacy planning. A study of graduates of public policy schools and of planning schools with a specialization in social policy suggests that the differing definitions of work and roles which occurred in advocacy planning are repeated in social policy. For example, planners who participated in the study disagreed on whether the planner's role in relation to clients was that of technical expert or educator/counselor. Those who adopt the counselor role charge that the technicians are elitist. Technicians admit the charge and claim that the counselors failed in their past planning efforts in programs of the Office of Economic Opportunity and Model Cities. Counselors retort that all planning fails (Bergman, et al., 1976:77). Some of the confusion about their role stems from the differences between the profession's self definitions of its role and society's view of the profession (ibid., 1976:77). There is also a gap between planners' own traditional and mainly technical definitions of what planning is and what they think it ought to be: "The something more that planning should be usually focused on the planner as facilitator of social change and thus inevitably involved with values" (ibid., 1976:70). The place of personal values in work remains a major unresolved issue in urban planning, with differing viewpoints expressed.

Another direction for advocacy in this cell is "inside advocacy," a form which developed largely because planners had such difficulties financing independent groups. It is based on the belief that planners can advocate the interests of communities while employed by government agencies. Social action programs like Model Cities provided planners with jobs in organizations whose goals were compatible with their own. Although employed by government, their mission was to help meet the needs of their clients. However, inside advocacy increasingly occurs within more traditional planning agencies, as community-based programs like Model Cities have ended or have been incorporated into established government agencies. This alternative future for advocacy planning will be examined in more detail below, since it is a likely way for the concept to survive but raises many difficult issues.

Groups in the lower half of the property space are less relevant to urban planning's future, given their emphasis on social and political action. Their members identify themselves primarily as activists or radicals rather than planners. The mission of such groups is to work for social change, either at the neighborhood or societal institutional level. In the third cell are groups oriented to organizing communities to gain control over developments in their neighborhoods. Planners in such organizations would probably not find their background skills essential to their work.

Cell 4 includes groups which identify with a social movement and are working for large-scale economic, social and political change. Early in advocacy planning's history, Peattie suggested that it might move in this direction if it allied itself with civil rights groups (Peattie, 1968:88). Advocate planners in this type of group would deal with issues of the general economic and social order, making proposals for radical change. Again, planning skills are not basic to this work. Rather than representing specific clients or constituencies, members tend to represent their own values and goals. A group in the metropolitan area studied which analyzes new economic policies, educational policy and housing belongs here. Some of its members have worked on plans for a new town which would embody egalitarian values. Its interdisciplinary staff includes specialists in taxation, economics, education, and housing.

The future for most types of groups is not auspicious. Most planners who want to use their knowledge and skills to help the disadvantaged will probably try to live with inside advocacy, since other planning jobs are scarce. A few will try to combine traditional jobs in agencies or consulting firms with voluntary spare-time work. Still fewer will commit themselves to careers devoted to advocacy and community work, with all the risks and uncertainties that this choice entails. How many will be able to maintain their commitment for long periods of time is not clear.

Inside advocacy has both supporters and critics. Becoming an inside advocate requires that a planner believe that he or she can achieve change by working "within the system." Many individuals find this hard to accept. On the other hand, supporters point to changes that have occurred in many planning departments. In Boston and New York, for example, neighborhood offices have been opened and staffed by planners whose job it is to respond to community needs and provide residents with services. Informants pointed to changes which have occurred in the metropolitan area studied which they believed made inside advocacy more feasible. For example, one city department which once had been the least receptive to social planning and advocacy was staffed by planners who worked with advocate planners and had become responsive to working with communities. According to another informant, agencies with long-established physical planning orientations wanted to introduce new programs and approaches, but did not know how to make the transition: "The staff of a lot of agencies feel the need to go back to school."

Even some planners who were critical of advocacy planning's accomplishments still saw the need for inside advocacy. One respondent considered advocacy within established institutions necessary because he was convinced that pressure from outside the system was not enough to bring about change. A former advocate planner agreed that a community needed people within the system to represent their interests. When he had tried to advocate the interests of the elderly in a neighborhood, he found that outside technical and organizing assistance was ineffective because it lacked the added push from within the agencies.

Some planners who see the need for advocacy view it as a temporary measure, necessary only as long as government does not represent the interests of all citizens. Optimists hope that advocacy planning will disappear in the future because large-scale economic and social change will make it unnecessary. In the past, support for socialist parties decreased when some of their demands were met by the New Deal programs introduced by the existing power structure (Rush and Denisoff, 1971:402).

Other planners are much more pessimistic about the feasibility of inside advocacy. There is some evidence to suggest that activists' fears of co-optation might be justified. Advocacy planning might suffer the same fate as citizen participation. Krause has traced how the ideology of citizen participation was adopted by agencies and programs as a means of justifying actions and policies (Krause, 1968:138–41). Communities were sometimes pressured to work with governmental agencies, even though their participation could have unanticipated and negative consequences for them. Thus, citizen participation sometimes placed communities in a double bind: they lost if they participated and also if they refused to participate (ibid., 1968:139). If groups refused to participate, leaving planning to the planners, bureaucrats were free to look after the interests of groups they favored. Then "who plans the planners?" (ibid., 1968:142). On the other hand, by participating communities agree to work within the limits set by the agencies. They accept someone else's definition of the rules of the game. It may be more in their interest to refuse to play the game, if they can present their case effectively to the public, gain support, and use this for leverage to get the government decisions they want.

Advocate planners face similar difficulties when they accept agency definitions of advocacy planning. Warren has asked whether the professional can work successfully for change while a "friend of the court" (Warren, 1971a:50–51). In considering advocacy in social work, he suggested that practitioners needed to go further and act as adversaries within the system. They would then oppose policies, in addition to guiding and counseling disadvantaged groups and representing their interests. But employees do not find it easy to adopt an adversary position within an established agency. The agencies usually interpret such a position as betrayal or hostility, as advocate planners who tried this stance soon learned. When planners in New York City's Planning Commission publicly disagreed with official policy at a public hearing, the consternation within the agency was considerable and fears of repercussions arose. Young social workers' demands that social welfare institutions support their clients and legitimate militant acts on their behalf constituted an insurrection within the occupation in the 1960s. According to Warren, agencies had to respond to these demands and to their clients' militancy if they were to survive. Individual social workers had to decide whether to help clients cope with their problems and to press for more effective service delivery systems or to concentrate on changing the institutions which perpetuate inequality (Warren, 1971a:51).

Krause's work on citizen participation certainly poses the issue of whether agency adoptions of advocacy planning may signify "form without content." Agencies may hire advocates and adopt procedures without giving planners or communities real influence. The rhetoric and processes of advocacy and participation may be introduced with much fanfare, but without substantive changes in who makes the decisions or what decisions are made. It is always possible for agencies to hold hearings and meetings with communities, give everyone their say, but not modify plans as a result. Moreover, the contest between community and advocates on one side and government on the other is an unequal one. As the experiences of many advocate planners and community organizers demonstrate, community groups can seldom maintain a high degree of mobilization over long periods if the battle is a long drawn-out one. In the view of one advocate planner, government always has time on its side. It can wait until the community tires itself out, then go ahead with its controversial plan when the opposition has died down.

One attempt to introduce inside advocacy in the metropolitan area studied was not a success. The local antipoverty agency, whose approval was necessary for IA's federal funding application, used its power to extract a sub-contract from IA as its price for approval. The agreement was for the agency to provide communities with social planning assistance while IA would concentrate on physical planning assistance. The project ended with the resignation of three of the advocate planners hired by this agency. They submitted a memorandum which stated in part that agency constraints made it impossible for them to act as advocates for the communities to which they had been assigned. With a flair for the dramatic, the resignation was timed for just before the submission of IA's application for its grant renewal. At that time, IA was confident enough of its strong position to submit its proposal without including the agency's subcontract. The failure of inside advocacy in this instance is particularly disturbing since it occurred in an agency whose mission specifically is to serve communities. Advocacy planning's potential for success in more traditional agencies would seem even slimmer.

So activists often found themselves frustrated in their attempts to reform agencies. As one respondent noted, young planners lacked power within the organization and had little voice in policy making. If they stayed and worked their way up the hierarchy, there was always the possibility that they would be co-opted along the way. As often happens when individuals join an organization with a view to changing it, they could become increasingly reluctant to jeopardize their position by speaking out against agency policies which conflicted with their personal values or the interests of the communities they wanted to represent.

Another major issue which inevitably arises with inside advocacy is the right of government employees to dissent. Planners for Equal Opportunity (PEO) has taken frequent stands in support of planners who have been fired for their views and actions. This organizaton was formed in 1964 to provide planners working in disadvantaged communities with a clearinghouse and forum for exchanging ideas and experiences. Its goals include informing the public about governmental programs and planning practices harmful to minorities and the poor. Its 1971 Annual Conference theme was ''The Planner's Right to Speak.'' Three levels of dissent were identified: ''1) channel 'inside information' to PEO which would publicize it through its own means and also pass it on to the press; 2) present the material to the press directly (as did Daniel Ellsberg); 3) declare 'reasoned' dissent in one's own name—the highest level'' (Planners for Equal Opportunity, 1971:5).

Although PEO members agreed that dissent should be encouraged, few reportedly wanted to take such action, given the risks involved. Most knew of colleagues who had been eased out of academic institutions or refused contracts because their views or actions were unacceptable to administrators. As long as no safeguards exist for public employees who engage in ''whistle-blowing,'' many planners will be reluctant to speak out publicly or perhaps even disagree with official policy privately.

In summarizing the possibilities for advocacy planning in the future based on the experience of the groups in this study, perhaps the most striking finding is that the one group which survived for more than a decade was the very one which changed its original mission and weakened its identification with urban planning. Much of its later activism and research were in the areas of industrial health and safety and, later, prison reform. The shift in IA occurred at least in part because staff members did not seem able to integrate planning knowledge and skills with their social activism to form a new synthesis, radical planning. The property space on p. 209 does not even include radical planning. Although radical planning was a much talked-about future direction, there were few examples of it in practice.

Numerous writers proposed that planners go ''beyond advocacy'' to some new form of planning based on radical politics, rather than the ''conservative democratic ideology'' on which traditional planning rests (Kravitz, 1970:266). Decentralization and participation are central values in these new planning orientations. However, apart from a few experiences drawn from other countries, most discussions of radical planning were set in some future time period when major societal change had occurred, making radical planning possible. It was not clear how society would move from here to there or what planners could do to hasten the transition. For example, Kravitz saw advocacy superseded by radical planning in the future. At this later stage, all members of society would have an equal opportunity to participate, because all possessed equal authority (ibid., 1968:44–46). He emphasized deprofessionalization and "anti-planning" as consequences of this change. In his view, "planning would be from the bottom up, rather than from the top down. People would become the planners; planning would be by the people with the professional serving as the catalyst or 'actualizer' of a communal planning process" (ibid., 1970:267). Yet the planner's actual work was not clearly described. One might even ask whether planners would be necessary.

In a somewhat similar vein, Robert Goodman, an architect disillusioned by his own advocacy planning experiences, proposed "liberation planning" for the future. Planners and architects would help a community improve its situation by evolving new cultural forms rather than by applying current theories at the community level (Goodman, 1972). Goodman also wanted people to be less dependent on experts. How planners and architects could help bring about this liberated society is not specified. His examples of what planners could do now to hasten the emergence of liberation planning were unlikely to lead to basic change. One proposal, guerrilla architecture, is directed toward combating apathy and hopelessness among community residents by having them take direct action to change their situation. The community would make the first move, forcing the bureaucracy to respond to it, whereas with advocacy planning, the sequence is usually reversed: the community responds to official plans or proposals. As an example of guerrilla architecture he cited the action of low-income families who squatted in higher-income, renovated apartments and, as a result, obtained lower rents and the promise of housing subsidies from the public housing agency. However, it is not clear why community groups need planners and architects to assist them in these activities, when those with other backgrounds might be even more effective. Another suggestion was that planners and architects design buildings with more communal living space. While he is under no illusions that these proposals are more than a start, he believes that they can help people successfully oppose bureaucracies. In his view, such actions are also preferable to having communities devote time and efforts to preparing alternate plans.

A Radical Environmental Designers Congress (RED) underscored the vague and confused state of radical approaches in planning and architecture. The following statement expressed the conference philosophy:

> Design can never be an end in itself and we reject the stance of those "professionals" who would insist that "good" architecture or planning can be defined in the absence of political criteria. For us, there can never be physical solutions to political problems. Our struggle is to

find a liberating practice, a practice that integrates our environmental concerns and our political beliefs. Only in such a practice can we truly serve the people, and we will serve the people or no one (Radical Environmental Designers Congress, 1972).

Although the conference theme was "practicing our politics," sessions resulted in few concrete proposals of how planners and architects could work for change. A familiar theme was that individuals could not effect change as technicians, but had to become organizers. At a workshop on architecture and ideology, comments made by architects and planners suggested that they might be just as elitist in their own way as traditional planners and architects. One speaker cited the following as an example of "subversive" architecture: Cuban housing which was designed without adequate kitchen facilities or places for families to get together so that people left their homes to congregate in designated community areas. Thus, design played a role in breaking down the strength of the nuclear family. When one participant objected to this procedure as manipulative, the speaker replied that people had been so brainwashed that they could only think along certain lines. Therefore, despite the talk of participation, people still seemed to be given little control over their lives or their communities. Other speakers and participants also suggested that architects "did not know it all" but just had certain skills. There seemed few concrete proposals for how these skills could be used for change.

Both Kravitz and Goodman seemed aware that radical approaches to planning had little chance of acceptance today, hence their focus on the future. Roland Warren's study of why antipoverty programs failed in attempts to develop new approaches to eliminating poverty seems relevant in explaining why (Warren, 1971b:469–491. Drawing on the sociology of knowledge for his analysis, Warren developed and applied two diagnostic paradigms to iner-city problems. Paradigm I was based on the individual deficiency approach to poverty; Paradigm II, on the "dysfunctional social structure" approach. The different conceptual frameworks underlying these paradigms lead to different recommendations for solving social problems (ibid., 1971b:472–473). However, the crucial point is that only Paradigm I, which focuses on the individual, is part of an institutionalized thought structure. The "helping professions," the antipoverty program, and advocacy planning are all largely oriented to this approach.

The belief system which supports Paradigm I holds that American society "*is essentially sound in its institutional composition*" but malfunctioning and causing problems (ibid., 1971b: 475. Authors emphasis). According to this belief system, these problems can be solved through a combination of democratic pluralism, science and, to some extent, organizational reform. Davidoff's proposal for advocacy planning is consistent with this belief system. His emphasis on services and improved delivery systems and programs is directed toward making the social system more effective, rather than toward changing the social structure.

Unlike Paradigm I, the belief system for Paradigm II is vague and its supporters disagree on the basic change needed. Even more important for explaining
advocacy planning's failure to develop is the fact that technical competence
developed within the prevalent paradigm has little relevance to Paradigm II
(ibid., 1971b:481). In the antipoverty program, groups which rejected Paradigm
I had few ways of expressing their disagreement, save for protests, boycotts and
other forms of dissent. These activities were often dismissed as "negative" by
their critics. Professionals were also criticized for not providing alternatives to
existing programs developed under Paradigm I, yet they lacked the technology to
do so. According to Warren, innovation derived from Paradigm II in the Model
Cities programs was opposed by institutions on the grounds that it was non-
professional, irrational, unscientific, wasteful, and potentially disruptive (ibid.,
1971b:480).

Furthermore, the technical competence which advocate planners offered disadvantaged groups was not successful because it operated only within the institutionalized thought structure. In Warren's view: "They do not have an articulated technology and expertness regarding alternate strategies designed to change
the institutionalized thought structure on the basis of Paradigm II. Even when
community groups acquired power to develop programs, they and their planners
reverted back to Paradigm I, since it had the only explicit technologies for
addressing problems" (ibid., 1971b:482) Warren's conclusion is that professionals lack the necessary skills for accomplishing change. In his view, the labor
union organizer and the minority party agitator probably possess techniques
which are more appropriate to developing a power base to challenge the dominant belief system than does the city planner, social service worker, or the
agency administrator (ibid., 1971b:490). Moreover, administrative rationales
like "participatory democracy," "power to the people," and "community"
which operate outside the prevalent paradigm are undeveloped and cannot be
implemented. Paradigm I's continued dominance is thus partly explained by this
lack of administrative and technological alternatives.

Therefore, Warren's analysis helps explain both why advocacy planning did
not develop into an accepted career choice within urban planning and why it took
two directions. Planners who defined their advocacy work in terms of technical
assistance accepted the dominant paradigm, but were unable to accomplish major
changes. Others who saw the limitations of this approach turned to social action
and radical politics. Some planners tried to use their skills for change by organizing communities around planning issues but those who became disillusioned with
their lack of impact then focused on ideology. They identified themselves as
radicals rather than professionals.

Another small group who did not want to give up their professional identification and skills tried to develop radical planning, but faced problems outlined by
Warren. They lacked a well-defined and accepted belief system and also the
necessary new technologies based on it. Since they did not believe that radical

professionalism could be developed on any great scale within the existing paradigm, their attempts to develop new roles and technologies were oriented to the future when an alternate paradigm had been institutionalized.

Given the obstacles in the path of planners who want activism to dominate their work, we might ask whether they might use their resources more effectively in other ways. One possibility would be to analyze planning theory from the perspective of the dominant paradigm in society as a first step toward formulating a replacement. David Harvey, a geographer influenced by Kuhn's work on scientific revolutions, seems to be taking this approach. He thought that his colleagues could make best use of their knowledge and skills by developing a new paradigm for social geography. His own work concentrated on the problem of ghetto formation. In developing a theory to explain their existence, he hoped to play a role in eliminating them (Harvey, 1972:11, 1–25). His work suggests that social geographers who take his advice might become rivals of urban planners in obtaining jurisdiction over the analysis of urban development and policy.

Consequently, since planners were unable to gain acceptance for an activist role as advocate planners, they too might develop a new paradigm.[13] The first step might be to develop a deeper understanding of how current planning theories reflect the dominant paradigm in our society. Furthermore, the creation of a new paradigm might begin as an interdisciplinary effort, with practitioners in various occupations and professions trying to reach a consensus. Then, members of each occupation could work out their own specialized theories and technologies based on a common paradigm. Finally, members of the various disciplines might work out a coordinated strategy for gaining wider public support for the new paradigm, admittedly not an easy task. Nevertheless, proponents would have the advantage of a common mission and mutual support. They might also socialize students to the new paradigm and give them a much greater awareness of how occupations and professions are influenced by the dominant thought structure.

CONCLUSIONS

The advocacy planning experience raises some serious questions about the potential for institutionalizing social action segments in occupations and professions. Efforts to develop an activist role for social workers ran into at least as many problems as did advocacy planning. However, *all* social action segments are not necessarily doomed from the start. Legal services, a social action segment in a full profession, may succeed.

As members of a full profession, lawyers have advantages over advocate planners. They work with a highly developed body of knowledge and possess well-defined skills which they are trained to use in a specific arena. Therefore, they are in a position to work for change "within the system." Legal services lawyers provide assistance to individuals by representing disadvantaged clients who previously lacked access to legal assistance.[14] They may also use class-action suits to obtain legal decisions with more far-reaching implications. Their prospective clients are likely to see the need for such services and to accept lawyers' claims of competence, as do officials and their legal adversaries in court. Therefore, lawyers do not have the same legitimacy problems faced by advocate planners. Some of their biggest opposition came from colleagues, solo practitioners who feared that their practices would be hurt by offers of free legal assistance. Although it is perhaps premature to conclude definitely that legal services has been institutionalized, it has survived for a reasonably long period during which many other social programs have been ended. It also seems to have gained the acceptance and support of a wide range of groups.

Lawyers who want to work for institutional change, rather than to provide assistance to individual clients, may use their skills in various ways. They may work for public interest law firms or they may defend radicals in court. These alternatives allow them to use their skill for change and to introduce new values into their work or honor those values often given only lip service. It is perhaps not surprising that several of the planners and architects interviewed indicated that they would choose law if they had their career decisions to make over. They saw more opportunities to work for change with a legal background.

It is evident that new specialties in occupations and professions like social work or law, as well as social action segments in any discipline, are tied to shifts in societal interests (Zald, 1971:27). Whether the demand for new services comes from clients or government, such nascent segments tend to need the support of powerful sectors in society to succeed. Social action segments particularly need allies because they seek to help clients without the financial resources to pay them directly or the power successfully to demand that government finance the services. However, since their goals are to assist the disadvantaged and to work for a redistribution of resources, they are to some extent challenging the rights and privileges of the powerful who may be reluctant to back them.

Social action segments also question the claims and status of the established segments in their own occupation or profession. Community health physicians, legal services and public interest lawyers, and advocate planners all raise the possibility that their own professions have misused their power and special status in society. Perrucci has even suggested that "the doctors, lawyers and clergymen who have chosen to define society, rather than the individual, as their clients face the possibility of having their professional status withdrawn by the professional associations" (Perrucci, 1973:124).

In contrast, segments in medicine like clinical pathology are often oriented to colleagues who are able to pay for their new services, or to well-to-do or influential groups in society. It is clear that social action segments must be able to mobilize widespread support if they are to succeed. Yet the problems are many: public interest is transitory and government programs come and go as national priorities are reordered. Genuine commitment to the success of new social programs is often lacking. Without constant and strong pressures to continue programs, funds dry up.

Segments which develop as a consequence of new knowledge and techniques have much better potential for survival than do social action segments. The public and affected groups tend to be receptive to such developments. Also, segments in full professions like legal services have advantages over segments in semiprofessions because of their higher status and more well-developed body of knowledge and skills. Social action segments represent a special case of occupational change, both because of their dependence on external factors and their origin in practitioner beliefs and values. Their chances of becoming institutionalized are enhanced if such values and beliefs are diffused throughout the society. Otherwise, the support of powerful groups in society seems essential.

This study also raises questions about whether attempting to develop a new segment is necessarily the most effective choice for practitioners who want to work for change. An alternative would be to work on new theories and analytical approaches and techniques, before trying to gain widespread acceptance for a concept which has not been translated into a well-defined form of practice. It may be that practitioners in some disciplines simply will not find it easy to make activism an integral part of their work. Then they face the decisions that planners in the study had to make: either to seek careers as activists or to separate their activism from their full-time occupations. In the first instance, activism and working for change are "central life interests"; in the latter, they are not.

FOOTNOTES

1. Among the many works which analyze the attributes of a profession, see Carr-Saunders and Wilson (1964) and Goode (1957:194–203). On the other hand, Bucher and Strauss adopt an approach to professions which stresses change and views them as "in process" (1961:325–334).

2. The collection of articles in Gross and Osterman (1972) provides an overview of changes in a variety of occupations and professions.

3. This research was the basis of the author's doctoral dissertation (Genovese, 1976).

4. During the 1960s and early 1970s, the *Journal of the American Institute of Planners* provided evidence of the growing interest in social planning with the publication of a number of articles on social factors authored by social scientists. Then, increasingly, articles on social planning were written by planners themselves, illustrating the growing orientation of the field in this direction. Now articles on social planning and advocacy have again diminished.

5. For a lively picture of early views on advocacy planning, see *Proceedings of the National Conference on Advocacy and Pluralistic Planning* (1969). Indications of the divergent orientations within advocacy planning are found in the *Social Policy* article by Piven (1970:32–37), "Whom Does the Advocate Planner Serve?" and the numerous replies in the next issue, including those by Hartman (1970:37–38) and Funnyé (1970:35–37). Also see the thoughtful article by Peattie (1968:80–88).

6. See Mazziotti (1975:38, 40–47).

7. Zald and Ash (1970:517–537) discuss social movement groups.

8. Fears about deprofessionalization seem stronger in semiprofessions than in full professions,

perhaps because professionals are more secure about their status. Similar concerns were voiced in social work with regard to new directions in that field, as Specht (1972:3–15) indicates.

9. See the discussions of mystification and demystification in Jamous and Peloille (1970:145).

10. The bases of legitimacy for social planning analyzed by Rein (1969:233–244) are extremely relevant to advocacy planning.

11. For an evaluation of advocacy planning's limitations, see Keyes and Teitcher (1970:225–226).

12. Among the articles on advocacy in social work, see Brager (1968:5–15) and Cloward and Elman (1966:27–35). For an analysis of the problems of introducing radical approaches into social work, see Rein (1970:13–28).

13. Some work along these lines has already occurred. See, for example, Fainstein and Fainstein (1971:341–362) and Grabor and Heskin) (1973:106, 108–114).

14. Numerous articles on legal services have appeared in law journals. See, for example, Wexler (1970:1049–1069) and "Neighborhood Law Offices" in the *Harvard Law Review* (1967:805–850). Also see the article by Moonan and Goldstein, "The New Lawyer," in Gross and Osterman (1972:117–131). For a collection of articles on radical lawyers, see Black (1971).

REFERENCES

"Advocacy Planning Is Alive and Well in Brooklyn" (1977) *ASPO Planning* (January:20–22.

Bergman, Edward M., et al. (1976), "The Practitioner Viewpoint: An Exploration of Social Policy Planning Practice and Education," Part 2: The Findings. Chapel Hill, N.C.: Department of City and Regional Planning, University of North Carolina.

Black, Jonathan, Ed. (1971), *Radical Lawyers: Their Role in the Movement and the Courts*. New York: Avon.

Blecher, Earl M. (1971), *Advocacy Planning for Urban Development: With Analysis of Six Demonstration Programs*. New York: Praeger.

Brager, George A. (1968), "Advocacy and Political Behavior," *Social Work* 13(April): 5–15.

Bucher, Rue (1962), "Pathology: A Study of Social Movements within a Profession," *Social Problems* 10(Summer):40–51.

_____, and Anselm Strauss (1961), "Professions in Process," *American Journal of Sociology* 66(January):325–334.

Carr-Saunders, A.M., and P.A. Wilson (1964), *The Professions*. 2nd ed. London: Frank Cass and Co.

Cloward, Richard, and Richard Elman (1966), "Advocacy in the Ghetto," *Transaction* (December):27–35.

Davidoff, Paul (1964), "Role of the City Planner in Social Planning," *Proceedings of the 1964 Annual Conference of the American Institute of Planners*, pp. 125–131.

_____ (1965), "Advocacy and Pluralism in Planning," *Journal of the American Institute of Planners* 31(November):331–337.

_____ (1973), "Working Toward Distributive Justice," *Journal of the American Institute of Planners* 39(March):317–318.

_____; Linda Davidoff; and Neil Gold (1970), "Suburban Action: Advocate Planning for an Open Society," *Journal of the American Institute of Planners* 36(January):12–16.

Elliott, Phillip (1972), *The Sociology of Professions*. New York: Herder and Herder.

Fainstein, Susan S., and Norman I. Fainstein (1971), "City Planning and Political Values," *Urban Affairs Quarterly* (March):341–362.

Funnyé, Clarence (1970), "The Advocate Planner as Urban Hustler," *Social Policy* (July/August):35–37.

Genovese, Rosalie G. (1976), "Advocacy Planning: An Attempt to Develop a Social Action Segment in a Semi-Profession,'' unpublished doctoral dissertation, New York University, Department of Sociology.

Goode, William J. (1957), ''Community within a Community: The Professions,'' *American Sociological Review* 22(April):194–208.

Goodman, Robert (1972), *After the Planners: Toward Democratic City Design.* Harmondsworth: Penguin Books.

Grabow, Stephen, and Allan Heskin (1973), ''Foundations for a Radical Concept of Planning,'' *Journal of the American Institute of Planners* 39(March):106, 108–114.

Gross, Ronald, and Paul Osterman, eds. (1972), *The New Professionals.* New York: Simon and Schuster.

Gusfield, Joseph R., ed. (1970), *Protest, Reform and Revolt: A Reader in Social Movements.* New York: Wiley.

Hartman, Chester (1970), ''The Advocate Planner: From 'Hired Gun' to Political Partisan,'' *Social Policy* (July/August):37–38.

Harvey, David (1972), ''Revolutionary and Counter-Revolutionary Theory in Geography and the Problem of Ghetto Formation,'' in *Perspectives on Geography,* Vol. II, Harold M. Rose, ed. De Kalb, Ill.: Northern Illinois University Press, pp. 1–25.

Hatch, Richard (1968), ''Some Thoughts on Advocacy Planning,'' *Architectural Forum,* 128 (June):72, 73, 103, 109.

Haug, Marie R., and Marvin B. Sussman (1969), ''Professional Autonomy and the Revolt of the Client,'' *Social Problems* 17(Fall):153–161.

Jamous, H., and B. Peloille (1970), ''The French University-Hospital System'' in *Professions and Professionalization,* John A. Jackson, ed. London: Cambridge University Press, pp. 111–152.

Keyes, Langley C., Jr. and Edward Teitcher (1970), ''Limitations of Advocacy Planning: A View from the Establishment,'' *Journal of the American Institute of Planners* 36(July):225–226.

Kirschner Associates (1971), ''A Description and Evaluation of Advocacy Planning Programs,'' report prepared for the Office of Economic Opportunity (January).

Krause, Elliott A. (1971), *The Sociology of Occupations.* Boston: Little, Brown.

—— (1968), ''Functions of a Bureaucratic Ideology: 'Citizen Participation,' '' *Social Problems* 16(Fall):129–143.

Kravitz, Alan S. (1968), ''Advocacy and Beyond,'' *Planning 1968.* Chicago: American Society of Planning Officials, pp. 38–46.

—— (1970), ''Mandarism: Planning as Handmaiden to Conservative Politics,'' in *Planning and Politics: Uneasy Partnership,* Thad L. Beyle and George Lathrop, eds. Indianapolis: Bobbs-Merrill, pp. 240–267.

Mazziotti, Donald (1974), ''The Underlying Assumptions of Advocacy Planning: Pluralism and Reform,'' *Journal of the American Institute of Planners* 40(January):38, 40–47.

''Neighborhood Law Offices: The New Wave in Legal Services for the Poor'' (1967), *Harvard Law Review* 80:805–850.

Peattie, Lisa R. (1968), ''Reflections on Advocacy Planning,'' *Journal of the American Institute of Planners* 34(March):80–88.

—— (1970), ''Community Drama and Advocacy Planning,'' *Journal of the American Institute of Planners* 36(November):405–410.

Perrucci, Robert (1973), ''Engineering: Professional Servant of Power,'' in *The Professions and their Prospects,* Eliot Freidson, ed. Beverly Hills, Calif.: Sage Publications, pp. 119–133.

Piven, Frances Fox (1970), ''Whom Does the Advocate Planner Serve?'' *Social Policy* (May-June):32–37.

—— (1975), ''Planning and Class Interests,'' *Journal of the American Institute of Planners* 40(September):308–310.

Planners for Equal Opportunity (1971), ''Fifth Annual Conference Proceedings,'' *Equalop* 5(Winter):3–9.

"Proceedings of the National Conference on Advocacy and Pluralistic Planning" (1969), Seymour
    Z. Mann, ed., Urban Research Center, Dept. of Urban Affairs, Hunter College (January 10 and
    11).
Rein, Martin (1969), "Social Planning: The Search for Legitimacy," *Journal of the American
    Institute of Planners* 35(July):233–244.
———— (1970), "Social Work in Search of a Radical Profession," *Social Work* 15(April):13–28.
———— (1971), "Social Policy Analysis as the Interpretation of Beliefs," *Journal of the American
    Institute of Planners* 37(September):297–310.
Ross, Robert (1976), "The Impact of Social Movements on a Profession in Process," *Sociology of
    Work and Occupations* 3(November):429–254.
Rush, Gary B., and Serge R. Denisoff, eds. (1971), *Social and Political Movements*. New York:
    Appleton-Century-Crofts.
Scott, Mel (1969), *American City Planning Since 1890: A History Commemorating the Fiftieth
    Anniversary of the American Institute of Planners*. Berkeley and Los Angeles: University of
    California Press.
Specht, Harry (1972), "The Deprofessionalization of Social Work," *Social Work* 17(March):3–15.
Warren, Roland (1971a), "Social Action and Change Strategies," in *Truth, Love and Social
    Change*. Chicago: Rand McNally, pp. 49–53.
———— (1971b), "The Sociology of Knowledge and the Problems of Inner Cities," *Social Science
    Quarterly* 52(December):469–491.
Wexler, Stephen (1970), "Practicing Law for Poor People," *Yale Law Journal* 79:1049–1067.
Zald, Mayer N. (1971), *Occupations and Organizations in American Society: The Organization-
    Dominated Man*. Chicago: Rand McNally.
————, and Roberta Ash (1970), "Social Movement Organizations: Growth, Decay and Change,"
    in *Protest, Reform and Revolt: A Reader in Social Movements*, Joseph R. Gusfield, ed. New
    York: Wiley, pp. 517–537.